Stan the man

Stan *the* man

A HARD LIFE IN FOOTBALL

**STAN TERNENT
WITH TONY LIVESEY**

JOHN BLAKE

Published by John Blake Publishing Ltd,
3, Bramber Court, 2 Bramber Road,
London W14 9PB, England

www.blake.co.uk

First published in paperback back in 2004

ISBN 978 1 84454 018 1

British Library Cataloguing-in-Publication Data:

A catalogue record for this book is available from the British Library.

Design by www.envydesign.co.uk

Printed in Great Britain by Bookmarque

3 5 7 9 10 8 6 4

Papers used by John Blake Publishing are natural, recyclable products made from wood grown in sustainable forests. The manufacturing processes conform to the environmental regulations of the country of origin.

Contents

'The nice thing about football is that,
if things go wrong, it's the Manager
who gets the blame ...'
Gary Lineker

To Kath, Chris, Dan, Yogi and Olivia
– the things I got right
Stan

Foreword

BY ALASTAIR CAMPBELL

I must have seen my first Burnley game around the time Stan Ternent joined the ground-staff at Turf Moor. I'm rather ashamed to admit it but I can't remember who we played that Saturday forty-odd years ago.

I just know that as an excited kid, everything about that afternoon with my dad – the crowd, the noise, the smell, the game and the famous claret and blue colours – was magical. I was hooked, and have been ever since.

In my case, it was luck that brought me to Turf Moor. My father, a Scot, didn't follow Burnley but Partick Thistle. I was brought up in Keighley and could just as easily have been taken to Leeds or Bradford for my first game.

In contrast, Stan made the deliberate choice to travel from his native North East to Lancashire as a 16-year-old. It is easy to see why.

At the time, Burnley was one of the great teams in English football. When I first saw them aged four, they had just been league champions, reached the quarter-finals of the European Cup and must have been on their way to the FA Cup Final. The team included names familiar to all football-mad small boys: Ray Pointer, Jimmy Adamson, Jimmy McIlroy, Alex Elder. Only the misfortune of reaching their peak at the same time as the great Spurs double-winning side stopped them dominating the English game.

But even then, Burnley was not a flash club. They were rooted in the town, their players coming through the youth ranks, their supporters fiercely proud. It was something which stood us in good stead when the good times came disastrously to an end in the Eighties.

And there is, as we all know, nothing flash about Stan. Not as a player and not as a manager. I don't remember seeing him play – though I suspect I might have done for Carlisle against us – but I know exactly what sort of opponent he must have been. Uncompromising, fearless, never giving less than 100%, never accepting defeat lightly. Exactly the qualities he brings to being a manager.

This courage and commitment wasn't enough to win him the playing opportunity he craved at Turf Moor – and, as this book reveals, he is still bitter it was denied him. But it made him the mainstay of the unfashionable Carlisle team that staggered the football world by fighting their way to the top division.

More importantly for Burnley fans, it also gave him the stomach for turning this club round, to win promotion back to Division One, to take us within touching distance of the top flight and to give us the hope and belief we'll be back there soon.

We have been away far too long. In the forty years I have been following Burnley, I've experienced some fantastic highs and some gravity-defying lows. We went from being champions, the very top of the pile, to the very bottom when we were just one defeat away from losing league status altogether. And over the last couple of decades before Stan came along, the lows certainly outnumbered the highs.

As we see-sawed between the divisions, Stan was learning his trade as a coach and manager. He, too, had his good and bad times. All are honestly and, at times, brutally described in this book. As you would expect, Stan ducks no tackles, pulls no punches whether he is talking about his success at Bury or his misery at Chelsea.

Throughout all this time and all the turmoil at Turf Moor, Stan's main link with Burnley was that he had met a local girl when he first signed for the club and had settled here after his playing career finished.

When the board finally turned to the manager on their doorstep, all supporters knew we were in bad shape and needed major surgery. It can't have been a comfortable time to be at this club for anyone. Stan doesn't so much ruffle feathers as pluck them out by the handful.

But slowly it brought results. Gradually, he built a team in his own image – committed and passionate. He gave the players the confidence to show they had skill too.

Just exactly how he achieved this has been spelled out honestly in this book – with too much honesty, I suspect, some will think. It's all here. How he cleared out the players he found wanting. How he brought Ian Wright to the club, a gamble which paid off so well. How he brought Gazza, which, sadly, didn't.

What also comes through is that Stan's belief that he deserves to be in the top flight and his ambition to test himself against the best in the land is still as strong as ever. So is his confidence that he has the talent and experience to succeed. Let's hope he gets that chance with Burnley soon.

A.C.

(10 Downing Street)

1

'You Know What It's Like with a Bird on Your Arm ...'

BURNLEY, 1998–99

My wife bolted upright in bed as ominously as a corpse with wind. The ringing of the telephone, now clamped to her ear, had woken us both. Her face paled as she registered the abuse pouring down the line.

'YOU FAT BAAASTARD!'

Kath leaned over and tapped me on the head with the receiver.

'It's for you.'

The caller had a point he wanted to make and seemed pretty insistent.

'YOU FAT BAAASTARD!' he shouted again.

Understand this: after 40 years in football, I have suffered. I've been spat at; pelted with beer cans; assaulted with turds (human *and* dog); locked in police cells; headbutted by my own centre-forward; hit with a brick; suspected of being the Yorkshire Ripper; the victim of an assassination attempt by two

13

Premiership stars and I've worked with a pair of the biggest shits in soccer.

So you would imagine I was immune to a touch of long-distance verbals.

Not so.

It was 11.00pm. I'd been in my pyjamas for over an hour and in a bad mood for longer. If I could have laid my hands on this lunatic phone-pest I would have knocked him clean out. Then it clicked. I recognised his voice.

'Hello, Jonah,' I said.

Vinnie Jones. The ultimate competitor. A gentleman. A man who shot down a plane for me. A man who comforted me as I approached a nervous breakdown at Chelsea during one of the lowest points in my life. Piss-taker *extraordinaire*. I relaxed.

> **Vinnie:** YOU FAT BAAASTARD!
> **Me:** I heard you the first time.
> **Vinnie:** I've just seen you on telly. I need a fucking widescreen TV!

Vinnie had watched Sky Sports on television and had stumbled across a story which barely made headlines beyond a five-mile radius of my farmhouse in the Lancashire hills. It was May 1998 and I'd just spent my first day as manager of Second Division Burnley.

Strangely, I was relieved to hear Vinnie's kind words. His call had rudely interrupted a self-pitying wallow as I digested the cancerous state of the club I had inherited less than 24 hours earlier. Too many of my new squad were worse than rubbish. As a young player for Burnley in the 1960s, the Turf Moor I knew was a stage for their championship-winning legends. That morning, it had resembled a knackers' yard.

I had to suppress the urge to be sick when it dawned on me that the centre-halves I'd been lumbered with were capable of being outjumped at corners by Jimmy Krankie and his little brother.

This was all doubly disturbing when I considered the Burnley fans I was supposed to satisfy. They are loyal, fiercely proud and loudly partisan. Some of them can be a tad judgemental, too. When ex-manager Jimmy Mullen led the club to immediate relegation the season after he took them to Division One in 1994, supporters tried to set fire to his wife in a chip shop.

> **Vinnie: Listen, Stan. Good luck. I'm off to LA**
> **tomorrow for filming. Call me, but not at**
> **4.00pm. I'm playing tennis with Rod.**
> **Me: Who's that ... Rod Hull?**

Vinnie was destined to move in different circles to me. He would be in make-up by the time I rolled out of bed to begin the most gruelling, depressing, punishing and exhilarating four years of my life.

Faced with nothing more taxing than months of Los Angeles sunshine and Hollywood pampering, Vinnie ended his gee-up call by bollocking me for not attending his *Hello!* magazine wedding and asking why I had accepted the job at Burnley. 'Where is it, anyhow?' he wondered.

Sadly, Burnley exists in a place neither Jonah nor many other Premiership stars will ever recognise. I, on the other hand, knew it well.

I had married a Burnley lass and made my home in the town 30 years ago after spending six years at the club as an apprentice and senior pro. I see it on sunny days when heather blanketing the surrounding moorland competes with the sunset to bathe us in a purple hue. I see it on autumn evenings when a badger will come snuffling through the wind-blown leaves piled against my garden fence.

Unfortunately, on the rare occasions those muppets from *Grandstand* come to town, they film cobbled streets, whippets and blokes with beer guts and their arses hanging out of their jeans.

The club has produced some stunning players – Tommy Lawton, Jimmy Adamson, Jimmy McIlroy, Leighton James, Trevor Steven, Ralph Coates – but if you want footage of them in action, the BBC cupboard is bare.

Ask the Beeb for clips of back-to-back terraced housing or an interview with a bloke in a flat cap smoking tabs and there are so many videos they have to be delivered by sweaty 17-year-old research assistants from the Home Counties using a forklift truck.

After a race riot a couple of years ago when the town's Duke of York pub was burned to the ground live on CNN, inspectors said Burnley had all the problems of an inner city with none of the benefits.

True, some areas in the centre consist of clumps of squalid houses owned by people whose weekly wage barely keeps their children in school clothes. Some homes are so damp they don't have rent books, they have tide tables. Drugs are dealt. Kids go hungry. Hardly news to anyone living in Britain today.

The crucial difference in Burnley those officials failed to recognise is that the town survives because its spirit has never been broken. And central to its fight against decline is Turf Moor, home of Burnley FC. It is the most important entity in town. It defines the place. Generations of locals have worshipped at its altar.

The stadium towers over surrounding streets like an aircraft carrier in dry dock. The club won the FA Cup in 1914 in the days when the coach on their home-coming parade was horse-drawn. It won the old First Division title in 1960 and has been champion of every other division at least once since it was formed in 1882. Burnley even reached the quarter-final of the European Cup in the Sixties.

It's easy to forget that, before World War II, Blackburn, Bolton,

Bury, Preston and Burnley won 14 FA Cups between them. Everton, Liverpool, Man City and Man United won five.

No one can question the club's pedigree. But it's all too long ago. The combination for the lock on Turf Moor's trophy cabinet remains set at Harold Macmillan's hat-size. Memories of those glory days are slowly dying with the stars and the fans who witnessed them.

In true Dunkirk spirit, Burnley supporters now hold slap-up dinners to commemorate a more recent historic victory, known as 'The Orient Game'.

When Football League bosses decided in 1987 to boot out clubs which finished bottom of the Fourth Division, they didn't imagine that on the last day of the season it would be Burnley, one of their own founder members, facing the chop. There was horrified embarrassment at the highest levels of the game. There was even talk of a compromise to let the club off.

But that was daft. Rules are rules. Burnley had only themselves to blame and, to be fair, they were crap. I'd bobbed down a few times from my home a couple of miles away to watch the lads training and it wasn't pretty.

On the day of their final game against Leyton Orient, that season's average gate of around 4,000 was obliterated as 17,000 fans poured in to watch. Most of the big-name newspaper, radio and TV members of the Claptrappers Union who packed into Turf Moor were desperate to see Burnley go under. They'd come to bury the club under a mound of meaningless drivel about 'sleeping giants' and 'the end of an era'.

But passions were stirred, and supporters who forgot what it was like to be aroused by 11 blokes in shorts were reduced to quivering wrecks, the way their fathers had been when Burnley competed for First Division titles almost 30 years before. There was a frenzy about the town that day.

Orient manager Frank Clark has since claimed that he was told before the match that police couldn't guarantee his team's safety if they came out winners. True or not, it was irrelevant.

Burnley won 2-1. A nation rejoiced. Lincoln dropped down to the Vauxhall Conference and no one noticed.

A revival of sorts followed. Burnley reached Division One again, although it took seven years, but it all ended in disaster when they dropped back into Division Two after just one disappointing season.

Fans turned on the Board. The Chairman at the time was Frank Teasdale, a plumpish fellow who blinked at you through large owlish glasses which made him look like the lovechild of snooker star Dennis Taylor and Toad of Toad Hall.

He was surrounded by directors who were well-meaning local worthies with either a few bob (but *never* enough) or big mouths ... or both.

Restless Burnley fans wanted revolution. After-match protests on the streets outside the ground went unnoticed, so they took their campaign inside Turf Moor.

During one game, at exactly 3.33pm, a firework exploded in mid-air behind a section of terracing. It was the signal for a bizarre display called 'Backs to the Board'. Seventy per cent of home supporters turned their backs on the game, and specifically the directors' box, as they stood in silence for one minute.

It worked. Fans got their change. But instead of quitting himself, Frank and his board clung to power while hapless manager Mullen was asked to leave.

Ex-Everton star Adrian Heath was persuaded to take the job after Mullen, but he soon sodded off to be assistant to Howard Kendall at Everton. He was followed into Turf Moor by England international Chris Waddle.

The team got worse. In their first season, Chris and his number two Glenn Roeder took Burnley to the brink of disaster. Only a last-match win against Plymouth saved them from relegation to the Third Division in the summer of 1998.

Chris left sharpish, supposedly by mutual consent. In

reality, the Board had played the celebrity manager card, been bluffed and wanted rid. Chris realised he could no longer rely on their support.

Finally, it dawned on Frank to offer the manager's job to the bloke who had lived up the road from the ground for years, who was bred to the Burnley cause, who had worked for Chelsea, Leeds, Crystal Palace, Bradford City, Blackpool and Sunderland, who had just won two successive promotions on a shoestring budget at Bury, and who was better qualified than the club's last six managers put together.

Me.

I was tempted to tell him to piss off.

I knew Chris was in trouble long before it ever occurred to Frank. I was busy keeping Bury in the First Division while he fought to keep Burnley in the Second on twice my budget. I didn't see them play a match that season. I didn't see why I should. There were enough long faces in my local country pub on the fringes of town, The Kettledrum, to tell me all I needed to know.

For years, I'd been expecting Burnley to offer me a chance to take them forward. But one spring night in 1998, when a phone call begging for help finally came, it wasn't from Frank at all. Surprise, surprise.

I'd doubted he even knew my number. It was Chris himself and he was desperate. He had six games left to save his season. He wanted to meet to pick my brain.

Ironic, really. His club could have been doing that for years.

I arranged to meet Chris up the 'Drum'; he wandered in with one of his assistants, Gordon Cowans. Over our first pint, it became obvious that too many regulars were taking an interest, so we went back to my house to talk.

Chris is a decent man. But despite playing for Newcastle and England, as well as coping with all the flak he received after missing one of the crucial World Cup penalties against Germany in 1990, he was finding the expectation levels at Turf Moor difficult to deal with.

He had spent over £1m, a small fortune by Burnley's standards, to bring new players in, but his signings let him down badly. They took six games even to score a goal ... and twelve to notch a win!

I'd heard there was trouble on the training pitch. One of Burnley's better players was Glen Little, a rangy 6ft winger with a cockney accent and a motor mouth, signed from Irish club Glentoran.

Little, a favourite of the fans, complained he was treated like a leper. He said, 'It was strange. When Waddle came to the club, all the players thought we would hit the big time. But mistakes were made. The players brought in were naïve. I wasn't allowed to be part of it. I was totally bombed out. The only two who knew why were Waddle and Roeder.

'Waddle didn't even speak to me for three months. I never trained with the first team. Players who'd never played a professional game in their lives were ahead of me. It was a nightmare. I was close to leaving.'

Glen said that he was alone in the boot room one day when Waddle walked in and stood there shuffling his feet in silence. Little said, 'He just mumbled, "All right", and walked out again. Other players were embarrassed by all this. I was depressed. I was a young bloke living a long way from home. I used to ring my mum a lot and she told me to just pack it all in and come back to London.

'I was close to going. When fans challenged Roeder to pick me, he said I wasn't fit to lace Chris Waddle's boots. The supporters were frightened to have a go at Waddle so they made Roeder the scapegoat.

'Training was a laugh and a joke. Waddle would say, "What's the day? Monday? Oh, see you guys Wednesday then." On match days, Waddle would say, "Go out there and play," and some of the lads would turn round and ask, "Where?" It seemed there was no game plan.

'Waddle's team-talks on a Friday morning lasted for five minutes, then we got the footballs out and that was it.'

As Chris's season collapsed around his ears and we sat round my kitchen table, I knew, out of respect, that I had to avoid telling him how to do his job.

Besides, I didn't know a lot about the players he'd signed, though you didn't have to be Anne Robinson to realise they were weak links.

I related my Bury experiences as the night wore on and worked hard to try to find common ground. It was impossible. His body language as he sloped out to his car that night illustrated how depressed he was.

Morale inside the club had already plummeted with separate factions vying for control. Director Clive Holt angrily claimed in the privacy of the Boardroom that Waddle organised training sessions around his media commitments.

Clive believed Chris was going to disappear to France that summer to cover the World Cup for the BBC, so he wrote a memo to Teasdale complaining, 'Quite frankly, this is not satisfactory. We have got to have some ground rules ... For God's sake, we need to sort this out. We need to organise a team for next season!'

At one Board meeting, Chris sent his pal Roeder along in his place. He was monstered by Clive. Roeder was attacked at the same meeting by another Burnley director, a former local Tory councillor called Bernard Rothwell. The pair of them laid into Chris's number two over the non-selection of Little.

The next day, Chris rang the directors to try to bollock them but Clive replied, 'Tough luck.' Saving Burnley's bacon on the last day of the season was never going to be enough to save Waddle's.

It was a real shame. Chris has plenty to offer football. He is charismatic and gifted, but a club as demanding as Burnley was always going to be too exhausting and bewildering for a novice.

When the end came, I was miles away, happily swallow-diving into a triple Bacardi and Coke in sunny Magaluf with my Bury lads.

I'd kept them in a First Division that included Charlton, Wolves, Sunderland, Middlesbrough and Manchester City and my Chairman, Terry Robinson, who looked like Bill Maynard's sumo-wrestling brother, was treating me and the lads to a taste of Bury's typical two-star luxury.

Terry wandered over to me by the pool one morning clutching a copy of the *Daily Mail*, his belly glowing bright red as though someone had opened the front door on a kitchen Aga.

'Waddle's gone,' he said.

Time to look inscrutable. 'Really?' I said. To be honest, I was astonished. I knew Chris was out of his depth but he was just cutting his teeth in football management. The only way to get experience is to hang on in there.

My career was littered with poxy chairmen, useless players and ridiculous expectation levels. I'm too proud to run away from any trouble and, after just 46 games, I wish I could have persuaded Chris to do the same.

Terry was paranoid about me leaving to manage Burnley. They had once tried to entice one of his ex-managers, Martin Dobson, and they had succeeded in nicking Frank Casper, his assistant boss, in 1989.

He said, 'Will you go?'

'No.' And I meant *no*.

As I thought more deeply on the flight home from Spain, I just couldn't see how the same Burnley Board who had blundered through the past ten seasons or so would finally see sense and knock on my door. Judging by their most recent decisions, I'd only get a visit from Frank Teasdale if I lived next door to Mr Bean and he wanted to ask the way to offer him the job.

However, a bit like my heroes in the SAS, who dares wins. Or is it the Scouts? Be prepared.

As we tucked into a rubber-flavoured breakfast at 30,000ft over

France, I sat myself next to my centre-half Peter Swan who used to play for Burnley. Time for me to do some brain picking of my own.

Eventually, the Burnley directors drew up a shortlist. For a shortlist, it was long on names. Usual ex-Burnley suspects they fancied included Jimmy Mullen, Adrian Heath, Brian Flynn, Mike Phelan (currently one of Fergie's coaches at Old Trafford), Dave Merrington and ex-player Jamie Hoyland. Candidates from outside were Frank Clark, Joe Jordan, Sam Allardyce, Lou Macari, Bruce Rioch, Neil Warnock, Sammy McIlroy and me.

If everyone got an interview, one of us could just have been appointed by Boxing Day.

Clive made the first move and telephoned Terry, my Chairman at Bury.

'Ah,' said Terry, doing his best impression of James Bond's nemesis Blofeld. 'I've been expecting you ... What about compensation?'

'Hang on a minute,' said Clive. 'Stan is out of contract. Are you going to stand in his way? We're a club he wants to join.'

'Leave it with me, I'll get back to you in ten minutes,' said Terry, who stomped off to see me in my office.

'Burnley want you. Do you want to talk to them?' he asked.

'Not interested,' I said.

'Look,' said Terry. 'I have to be honest with you. There's no chance of a rise next season.'

Terry was tight. We once toured the Isle of Man with Bury and I wanted to go to bed after a long night but he refused. Short-sighted punters in the hotel bar had mistaken him for Clive James and were buying him free drinks by the barrel.

He became impatient. 'Are you going to speak to them or not?'

I thought, No rise ... no stay, you skinflint.

God help me. I knew I was the Last Ditch Hotel for Burnley. I knew I should have had the job five years earlier. I knew they were a division lower than Bury. I even had some inkling of the awful state of affairs at Turf Moor.

'Yes,' I said.

Terry turned and walked away. Minutes later, I had my first phone conversation with Clive Holt.

> **Clive: Morning, Stan. We'd like to talk to you about the Burnley job.**
>
> **Me: Go on.**
>
> **Clive: We'd like you to come to an interview at the ...**
>
> **Me: A what?**
>
> **Clive: Er ... an interview?**
>
> **Me: I'll come and talk about the job. If you want me to do an interview, you know where you can stick it.**

I met Clive at the Trafalgar Hotel on the outskirts of Preston, and then met Frank Teasdale at the house of another director.

He said, 'Stan, I'd like you to manage the club. And I'd like to offer you fuck all to do it.'

Alarm bells. He didn't actually say 'fuck all', but it sounded like it to me. £70,000 was on the table.

'Hang on,' I said, 'that's less than I'm on at Bury.' I needed to sleep on it. Were they taking the piss? Did I even want to leave my comfort zone at Bury?

I knew Kath and my lads Chris and Dan were still angry with Burnley for ignoring me over the years. I also knew that taking the job would change our lives for ever. We lived locally, like long-suffering ex-managers Jimmy Mullen and Frank Casper. Setting fire to Mullen's wife in a chippy had not been enough for some Burnley morons, who had also abused the couple in a restaurant. One of Casper's sons was spat at in the face when results were poor.

I'd kill the first fan who ever thought of hurting my wife, but when I woke the next morning, I chose to be positive.

We convinced each other over cups of coffee at a family conference in the kitchen that if I took the job it would have to be for the right reasons. I wanted to take Burnley to the Premiership and then retire. Job done.

It was obvious from discussions with Terry that I'd reached my wage ceiling at Bury. Sod it. I rang Frank to say I'd accept the job for £130,000 and the same car I had at Gigg Lane, a Mercedes E class.

I had to haggle over the Merc.

> Frank: Wouldn't you be better off with a Vauxhall?
> Me: If you want a Vauxhall club, get me a
>   Vauxhall. If you want me turning up at
>   other clubs looking like one of the
>   Clampetts, give me a Vauxhall.
> Frank: OK, have a Merc.
> Me: By the way, Sam wants one, too.

That came as a surprise to Frank. Only I knew I wanted my number two at Bury to follow me to the Turf. Neither Frank, Terry at Bury or even Sam himself had a clue.

Sam Ellis is one of my closest friends in football. He's a ruddy-faced bull of a bloke with a ready smile. It's hardly surprising. He only has to remember the day in 1967 when we both made our professional debuts in the same match and he wets himself laughing.

I was playing for Burnley at Sheffield Wednesday, against Sam who was their teenage centre-half. I'd spent five years fighting for a passage through the youth team, A-team and into the reserves at Turf Moor, where we often played in front of crowds of over 10,000 who paid to watch the second XI. Finally, manager Harry Potts gave me my chance with the first team.

It was the reward for rolling up my sleeves and not walking away when things didn't go my way. I'd seen countless other youngsters play alongside me for the reserves and then get their chance with the first team while I'd stayed put.

I'm a stubborn sod, though. My pride and determination drove my desire to make the teamsheet. When we arrived at Wednesday's ground, I glanced around the dressing room, watching brawny Andy Lochhead, Ralph Coates and Willie Morgan pull on their claret shirts. I thought, This is it. Big time, Stanley.

A little lad popped his head round the door and handed me a telegram moments before kick-off. I hoped it wasn't the gaffer's way of telling me he'd changed his mind.

'CONGRATULATIONS. BEST OF LUCK.' It was from some family friends. I've still got it.

I kept the match reports, too.

BURNLEY BEATING WORST IN DECADE

It should have been a day to remember. But 90 minutes after it started it became a day Ternent will want to wipe from memory. A nightmare of confusion, uncertainty and panic as Burnley crashed to their biggest hiding in a decade.

DAILY EXPRESS

WHITEWASHED

Burnley looked like a disaster area when it was all over.

BURNLEY EXPRESS

We got stuffed 7–0. They even missed a penalty. The following Saturday, I was the only player dropped.

So Sam saw me lose my first fight from close quarters, but he's been alongside for many years since and I haven't let him see me lose many more.

As soon as the deal for us to come back and manage Burnley had been hammered out, I did what every self-respecting football high-achiever does. I got straight on the phone to Terry at Bury and told him that although I'd said 'yes' to Teasdale, I'd stay with him if he could match the offer.

He shot off to talk money with Bury's penniless backers while I pulled Sam to one side and said, 'We're off.' I knew Bury couldn't afford us both, so I was anxious to see how Terry would respond. He called me back.

'We'll match Burnley's offer.'

Shocked, I realised I was now in a corner with a big decision to make. By this stage, I was bluffing both Burnley and Bury. You do what you can to get the best deal; what I hadn't anticipated was that Terry would bluff me! It was like a scene from *The Sting* with 'ey oop' northern accents.

While I was secretly plotting my and Sam's future away from Bury, Terry had felt certain that Sam would stay loyal. He planned to offer my deputy a job as 'Director of Football' and recruit former Wimbledon FA Cup-winning hero Lawrie Sanchez as manager.

Sam never mentioned this but reassured me, 'I'm going wherever you go.'

On the morning Frank Teasdale was to arrive at my house with the Burnley contract, I was all set to tell him the deal was off. Then, at the very moment I heard his car coming down the drive, my phone rang. It was Terry.

The Bury offer was withdrawn.

'Our deal's off, Stan,' he said. 'We can't raise the cash. You'll have to leave.'

My mind was made up for me.

Unaware that he had been 60 seconds from losing his new manager, Frank tapped on my front door, sauntered in and walked away with my signature.

I'd got Sam a great package. The Merc was top class, although he's such a scruffy sod I should have negotiated him a skip on wheels. When I later discovered he had been speaking to Terry about being Director of Football, I felt betrayed.

I knew that Sam was loyal and that he had every right to explore his options. But I hate the unknown. The thought of his secret dialogue with Terry was costing me sleep. At 4.00am one morning, I telephoned and woke him up.

'Why didn't you tell me you've been talking to Terry? You've been ducking and diving behind my fucking back.'

I soon cheered up when Terry realised I'd beaten him to Sam and went potty.

He had said to us, 'I give you my blessing,' when we'd left. Now he was suing the Board at Burnley for illegally approaching my number two.

He told anyone who would listen, 'It left a bad taste in my mouth. I wasn't 100 per cent sure that Stan would go but, even if he did, it never occurred to me that he'd take Sam with him. I wasn't sure Burnley could afford them.'

Terry was convinced we had jumped ship and shafted Bury purely for the money, so he tried to claim £100,000 compensation. A Football League tribunal paid him £20,000.

But he still managed to have the last laugh. Barely three months after my dreadful first day at the Turf Moor office, when it dawned on me that I'd walked into a madhouse full of weak, third-rate players, we were drawn to play Bury in the Cup.

* * *

My first week in the job at Burnley was a whirlwind of mental anguish and pain.

When I was a professional player, I would rather lose a leg than a tackle. As a manager, I was used to discipline, aggression and organisation from the players under my control. So when the out-of-shape lumps in my new squad finally sauntered back from their summer holidays, I ranted at them like a lunatic.

I was dealing with a bunch of overpaid footballers who expected to get days off from training if they managed to string two passes together. I attempted to test their mettle by devising SAS-style runs over the moors near my house but, within minutes of setting off, I was savaged by three sheepdogs which bolted out of a cottage garden. As I wrestled with them, I told the owner I'd be back to shoot them, but she just shouted, 'Sorry, luv, they don't like joggers.'

Within a week of starting our pre-season fitness schedule, I realised the players weren't even close to Second Division standards. Three of them – Glen Little, a young gutsy midfielder called Paul Weller and the club's top scorer Andy Payton (who at least was honest enough to admit that the team was crap) were the only decent players. Most of the others were fucking hopeless.

As they had fought to save their skins towards the end of the previous season, they had to beat Oldham at Boundary Park to stay up. Leading 3–1 against 10 men with 14 minutes to go, they bottled it and folded, drawing 3–3 in front of 5,000 travelling Burnley fans. Manager Chris Waddle admitted, 'We lacked leaders.'

Leaders? Physically and mentally, they lacked everything.

Away from the playing side, I discovered a club in chaos, too. There was an awful cancer of indifference and neglect gnawing away at Burnley FC from the inside. Mail had been left unopened for weeks. Players had been handed contracts by Frank in Chris's absence. Ex-England goalkeeper Chris Woods was still on the books ... and he was 38!

The first chance I got, I pulled him into my office. 'Sorry, Chris, you are never going to play in goal for me.' I didn't want him wasting his life driving 55 miles to Turf Moor from his home in Sheffield every day. There was no point. It may have seemed harsh, but I felt I treated him with respect. It actually gave me pleasure to feel someone was starting to do a bit of straight dealing with the staff.

I couldn't believe that so many squad members were out of

contract. It was breathtaking incompetence which should never have been allowed to happen.

One player, Jamie Hoyland, fancied himself as a coach and refused a new contract. I got rid of him on a free transfer. I think some of the supporters wished they could have done the same to me. Letters protesting about my selection were written to the *Burnley Express* asking, 'Stan who?'

These deluded followers hardly cover themselves in glory. They see their club as massive. To them, I wasn't a big name. What do they expect? They think Fergie, George Graham or Bobby Robson will take the job. They need to learn a simple lesson – it's Burnley, not Barcelona.

Too many fans have misguided loyalties. Every ex-Claret who comes back to play at Burnley gets a standing ovation. It's pointless, even damaging, as they cheer on our opponents.

John Ward, once an assistant at Turf Moor to Adrian Heath, gets an encouraging round of applause whichever new team he brings here to beat us. Why? He soon went to Bristol City and left Heath when he got a better job offer. For now, my loyalty rested with Burnley and I couldn't waste any time worrying about what idiots wrote to the local press.

When I sat back for five minutes to survey the weeks ahead, the next cock-up to come to light was a distinct lack of pre-season matches.

I wasn't sure it was even worth the effort. The attitude of too many of the players appalled me. They whinged from day one that an ex-squad member who'd left Burnley to play abroad had nicked £400 of their 'pool' money, cash they collect off each other during the season to fund a Christmas party.

I knew this bloke had returned to England, so I deliberately leaked the news to my players fully expecting them to show some spirit, hire a minibus and go over and chin him. They shrugged their shoulders.

Had they no balls? If it was my cash he'd stolen, I would have hunted him down. He broke sacred team rules. If you kick one player, the whole team should limp.

Not at Burnley it seemed. The squad was listless and disinterested. Leading scorer Andy Payton said that if the team had won on Saturday during the previous season, the attitude from management was: 'See you Tuesday, then take a day off on Wednesday.' Andy was professional enough to understand that, playing by those rules, the club was never going to win anything.

I spent my first week wrestling with mixed emotions of overwhelming regret at accepting the post and thrill at the prospect of grabbing the squad by its bollocks and knocking some sense into it.

Most afternoons, I tended my garden at home, mowing my lawn, strolling around in a T-shirt and Y-fronts, pondering our next move. We needed a pre-season tour.

As I picked grass cuttings from between my toes, I accepted a few facts: (a) We were not seeking sun; (b) We were not seeking fun; (c) We were not seeking an easy life.

I knew a man in Devon. We would yomp over the moors and sleep in a spartan dormitory at Exeter University. It was time to ask some serious questions of my squad. Perhaps the players would finally summon the balls to object to a military training regime. If so, I was ready to chop them off.

On the doorstep of the team bus heading to Exeter, I gave my first meaningful press conference to local reporters in Burnley. They are a busy bunch who get where water can't.

Journalists have a right to air their views but they have to answer for it. I like to ambush them with telephone calls to their homes. It concentrates their minds if they pick up the phone on a Monday night to hear me on the other end asking politely, 'What fucking game were you at?'

I refuse to suck up to football writers. At best, if things go badly, they can buy you three games to try to save your neck by holding back on the SACK STAN headlines. But I'm not prepared to sacrifice my privacy and integrity by bumming up to that lot for the sake of three games.

As we left for the South-West, it was vital they didn't get a hint of the screaming demons swarming around in my head cursing all things Burnley, so I said all the right things.

'This is the start of the job I always wanted,' I enthused. 'We've now got five weeks of pre-season training ahead of us. Listen, we are not big, bad wolves. I'm looking forward to training, and so should the players, because it will be fun. They must have no fear. If they want to be part of what's going on, that's fine with me. If they don't, that's fine also. We'll have to find a way of replacing them with others who want to do it my way.'

'But, Stan,' asked one of the hacks, 'can you turn the club around?'

Sometimes in interviews, I avoid answering questions directly by saying too much. I'll travel to London via Glasgow and Cardiff to lead reporters off the scent of a story. This time, I drew upon one of my favourite conversation stoppers.

'Look,' I said, as I prepared to shut the door, 'it's a tough league and we've got to play everyone twice. See ya, fellas.'

We were off. Just as the players began to relax, about 100 yards from the gates of the Turf, I stood in the aisle and announced, 'You lot have got a choice over the next five days ... get fit, or get out.'

After distance runs around Exeter over the first 24 hours to stretch our legs and avoid deep vein thrombosis from the charabanc trip, we faced our first big game, an evening kick-off against Dawlish Town of the Screwfix Direct Western League.

We won 4–0 but it could have been 9–4 to them. Afterwards, some of the players spent half-an-hour swanning around like internationals, signing autographs for 60-year-old groupies in Burnley shirts. They acted like superstars, even if they couldn't play like them.

We beat another local team, Elmore, 4–0 a few days later, but nothing had improved. I was beginning to fear for our future in the Second Division, but some of the players had other things on their minds. A deputation came to see me on Friday afternoon.

> Deputation: We'd like a night out.
> Me: OK.
> Deputation: Really?
> Me: Really. But I want you in by ten o'clock.
> Deputation: OK.

They left, seemingly satisfied. The same deputation shuffled back within five minutes after a conference with the rest of the lads.

> Deputation: What if we're back for 1.00am?
> Me: Midnight. That's it. Don't be late.

The stench as the big girls' blouses prettied themselves up that night was as stomach-wrenching as if they'd blobbed on their aftershave using a crop-sprayer.

I popped out for a civilised pint with Sam and we were back by 11.30pm. It was time for my patrol. The waiting game began.

Payton knew me from a previous club, so he was one of the first to arrive back. Payts appreciated that a midnight curfew still allowed for a good night out. His experience warned him that tonight was not one to take risks.

Other players returned in small groups, braking in panic like speeding cars approaching a traffic camera as they caught sight of me having a fag in the doorway.

'All right, lads,' I said, 'get to bed.'

I checked my watch. It was midnight. Bang on. I pulled a seat from behind a desk in the entrance hall, sat down and pulled out a pencil and paper. I knew the wasters who would be late, but I still wanted to record their names as they trickled home.

Sam yawned. 'I'll be off to bed then, gaffer.'

'No chance, Sam. We'll watch them come home.'

Like the BBC bod during the Falklands War, I'd counted them all out, now I was going to count them all back in. I made Sam sit with me. When I verbally ripped their heads off later, I knew he would be equally as pissed off as me.

The first two latecomers wandered in at ten minutes past midnight.

'Sorry, gaffer.'

I expelled a mouthful of Silk Cut. 'See me at 8.00am.'

It was well over an hour before we saw the next sign of life. It came from bushes in a garden area in front of the dorm. I'd locked all the doors and windows in our building as soon as I'd returned from the pub. This was the only way in. Straight past me and Sam.

The rustling in the bushes became more intense. I motioned to Sam to go to one end of the hedge while I covered the other, crouching down inside some shrubbery. Moments later, like a bloated stoat on the hunt for grub, one of my dodgy defenders emerged from a bush crawling on his knees and elbows.

'Where the fuck have you been?'

At the sound of my voice, he blinked up at me through a haze of alcohol and a veneer of mud. He struggled to his feet and brushed patches of dirt off his trousers.

'You know what it's like when you've got a bird on your arm, gaffer. Your luck's in.'

I turned away in disgust. Sam packed the imbecile off to bed.

I settled back into my chair to wait for the rest. The directors were fortunate to be staying in a hotel a couple of miles away from the campus, otherwise I'd have dragged them out of their rooms to witness the disrespect some of their players felt they could show our club.

The final pair of stragglers staggered in at 4.00am. They

sobered up instantly as they stumbled across me and Sam with a dozen cigarette butts layered around our loafers.

As I ticked them off my list, I hesitated. I had the names of my 17-man squad in front of me. Only 16 were scribbled out. I was still missing a man.

He finally came back at 7.00am.

He was too knackered even to attempt an explanation. I was too disgusted to speak to him.

'Sam,' I said, 'send him to my room.'

Minutes later, I heard a knock at my door and in walked the dirty stop-out.

> **Me: Where have you been?**
> **Stop-out: I slept out.**
> **Me: You're finished.**
> **Stop-out: What shall I tell my wife and kids?**
> **Me: Just go to the station. You're finished.**

I turned away to wait for him to leave the room. Instead of a door slamming, I heard a sound I'd never heard before from a professional footballer. He was crying. And not just a muffled sob.

Here was a so-called 'man' the fans back home hoped would win us promotion next season bawling like a little girl who's not been caught at kiss-chase. It told me everything I needed to know about the calibre of the characters I was dealing with.

Naturally, I treated him with as much sympathy as I could muster. 'Piss off.' This time, as I busied myself preparing for the day ahead, the door did slam.

Before long, the other four players who were bollocked for coming back late appeared in my room to plead for their mate. I delivered my verdict.

'Right. I want the lot of you home. Now.'

They panicked. 'How are we going to get there?'

'I don't give a toss. There's a taxi rank in town, isn't there?' I was prepared to play our remaining matches on the trip with a team of eight if I had to.

Eventually, the rest of the squad asked me to reconsider and, out of compassion for their families, I let them stay. For the rest of the trip, though, the players were numb. One of the decent lads, Chris Brass, told me later the verdict in the dressing room had been: 'We won't get away with any bullshit with this manager.'

Mission accomplished, as far as I was concerned. I had learned quickly during my time at Chelsea with Vinnie and Dennis Wise that if players find a weakness they will exploit it.

I was pleased this lot had responded when I'd drawn a line in the sand. My only other option was to knock the lot of them out.

2

'I Would Like to Apologise ...'

BURNLEY, 1998–99

Fresh from our triumphant tour of the West Country, I sat at my desk above the Turf Moor souvenir shop to savour the remaining high-profile friendlies I had managed to arrange at the last minute: Halifax, Morecambe and Rochdale.

The way my lot were shaping, I couldn't be sure that we would win any of them. So I had spent the previous 48 hours bruising my dialling finger trying to find players of quality willing to join us.

When I accepted the job, I'd been made promises by Frank Teasdale that I would be given money to make signings. A bit like our back four, they soon evaporated.

I needed quick dough to have any chance of cracking on, but things were truly hopeless. I lined up three players who had served me so well at Bury recently – Paul Butler, Chris Lucketti and Dean Kiely. They would have provided a solid base that might offer us a fighting chance of survival.

But Frank's excuses and refusals all boiled down to one thing – we were skint. I could have hustled and haggled and kept supporters' dreams alive for weeks in the hope that the Chairman might win the National Lottery, but I refused to let these loyal boys suffer the insecurities surrounding transfer deals that have no chance of coming off. Reluctantly, I told them to look after themselves and their families the best they could. That didn't include transfers to Turf Moor. Instead, Butler and Kiely went into the Premiership with Sunderland and Charlton and Lucketti is now Preston's commanding centre half.

Frank seemed afraid to admit that any spare cash had already been spent by previous managers on a string of sausages in shorts. As a result, the side I chose to play away at Third Division strugglers Halifax was practically the same team that embarrassed me so painfully in Devon. I had no option.

As we boarded the bus outside the ground and it pulled away, I settled into my usual seat behind the driver and contemplated tactics that might overcome my players' limited ability. Then we turned right instead of left. Did I have to drive the bloody bus as well?

    Me: **Where are we going?**
  Driver: **To pick up a couple of the directors at home.**
    Me: **No we're not.**
  Driver: **But they are expecting us.**
    Me: **Bollocks! We're a professional football team on the way to a match, not a golf club on its fucking Christmas outing!**

We turned round and drove to Yorkshire without those directors. I still don't know how they got to the game. I hope they had to thumb a lift in their best blazers. The place was run like an old buffers' club. I was sickened but not surprised.

During my contract negotiations, I fought to manage every

aspect of the club that came within touching distance of my players, from the selection of hotels to the brand of chewing gum we ordered for the dressing room. To salvage a wreck, attention to detail is vital.

One match day, as I inspected packed lunches loaded on to our coach before a gruelling motorway journey to Bournemouth, I discovered that the tops of our soup flasks were covered with cling-film instead of proper lids. I ordered the driver to take the bus 500 yards around to the main stand, marched up to the kitchens and flung the lot at the chefs.

Picking bits of boiled chicken out of their hair, they heard me say, 'This club revolves around the players on that bus! Do you understand that? Nothing happens here, including jobs for you Gordon Ramsays, if it's not for them. I want them treated like royalty.' Needless to say, the team didn't deserve any of it.

We were winning 3–1 against 10 men with 15 minutes to go at Halifax, but only managed to draw 3–3. It was exactly what happened under Chris Waddle when he needed to win the crucial relegation match at Oldham. I was livid.

When I spoke to the press, it was vital to let the fans know I wouldn't tolerate it like Chris. I ranted, 'It was feeble defending from a load of rubbish. We were abysmal at the back. There's a problem here and it's been here for a while. I'll do something about it, don't worry. I'm not having it. They were like schoolboys. A blind man on a galloping horse could see that we are not improving.'

My point was proved a few days later when we lost 1–0 at non-league Morecambe, and some of the 1,000 Burnley fans had a go at me. 'Bloody rubbish, Ternent. You're worse than Waddle!'

I turned round and had a row. 'It's been rubbish all along and I've still got the same players. Do you think I've got a magic wand, eh?'

To add insult to injury, Morecambe tried to make us pay for the bus to take us home when we'd been doing them a favour. The humiliation was complete. Or so I thought.

A win in our opening league game against Bristol Rovers was marred when Lee Howey came to our dugout after 30 minutes and begged, 'Can you take me off at half-time, I'm knackered.' It was hardly a good omen for the games to follow – our dreaded two-legged Littlewoods Cup tie against Bury.

Terry was out for revenge, and they were now managed by someone I don't get on with, Neil Warnock. In the past, when I was manager of Hull City, Warnock accused one of my players of assaulting him after a game, only to drop the charge when the police were brought in.

Our long-running feud would eventually lead to my biggest punch-up at a professional football match but, for now, it galled me enough that he had inherited the successful Bury team I spent years developing. Worse, he was about to play against my awful new team. We needed a miracle to avoid a mismatch.

We scraped a lucky 1–1 draw at Bury in the first leg, but the return at Turf Moor became a rout. Warnock's team, my old boys, tubbed us 4–1.

During heavy defeats, I deliberately stand at the outer edge of my dugout area, ramrod straight, in full view of the stands. I'll never be accused of hiding. I always walk purposefully to the touchline on these occasions. People mistake my deliberate movements for pride. It's actually caution. I once ran from the dugout to challenge a linesman and slipped on my arse in front of 20,000 people.

As Bury's goals went in, I tried to stand tall. The Bury substitutes warmed up in front of me, taking the piss at full volume. 'He's thinking of putting me on but I don't think he needs me.'

They were stronger mentally and physically and had superior skills. They also had a few breaks. Nicky Daws normally couldn't hit a bull's arse with a shovel. If you put three goals on top of each other he'd usually miss, but that night he bagged a screamer.

When Gordon Armstrong scored for them, he shouted as he ran past me, 'What about that then, gaffer?'

I felt proud of the Bury lads and suicidal about Burnley. As I walked off the pitch, refusing to shake hands with Warnock as usual, I wondered for the hundredth time whether, by swapping sides, I'd made the biggest mistake of my life.

Ironically, secret phone calls I received from some of the Bury players interested in transferring to Turf Moor were the only signs of hope that saved me from complete despair. I knew, as they knew, that Burnley was a bigger club than Bury, but I had to act quickly to turn the team around and avoid complete disaster.

It took me a year to get over that 4–1 defeat.

Thanks to the incompetence of a group of Burnley players, it only took me four more days to find an excuse to stick the boot in and finally sort them out in a way that shocked the whole of the town.

We were losing 1–0 at home to York. The match was awful and the atmosphere matched it. I finally snapped. Propelled by fury, I beat most of the team to the dressing room when the final whistle sounded and waited patiently until they were all inside and the door was closed.

I spoke for two minutes before I left them to their thoughts and marched down the narrow corridor to the press room where hacks were waiting to add another few lines to my obituary. I wouldn't let them speak until I had finished what I had to say first.

'I would like to apologise to the Burnley fans. It is nothing personal. It is business. But Steve Blatherwick, Lee Howey, Mark Winstanley and, to a lesser degree, Michael Williams, because he will never win the fans over, will not play for Burnley Football Club again. We can sink or swim. I will swim and get Burnley where they rightfully belong.'

It was unprecedented. I had just sacked four players live over the airwaves of BBC Radio Lancashire. Minds were focused at last.

The decision was not preconceived, but as the débâcle on the pitch wore on that afternoon, I realised that, if I was ever going to get on with this job, I had to move my arse.

Howey and Blatherwick, two of the defenders brought in by Chris Waddle, were the first to suspect I'd reached a watershed.

I substituted them at half-time, preferring to replace them with Matty Heywood and Chris Scott, two willing but totally inexperienced kids. In front of their team-mates, I told the pair I'd hauled off that they would never play for the club again. I watched as expressions of shock washed around the room like a Mexican wave at a social night for manic depressives.

If I'd thought the referee would permit it, I would have strode to his office during the interval and asked him if I could take all four players off. I would willingly have played the second half with ten men.

After the final whistle, I took Blatherwick and Howey, plus Williams and Winstanley, to an ante-room opposite the referee's area. They had to be in no doubt that they were not good enough.

It was nothing personal. The club needed major surgery. Not just an incision, an amputation. My main responsibility was to the Board and fans. I didn't give a toss how the players reacted. If these four had put their heads down the toilet a few weeks earlier, it would have saved me a job. I felt a few pangs of sympathy for Williams because he was a nice lad. He just wasn't going down well with the crowd. Winstanley, on the other hand, seemed disinterested.

Howey had an unbelievable clause in his contract which allowed him to commute to Burnley on a 70-mile round trip from Harrogate every day, even though he was constantly moaning about his bad back. There was no way I could ever override this clause, even when he sold his house in Yorkshire and started to drive to work each morning from Sunderland!

I wasn't unnecessarily harsh. There was no queue of scouts outside my office desperate to take any of them off my hands. I made my way to the Boardroom immediately after the radio interview to tell the directors what I had done.

I could see they agreed. They would have had to have been

idiots not to. But Clive Holt pointed out, 'Thanks a lot. How are we supposed to sell them now you've publicly devalued them?' I could see some of the directors were developing the impression I was worse than Waddle.

Some fans surprised me with their reactions, too. Burnley supporters can be great, but they can be brazenly two-faced. A few signs of success and they ask me to autograph everything from their packets of Benson and Hedges to pet dogs.

A survey once asked them to choose between a fantasy night out with Stan Ternent or a night with Elvis ... and they picked me.

After my radio revolution, some supporters turned their backs. I was once so pissed off with the players that I locked the dressing room doors and sent them straight back on to the pitch in the rain for the 15-minute half-time interval, telling them, 'Go and stand in front of the people who you've just let down.' I couldn't believe it when a group of fans wrote to the local paper complaining I was being cruel!

What mattered most now was the reaction of the squad. Payton said he'd never seen anything like it. Others thought it caused friction until the day the fired four actually left. I prefer Glen Little's verdict. He admitted, 'We felt sorry for the players because they were our friends, but we knew they weren't good enough.'

I jumped into my motor that night and left for home without a hint of regret, relieved that I had acted on my gut instinct and convinced, finally, that things could not get any worse. I was wrong on so, so many levels.

The reserve team kids I drafted in to shore up my side fought hard for their shirts but their lack of experience sapped our strength.

After a 2–1 defeat at Gillingham, which left us firmly in the bottom half of the table, I tore into the lot of them. To emphasise my disappointment, I booted a 'plastic' litter bin across the dressing room floor. The journey home was excruciating as I tried to hide my agony from the players. The bin wasn't plastic, it was metal, and I'd broken my fucking toe.

As punishment, I resorted to my usual method of torture for the players, slipping my favourite Joseph Locke cassette into the machine in the dashboard and blasting it out at full volume. The lads hate it. Sometimes, after very heavy defeats, I use Boxcar Willie. I always tell them the same thing – 'It comes off when you win another fucking away game.'

The team limped on, earning a point at Manchester City and three for a 4–0 win away at Colchester. But God, and just about everyone else, conspired against us.

Macclesfield beat us 2–1 and, when we were all on the bus ready to leave, my lads Dan and Chris pulled me to one side. Towards the end of the game, my striker Andy Cooke was sent off for a second bookable offence after challenging their defender, Effe Sodje, for a high ball. Sodje performed a triple salco with full pike on his way to the deck and rolled around like he was trying to put out a fire up his arse until the ref had little option but to show Cooke a red card.

Dan and Chris were having a quick pint in the bar afterwards when they overheard Sodje bragging to his mates about Cooke's dismissal. As soon as they told me, I hurtled off the coach to confront him.

He still says 'Good afternoon' to me every time I see him, but I can't help blanking him. I never forget that the livelihoods of my players and their families, plus the fantasies of our fans, are entrusted to me. If people are brave enough to cross me, I take it very personally. I bear grudges as determinedly as David O'Leary bears his suntan. When any team of mine is at war, it is total conflict, and enemies outside the camp must be dealt with brutally.

Unfortunately, in the grand manner of Captain Mainwaring, our own Commander-in-Chief chose this precise moment to fall on his sword.

One winter morning as I arrived at the ground, I was told to go to Frank Teasdale's house, a stable conversion he called 'The Project', on the outskirts of Accrington. I told Sam, 'Get your coat, you're coming, too. Say nothing.' I had no idea why the Chairman needed to see me, but I felt I needed a witness. For all I knew, his place was bugged.

As I made the short journey along the M65, I reflected on my three-month relationship with Frank. He was a shy bachelor who was difficult to get to know. He threw the odd party at his place, centred around his bar and pool table. While his methods of running Burnley FC occasionally left me cold, I was impressed by the fact that he could eat eggs whole without removing the shells.

During a meal at a Chinese restaurant near Blackburn, he challenged one of my coaches, Mick Docherty – son of legendary manager Tommy – to a flower-eating competition. Mick lost when he puked after five.

Frank promised me money; I never got it. He promised me players; I never got them. Our relationship was stressed from the start and we had our blowouts.

Before one away game, all the players had gone to bed and we were in a bar with his co-directors when Frank indulged in another of his weird pastimes, topping other people's stories. If I'd jumped over the moon, he'd done it a week before.

This time, he had been on better, bigger, more expensive holidays than the rest of us put together. I'd had enough.

I said, 'Do you know what, Chairman? You bore the arse off me.'

Around the table, everyone suddenly developed an 'Oh fucking hell' look.

I said, 'We're supposed to be here enjoying a good time, but everything we've done, you've done before.'

Sam's face went bright red. 'I'm going to the toilet,' he said.

'No you're not,' I told him. I knew everyone agreed with me. No one was getting an early bath. They could all sit there and suffer. Frank didn't speak to me for weeks.

In fact, our sudden meeting at his house that morning was to be the most meaningful chat we'd had in a long time. It seemed quite obvious to me he had been in tears.

'I'm quitting,' he said.

I knew the club was losing £10,000 a week; the team were losing more games than we were winning and fans had targeted him personally. Weeks ago, some toe-rag had blocked his gas flue with bricks and tried to poison him. A police officer was posted outside his front door. Most Burnley supporters thought he had a double-barrelled surname – Teasdale-Out. Despite all this, I was stunned by his decision to go.

He repeated, 'Stan, I'm packing it in.'

I said, 'I've only been here for three months of a three-year contract. Where does that leave me?'

Frank offered to amend my contract so that I could walk away at the same time as him with full pay. He said, 'I want to look after you. I'll get the Board to agree.'

He didn't have to do it, but I would have been a fool not to accept. For weeks, however, he failed to act on his promise to quit. I became uncertain. How did he expect me to encourage players to fight for their careers, not knowing from one match to the next if the Chairman was going to pack his bags?

The fans left him in no doubt. After a miserable home draw against Notts County, supporters held a protest sit-in at the ground. Their anger was aimed directly at Frank. They knew he had no vast personal wealth. And they resented it.

His fellow directors equally lacked huge wads of spare cash to pump into the club. They spent the duration of the demonstration tucked up in the Boardroom.

I sent my players out to warm down and, as the police moved away the last yelling stragglers, we applauded the supporters. I ached to tell them salvation could be at hand. My sources had informed me that a wealthy local printing magnate called Barry Kilby was pondering a take-over.

Time would tell if he was to be the man to save Burnley, but time was running out for Frank who, despite his best intentions, patently had no resources to improve my third-rate team.

A nightmare 4–1 hammering at Preston, which could easily have been 10–0, illustrated the gulf between us and one of our closest neighbours. I was so angry and self-absorbed I sped away in my car after the final whistle and completely forgot to take Kath home with me.

A further defeat to Stoke was followed by an FA Cup tie away at Third Division Darlington. Unbelievably, disastrously, vomit-inducingly, after leading 2–0 with ten minutes to go, we lost 3–2. Throughout my career, I had never worked with such a spineless bunch.

I travelled home that evening to speak to my family, intent on packing the lot in. They talked me round, but the inner strength and mental toughness which had sustained me through over 30 years of turmoil in football was being painfully leeched by each performance.

For a trip to Bournemouth that weekend, I tried to revitalise things by signing a new goalkeeper, Paul Crichton.

The game was goalless at half-time. Not bad. As I barged into the dressing room, I recalled one match at Turf Moor when I was still boss at Bury. I'd been stunned to hear one of the Burnley backroom staff shout at their winger Paul Smith, 'Smithy! They're taking the piss out of you. They're laughing at you!'

I don't believe in humiliation as a motivational factor. So, face to face with my players as I paced the room at Bournemouth, I yelled, I cuddled, I motivated, I cajoled, I inspired, I instructed, I reminded, I enforced, I cuddled some more and I told them to go out and play with a chuckle in their boots.

We *lost* 5–0.

It was now, officially, hopeless. If they were not humiliated, I was.

I became convinced that one of my centre-halves was colour blind. The other one, presumably, was just blind. Our young players desperately needed help but the senior players' arses had dropped out. If we didn't get in a few new faces within weeks, the team would be dead.

Players only work for 69 hours a season. That's the total time they play competitive football. If they can't be ready for that, they don't deserve a shirt.

I was strung out, and when Glen Little shouted across the dressing room afterwards to our new keeper, 'Nice debut, Crichts!' I took the only course of action left open to me – I hit him over the head with a bottle. It wasn't the first time I'd battered Glen.

One morning, during training in the Turf Moor gym, he'd got the hump with a refereeing decision I'd made and it was ruining the session. I told him, 'Go on, get out.'

Little booted open a metal emergency exit door which slammed back against a brick wall and crashed loudly. A dozen people in the car park outside turned to stare.

'Get him back, now,' I told his mates, but Glen refused to return.

I wasn't having my authority flouted in front of witnesses. I barged outside, caught him by the arm and clipped him around the head. 'Get back in there, you t**t!'

He did.

Now, on the coach journey home from Bournemouth, I felt a similar sense of fury fermenting.

I overheard one of the players I'd inherited, a midfielder called Mark Ford, brag to the other lads about his days at Leeds United. He gave it large ones about how he'd played with David Batty and other stars. He went on ... and on ... and on.

I had a word in front of his mates. 'If you're so good, what are you doing swanning around the old Third Division then, eh?' Ford had cost Burnley £250,000, a small fortune, but he was never above mediocre. 'What exactly can you do?' I asked him. 'What strengths have you got? Can you pass? Can you head? Are you quick? Can you beat three men at once? Do you score 20 goals a season? The answer is no, no, no, no and no in my opinion, pal. What exactly do you give us' I was sick of makeweights crippling the club.

Back home in Burnley, I rang Vinnie Jones who was playing for

QPR and he offered to pop up and see us. 'You could do with the Jones boy,' he said.

In truth, at that point I would have paid Vinnie out of my own pocket to set him loose among my lot for just five minutes during training. Life at Turf Moor would have driven him potty. It was infested with weak characters incapable of dealing with first class professionals like Jonah. I wouldn't have minded him as a bodyguard.

On the run-up to Christmas, my personal stock in Burnley was lower than a man at a wedding in a Blackburn Rovers top hat. In the seventies I had become one of the Football League's youngest managers when, aged 32, I took over from Bob Stokoe at Blackpool. There were more rats than traps behind the scenes, all of them trying to run that club and I was soon thrown out so they could bring back local hero, Alan Ball.

Their fans never forgot me though. When I walked past them before we played Blackpool at Turf Moor one lad, showing more accuracy than any of their strikers, gobbed straight in my face.

I lurched forward and tried to knock him out. A steward, who did nothing to stop the dirty sod gobbing in the first place, restrained me, so I spat my chewing gum back into the crowd. Typically, the moron escaped and I was reported to the FA, who fined me £500. To save my neck, I was advised to say that I'd coughed and the gum came out accidentally. But I refused to lie. It would have been some cough. It travelled 20 feet!

I'm commonly covered in spit at Turf Moor. The players' tunnel at Burnley is in the middle of the 'away' end making it the only ground in Britain where the home team gets booed on. Animal scum among visiting fans gob at me so often I need a rub-down with the magic sponge before we even kick off.

After we lost 2-0 at home to Northampton three weeks later, when were booed *off* as well as on, some of our own fans started to stick the knife in, too.

Any sucess the club has enjoyed over the years is *despite* some sections of the Turf Moor crowd. Ninety-nine per cent of supporters are blinding and will follow us through thick and thin. The rest are dickheads. Even if God Almighty was manager with the Holy Spirit sat beside him in the dugout, they wouldn't be happy.

One bloke strode up to me one afternoon in a garden centre and said, 'Bit of a struggle on Saturday, Stan.'

'You what?'

Luckily for him, I had a 10ft Christmas tree over my shoulder or I would have speared him with a pruning fork. If I had walked into his factory and told him his work was shite he would have told me to get stuffed. Quite right, too.

I don't mind criticism from the stands on match days. I'm paid to run the gauntlet for those 90 minutes. But suddenly I caught flak from all sides. Kath bought a sandwich for her lunch when she overheard a bloke in the queue say, 'That Ternent will have to go.'

To cap it all, the next morning I found a letter on my office desk. It read:

Dear Stan,

I think you set a disgusting example to juveniles who are in a sporting arena to witness excellence yet are subjected to the sight of you smoking on the touchline. I have a 14-year-old son and I've been trying to steer him away from the vice of tobacco.People like you are a disgrace.

I replied:

Bollocks.
Love Stan.

I enjoy smoking. I always spray aftershave on my hands after a tab to get rid of the smell, and I can bum fags for England. I haven't bought a packet in 22 years! But I refuse to be lectured by politically correct prats. I tried to give them up once at Bury but my players got so sick of my vile temper they requested a team meeting and begged me to start smoking again, even if they had to pay. The odd tab was the only activity keeping me sane at Burnley.

One morning, I took my last drag on a Silk Cut and flicked it out of my first floor office window.

Moments later, I heard a commotion in the club shop directly below. I barged downstairs to find a fan shouting, 'Some bastard's set my hair on fire!' My discarded fag had landed on his head and I admitted it. 'Oh, was it you, Gaffer?' he asked. 'That's alright then.' He smiled, patted his hair out and left. In the light of all this stress, I still wonder to this day why I accepted an offer to switch on the town's Christmas lights.

I awoke on the morning of the big day to an encouraging start. Sports journalists at the *Burnley Express* had chosen that very moment to question my judgement, and even my appointment. Their jibes didn't hurt and I would enjoy ramming them back down their throats, but I ought to have felt a jolt of unease as I drove into town that evening to be a VIP.

The second bad omen of the day greeted me as I emerged from my car. I was met by a 10ft-tall Postman Pat with a prat inside trying to shake my hand.

As I clambered on to a bandstand in the centre of the shopping arcade to throw the switch, the crowd offered me their own heartfelt Christmas welcome. 'BOOOOO!' 'Fuck off, Ternent!' 'BOOOOO!' 'Fuck off back to Bury!'

Call it the season of goodwill? I stood there like a lemon next to Postman Pat while half of Burnley abused me. I thought, This is the job for me, all right!

If I hadn't had my nephew alongside me, I would have waded

in and knocked the lot of them out. The majority of the idiots were typical Burnley chip-eaters who pay the same attention to the club whether we are winning or losing – none.

As I finally escaped to The Kettledrum for a last-orders pint, I received the important news of the day ... Frank Teasdale, Chairman of Burnley Football Club for 13½ years had finally, irrevocably, quit.

Over the previous ten years, apart from a disastrous season in Division One, Burnley had crawled out of the Fourth Division and reached the final of the Sherpa Van Trophy. Not much reward for a lot of time and effort. The club's legacy had been squandered. It was a relief for Frank to get out. He wanted the best for BFC but it had clearly not worked out. As well as vandalism from fans at home, his car had been scratched, too.

He didn't deserve the dog's life he had led at the end of his stint. He is a loyal Burnley fan who still attends games, but the club's future was in doubt. It didn't need another fan. It needed finance.

Frank's successor was the man I'd been tipped off about, Barry Kilby, a softly-spoken entrepreneur who had made his fortune printing promotional cards and lottery products for *The Sun* during the 1970s and '80s. If he hadn't taken over, the club would have foundered and I would have quit.

Kilby vied with Ray Ingleby, an American-based financier, for overall control of the club and won. The pair of them promised to work in partnership. Almost immediately, their wallets were out.

After spending £75,000 on bit-part players over my first six months, I was able to bid £750,000 to land Steve Davis, a towering centre-half who had spent his early career at Burnley before moving to Luton when he tired of underachievement.

I drove to a hotel in Chester where I met with Steve, his agent and Barry. Immediately, Davis told us he wanted better wages than Burnley were currently paying. I prayed that Barry would be brave. He wanted time to think. In my view, it was a no-risk signing and I would be seriously brassed off if we missed out on the man I wanted to make my captain.

While he deliberated, I took a call from Charlie Woods, a scout at Spurs at the time, who currently works for Bobby Robson at Newcastle. He said, 'What about that guy Steve Davis ... he used to play for Burnley, didn't he?'

I went cold. We had to act quickly. If Charlie got his hooks into Steve about a move to White Hart Lane, I knew I could not compete. This was a vital signing if I was ever to start encouraging the Burnley fans.

'He's not quick enough for you,' I blurted out.

When Davis signed on *my* dotted line 24 hours later, Charlie called me at home to congratulate me. 'You crafty bastard,' he said.

Unopposed by Charlie, I also signed Mickey Mellon from Blackpool and Lenny Johnrose, one of my old boys from Bury. All of them were strong men with enough aggression to motivate the rest of the players and start extricating us from the relegation zone.

Barely two days after he arrived at Turf Moor, Johnrose was aghast. He told me, 'I'm amazed. Everything I ever heard about Burnley was that it was a big club. But it ... it's shocking here.'

Johnrose knew me well. I can excuse players not being brilliant; I cannot excuse them for not trying. Yet over the next nine matches, with his help, we were only beaten twice. We won away at Bristol Rovers and Millwall. My team began to achieve at last.

With the prospect of three consecutive home games looming against Gillingham, Manchester City and Preston, I imagined we'd emerge comfortably in mid-table, with the débâcle of the opening to our season becoming a very distant memory. It wasn't too much to ask. Surely?

Apparently it was.

After the first two matches, I left my dugout in shock, mortified by performances which threatened to end my career in shame and make the club I love a laughing stock.

When Gillingham walked out to face us at Turf Moor on a blustery February afternoon, we had not won at home for seven games. Even so, I was not too worried. They were pushing hard for a play-off spot against more fancied teams, but I felt my players had begun to understand the levels of effort and dedication I required over 90 minutes. I accepted that none of them would break into the England set-up in the very near future. Pure footballing skill is a gift from God. But fitness can be acquired and maintained. Over my first six months, I'd worked them hard.

I obeyed my instincts and shipped out the remnants of the previous backroom staff. Gordon Cowans was removed as coach and I told ex-Everton player Alan Harper that he was no longer required to run my youth teams.

Instead, I recruited a family of ex-Burnley players to run the club. Jimmy Robson, who played for Burnley in the 1962 FA Cup Final against Spurs and scored the hundredth goal in a cup final at Wembley, joined as a coach. I also appointed Mick Docherty, a young full-back at Turf Moor in the days when we were dubbed 'the team of the Seventies', to work with the youth teams.

I was in management with Doc at Hull. He was a scrapper. I admired his fighting spirit although he could go over the top. On one away trip as we arrived at the ground, he stood up at the front of the bus and gave an inspirational speech to the players that Churchill would have been proud of, and then dismounted with a flourish.

I got off after him. 'Can a manager not take his own team off the bus?' I asked.

Doc burbled, 'I was only trying to ...'

'Never mind that,' I said 'I'm the manager. I get off the fucking bus first.'

Despite his over-enthusiasm, I like Doc. His balls are so big he needs saddlebags on his jockstrap.

Doc was alongside me and Sam in the dugout as we kicked off against the Gills to spur on the team.

By the final whistle, we were hoarse. We had also been beaten 5–0. Their veteran striker Bob Taylor scored all five and by the end of the game sections of our fans applauded him, which pissed me right off.

Our dressing room afterwards was quiet. Too quiet. I wanted to walk in and find players arguing and rolling around on the floor punching each other. At least that would have showed they felt the drubbing as keenly as I did. Instead, there was only one emotion on display as they sat with their shoulders hunched.

Fear.

I didn't rant. It would have been like kicking puppies. All their inadequacies were exposed. They were raw, they were humbled and, worst of all, they were going to have to return to that dressing room for their next game in ten days' time, against Manchester City.

I suffer fierce mood swings if my professional life threatens to spiral out of control. The first morning we were due back in training, I tore into my family over breakfast like a pitbull.

I live 15 minutes' drive away from the training ground so, as I often do, I took a 30-minute detour to help clear my head. Kath, as she often does, telephoned Sam and warned him of my mental state.

When I barged on to the training pitch, the players scattered to their positions. More fear.

We worked hard on defensive discipline over the following days. There was no point inventing daft Christmas tree formations for my lot. In order to succeed at any level of football, you have to adapt your game to your players' abilities, not the other way round.

We concentrated on basic tactical awareness and tried to solidify the starting 11 as a unit which would not crumble and could, perhaps, threaten City in their vulnerable defensive regions.

Come the night, come the kick-off. Wallop. Thump. Whack. Hat-trick. Screamer. Prod. We lost 6–0.

When I walked the 20 yards between our dugouts after the final whistle to shake hands with the Manchester City manager, my old pal Joe Royle, I was dazed.

He gave me a hug and said, 'I'd rather it had been anyone but you, Stan.'

I hardly heard a word.

Of the fans who had waited until the end, those who didn't boo me looked on in pity, as though my budgie had just died. I glanced up to Kath in the directors' box. Her face was full of pain. I tried to reassure her with a little nod that I would be all right, but I didn't even believe it myself.

I thought about my sons. Those lads have taken abuse all their lives because of my job and, once more, I knew I would need to warn them not to go drinking in the town centre for weeks for fear that some moron might take his disappointment out on them.

I made my way towards the tunnel to find it surrounded at the entrance by jubilant Manchester City fans singing, 'Can we play you every week?'

I glanced into our dressing room and registered a scene of desolation and mayhem. The players were animated at last but, despite all the noise, nobody admitted any part in the fiasco. They stood around and pointed at each other. They shouted. They bawled. They accused each other of cocking it up.

I closed the door and made my way down a narrow passageway running under the stand towards my office. There was no escape from the noise of joyful City supporters. Every insult could be heard clearly at top volume through wafer-thin cladding on the roof and walls.

Beckoning Sam inside with me, I sat down heavily, opened a beer from the fridge and gave him my verdict. 'Go and get the Chairman ... I'm calling it a day.'

Sam, almost in tears himself with frustration at the night's events, tried his best to look surprised but I knew he feared, along with some of the senior players, that I had taken too much punishment. Perhaps I wanted success too much.

He tried to persuade me to stay. 'You can't do this.'

I could. I had to. I was overwhelmed by a sense of honour which meant I felt obliged to offer Barry the chance to ditch me. I wasn't his choice, after all.

Stand by your man, sings Tammy Wynette.

Only I wasn't Barry's man and it ate away at me. I wasn't prepared to continue in the job if the Chairman and his Board privately felt the same about inheriting me as I did when I inherited Waddle's team.

'I've got to go,' I insisted. 'I owe it to them. It's time for someone else.'

Sam continued to plead. 'It's the players who are letting you down. There just isn't any quality here. If you go you'll let me down and the others you have brought in. Get your tin helmet on and go and face the barrage. You and I know you'll get it right if you have time.'

I was knackered. Only a season ago I was labelled 'Fergie of the Nationwide League' after achieving a miracle double promotion at penniless Bury.

Deep within me, I knew I had the guts and ability to do the same for Burnley. But 11 goals against in two home games allowed for doubt on the part of others.

'Listen, Sam, go and get the Chairman, eh?'

He left reluctantly and my lad Chris came to see me. We talked about things. He was proud of me. I smiled in gratitude but, when Barry arrived, Chris patted me on the shoulder and left.

'You wanted to see me, Stan?'

'Listen, Chairman,' I began, 'I'm not your appointment. If you want a new face, you have that right and I'd fully understand.'

He didn't reply. I hoped he appreciated that I was making it easy for him. I could have showered, changed and driven home that night, happy to sit tight and wait for the sack. Financially, it would have made more sense. By offering my head on a plate, I made it clear if he wanted rid, I would not be difficult to deal with.

I would do a deal that wouldn't paralyse the club.

Barry remained silent. Thinking.

I spoke again. 'Look, Chairman, if you say the word, I'll be off. But I don't *want* to leave, you know. Give me a chance and I'll turn it around.' I wasn't pleading for my job. I don't beg. I was simply stating a fact.

Barry said, 'See me tomorrow,' and walked out.

The next morning, I drove to his company HQ in Blackburn. A photographer hid in the bushes to take my picture as I walked alone like a condemned man up the drive to the Chairman's office. The picture appeared in that night's paper under the headline TERNENT TO BE SACKED.

Once inside, our meeting was over in minutes. Barry told me, 'I'll get back to you. Give me a day.'

In fact, it took a little longer. He went to London on business and called a Board meeting in plush offices behind the Hilton Hotel on Park Lane, the first time our directors had ever met officially outside Burnley.

Signs of a revolt appeared. There were mutterings around the table about ditching me to recruit a big name but there were enough dissenting voices who supported stability. Burnley had been notorious for changing managers over recent years. Between 1958 and 1976, the club employed two bosses. Since 1977 they had had 13.

Barry did his homework. He even consulted a group of senior players and asked them for their verdict on my reign, and our possible future together.

I don't know who the Chairman talked to in the dressing room but it worked. My job was declared safe. When the flak had begun to fly, Barry had been strong.

I called a press conference immediately and came straight to the point. 'Resigning never crossed my mind. I have no intention of stepping down. I am still the man for the job. I'm not walking away with it unfinished, like Chris Waddle and

Adrian Heath. I came here to do a job, and you don't become a bad manager overnight.

'I had no control over the decision the Chairman and the Board have made. What did concern me was that if the Chairman didn't back me, I couldn't do the job. But he *has* backed me and I appreciate that. I'm the man for the job and I believe I will turn this club around. In fact, I guarantee it.'

Other managers telephoned to express their support for me. Joe Royle re-emphasised, 'Stan, it was business, you know that. Not personal.'

Five days later, another set of play-off candidates, Preston North End, arrived at Turf Moor ... and duly left with three points after a wonder-goal from their ex-Burnley striker Kurt Nogan.

But our performance was better. Sections of our more objective fans even began to appreciate it. Others didn't.

In a bizarre protest against me, my son Dan was dropped from his local pub football team in favour of a 16st bloke who could hardly bend down to tie his own boots.

I was out walking on the outskirts of Burnley one afternoon when a bus, packed with passengers, screeched to a halt beside me. The driver tooted his horn, wound down his window and leaned out towards me.

'Oi, Ternent. I wouldn't have your job for a gold clock,' he said as he engaged first gear and rumbled off.

Radio phone-ins held 60-minute debates over whether I ought still to be in work. Even worse, live on Granada TV, a presenter called Elton Welsby openly touted my job.

During an interview with Steve McMahon on a Sunday afternoon football highlights show, he asked, 'Burnley are having a bad run. I have heard that Stan could be going. Is that the kind of job you'd be interested in?'

To his credit, Steve, who was in an impossible position, ducked the answer. Quite right, too. Fellow managers – most of them anyway – do not apply for jobs that are already occupied.

Later, after our penultimate game of the season, at Wigan, I bumped into Welsby, who had the bare-faced cheek to ask me to appear as a pundit on his crappy show.

I tried to be diplomatic.

'Will I BOLLOCKS!'

* * *

'There's something uneasy down at the club, Stan.'

I said, 'Yes, it's probably our back four.'

Kath and I tucked miserably into an Indian curry three hours after Preston had become the third club in a row to beat us at home.

She stared at me across the kitchen table, deadly serious.

'I haven't liked the feeling down there since the first day you took over,' she went on. 'There are evil comments during games. Just a nasty spirit about the place. I can't explain it, but we need to do something.'

Kath is not a religious fanatic, prone to hysterical over-reactions. She thought deeply about the problems we faced and came to the conclusion that factors outside football might help.

I have superstitions. For three years I have worn the same pair of socks on match days. I stole them off my lad Dan because they have 'LUCKY' stitched around the ankles. They work ... sometimes.

What Kath suggested went way beyond superstitious rituals.

I looked up and mumbled, 'I think I know how I can get my hands on some Holy water.'

'That's the stuff,' she said, matter-of-factly.

The rest of the meal passed in silence.

We had formed a small alliance, half-afraid of being condemned for being daft, but exhilarated at the prospect of a positive gesture to end nine months of misery.

It took me two days to acquire a five-gallon container of water from Lourdes. I struggled to carry it through the kitchen where we both sat and stared at it after wedging it in a cupboard under our microwave oven.

Eventually, Kath poured half a pint of it into an empty milk bottle and gripped it firmly as she climbed into my car so I could drive us both to Turf Moor.

It was a Tuesday afternoon and fine drizzle slanted across the pitch. Apart from a handful of office staff, the place was deserted.

We climbed the stairs to my office. Instead of tuning right into the ante-room used by Sam and Chief Scout Cliff Roberts, we continued down the passage and emerged into the stadium itself alongside the police's match day control point.

We strolled around the outer edge of the playing area for minutes as we debated what to do next.

Ought I to say some sort of prayer? Instead, we sprinkled the water around the centre circle, both goalmouths and on the spot next to my dugout where I normally stand and chain-smoke.

Back home, an hour later, I found a small sherry glass and placed it on the windowsill behind our sink. I resolved to drink a mouthful of Lourdes water before every match for the rest of my career.

The following Saturday, we travelled to Wrexham. Before Sam picked me up to meet the team coach, I gulped down mouthfuls of the six-year-old Lourdes water. It tasted fresh. And we got a point.

Next game – home win. Next game – away point. Next game – home win. Next game – away point. And so it went on. Was somebody smiling on us?

We won 2–0 at Blackpool.

We won 4–1 at play-off-chasing Stoke City where the new-found spirit of the side was embodied by Ally Pickering, who was desperate to play and scored a 20-yard screamer in the same week he'd had to bury his father. When he ran to the bench, although it is not normally my thing, I hugged him senseless.

We beat runaway league leaders Fulham 1–0 to confirm we were staying up.

It was implausible, but we were unbeaten for the final 11 games of the season. My side was showing promotion form and finished almost in mid-table, five points clear of the drop.

On most days we could have been beaten by any Raggy-Arsed Rovers. I couldn't sleep and I wasn't used to that.

It had been close, too close. Without the amazing run-in, we would have been relegated by April. It was the water. It was the players who were getting stronger, taking shape as a squad. It was the ghosts of Burnley Football Club refusing to allow yet another humiliation. Most of all, it was my trusted ability to forge a fighting unit in my own image.

It took Bobby Robson five years to go grey when he was manager of England. For me, one traumatic season at Burnley was enough.

Without doubt, it was the toughest spell of my career. The relief I felt when we survived was as tangible as the joy I experienced when I had previously won promotions.

It had been a horrible 12 months. I'd cleared some shite out, at least 14 players. But was it the worst period of my career?

Nah!

3

'It's Only an Hour up the Road ...'

BURNLEY, 1962–68

I first knew Ralph Coates when he had hair. Not much, I admit. But more than the flowing string vest that passed for his barnet when he was flying down the wing for Spurs in the Seventies.

We were both 16 and had been thrown into bed together like Eric and Ernie in our first official digs. Along with Willie Morgan and Sammy Todd, we formed the intake of groundstaff at Burnley in 1962, the year they reached the FA Cup Final at Wembley. We shared a damp room on the top floor of a freezing terraced house on the outskirts of town. The landlady, a plump widow, met us at the front door after we'd made our way to her home from the railway station.

'No girls or I'll tell the club. No drink or I'll tell the club. None of your own food. Make your beds. Be in by 8.00pm weekdays, 11.00pm weekends. No smoking or I'll tell the club. I don't have a TV. No music. Hope you enjoy it. I'll show you to your room.'

As we trailed behind her through the kitchen, in contrast to her sparse reception, a mouthwatering smell of roast chicken wafted from the oven. The thought of a heartening meal stopped us breaking down completely when we were shown into a threadbare attic room with three beds and a hole in the roof. We'd barely had time to unpack before we heard our new hostess's forbidding cry, 'Tea's ready!'

We were so hungry we crushed into an unruly conga line as we fought to get out of the bedroom door and be first down the stairs to sink our teeth into succulent chicken breast with all the trimmings.

She waited, poised over her kettle. 'Tea?'

We were speechless.

'Go on then, eat. There's beef spread on those butties, salmon spread on those and the sandwiches over there have a bit of tomato on them.'

We picked mournfully at the bread as all of us, simultaneously, missed home.

Where had the bloody chicken gone? We knew landladies employed by the club were given a budget to feed apprentices. Surely Burnley could afford more than fish paste and Hovis?

Back in our rooms, we were overcome by hunger pangs and became obsessed with the missing chicken. We were starving.

A door slammed. Coates raced to the window and peered out into the early evening gloom.

'It's her, she's gone,' he mumbled.

He wandered back to where we all sat. After a few seconds of silence, we gradually met each other's gaze. Chicken time!

It wasn't in the oven. It wasn't on the table.

Perhaps she's taken the bloody thing with her, I thought. Maybe that's what people do in Burnley.

It wasn't in the dining room. There were no bones in the bin so she couldn't have eaten it yet. A small, shelved cold store doubling as a parlour boasted a few jars of some unidentifiable slush – probably our fish paste – but no bird.

We split up to search the rest of the house.

Moments later, Coates yelled, 'Lads, in here!'

He'd had the task of searching the landlady's bedroom and struck gold under her bed.

'Have a look,' he said.

We got on all fours, lifted the bedspread that trailed on the floor and craned our necks to see under the dusty frame.

'Bloody hell.'

There was the freshly cooked chicken, safe from our hungry mouths in the only place she knew we would never dare venture.

It sat right in the middle of her pisspot.

I spent my first month in Burnley dreaming of sausage sandwiches. Most Saturday nights back home in Felling-on-Tyne, across the river from Newcastle, they were reserved as my special treat.

I was born in Gateshead in 1946 but, because of my dad Mick's allegiance, I was never going to be anything other than a Sunderland fan. After each match at Roker Park we made our way home to our modest terraced house to the familiar theme of the BBC's *Sports Report* blaring from the radio and the biggest butties imaginable waiting for us, dripping with onions, gravy and melted butter. Mam Peggy knew we needed them to maintain our energy levels.

Match days at Sunderland were exhausting expeditions. The day began as Dad heaved me on to his shoulders to carry me to a graveyard near Heworth. He'd plonk me down on a stone wall and disappear around the corner to a pub called The Swan. Like my mam, Dad didn't drink. Never touched a drop. But outside the pub was the best place to blag a lift to the ground.

For too many people in the North-East in the early 1950s, cars were a luxury they could not afford. At least five hours before kick-off, a huge scrum of more than 70 supporters would gather at The Swan, throwing themselves at any passing vehicles heading remotely near the ground.

'Are you ganning to Roker Park, mate?'

'Gi'us a lift then!'

'Ah, bollocks to ya.'

If Dad succeeded and scrounged a free ride, he would dash back to collect me and throw me into the back seat. His next job was to persuade the unsuspecting driver to give us a lift back to The Swan afterwards.

I still cringe when I recall the image of Dad emerging from the car as we arrived at the ground and shouting to the driver, 'Right, mate, what time are we setting off back?'

If no one stopped to offer us a lift, and kick-off ticked closer, Dad threw me back on to his shoulders and carried me the whole nine miles to the ground.

Once inside Roker Park, he sheltered me with his arms as we fought our way through crowds of over 60,000 towards a huge wooden fence at the back of the Fulwell End. After he planted me down, Dad, who was deaf in one ear, would yell, 'Now stand still until I come back for you,' before he disappeared deeper into a swarming throng of flat caps.

Once alone, I used to strain my neck to try to read a programme through a fog of tobacco smoke over the shoulders of men in front of me before I soaked up the performances of legends like Len Shackleton, Stan Anderson, Charlie Hurley and Charlie 'Cannon Ball' Fleming .

If Sunderland played away, we made the short journey to watch Newcastle United instead.

After matches at St James's Park, we would emerge to meet my mam, who worked in a store nearby. Together with my sister Kathleen, we would race into the steaming warmth of Bower's fish and chip restaurant for our tea. When the feast was over, Kathleen and Mam buzzed off home while Dad took me to St James's, just around the corner from the Newcastle ground, to watch Les Kellett and the terrifying Mask knock each other senseless during thrilling wrestling shows.

In my adolescence, pleasure became synonymous with football. I devoured match action each weekend over winter as much as I savoured our family time in the hours either side of kick-off.

During the week, I saw little of my dad. He was off to work by 7.30am as a cabinet-maker for a company in Pelaw, so, despite his best attentions on Saturday afternoons, I was forced to find other company outside the school gates.

I knew my parents disapproved of some of my pals but, at the age of 12 and 13, who listens?

None of us ever imagined it would end in police cells and death.

Temptation to stray first struck me on the way home from school one night when I played around on a slagheap with three friends, looking for fun.

Half buried in the dirt we found a wage packet bursting with cash. Quickly leafing the fresh notes with our grubby fingers, we realised we had discovered £28, a treasure haul for a bunch of North-East lads in the days when a portion of chips cost a few pennies.

We weren't completely without morals and took it, eventually, to the police station ... but not without first removing a four quid finders' fee.

I kept my pound share under some oilcloth at home. It didn't stay hidden for long. We blew the lot and spent a full week holed up in the anonymous gloom of the local cinema.

We were horrified when the ungrateful sod whose wage we had recovered realised he was a few quid down and complained. I was collared, along with my mates, and sent home by the police with a bollocking.

Dad, normally a calm and phlegmatic man, was horrified. He could tolerate all sorts of hassle from his kids, but when his patience was stretched too far, he would knock you out. When he heard I'd helped myself to another working man's hard-earned money, he took to me with his belt and gave me a right good pasting.

It didn't stop the stakes getting higher. I was a hard-nut. I had an evening job selling sports papers called 'Pinks' on street corners at weekends in Felling. I was always happy to scrap for the best pitches.

I got roped into a burglary. I was told that if I didn't join one raid on a factory as lookout, then they would end any hopes I had of a career in football.

'If you run off, we'll break your legs.'

Later, I helped to steal a dumper truck with some mates but we were caught and I found myself locked in police cells. My parents despaired. Once again, I felt the sting of the belt.

Soon after, my pal Darkie Smith ensured that my life beyond the despairing reach of my mam and dad was over for good.

We used to cycle near the banks of the Tyne – me, Darkie, Eddie Heads, Alec Cassey and Bunter Russell, a bulky lad who used to row ferries across the river. Like demented fools, we charged around on our pushbikes, trying to knock each other off as we hared along pathways close to the river.

We found a steep hill which led down to the water. We made a pact. We pushed our rusty second-hand cycles to the top of the slope, climbed into the saddle and took it in turns to career downwards. At the bottom, faced by a low wall, we slung our bikes to one side and ourselves to the other. The dare, without using brakes, was to get as close to the wall as possible before jumping for our lives.

Time and again, we sped down the hill, legs outstretched as we yelled and shouted. As Darkie made his way to the top for his fifth or sixth attempt, I sat to one side on the wall at the foot of the slope to watch his progress.

Down he came. He raced over the grass. There were no brakes. Not allowed in our game. I'm not sure his bike even had them. Closer to the edge, perhaps the closest of us all. Yes!!!

But he didn't jump. Darkie clung desperately to the handlebars and scraped his feet into the ground. He left it too late. He crashed into the wall at a section where the brickwork was loose and much lower than elsewhere. His bike juddered through the gap and he disappeared over the other side.

Stunned, we raced to the wall and peered over. Darkie was in the freezing water. His bike had already been carried away by the roaring current. We pelted down a set of steps leading to the water's edge and stumbled and slipped on mossy patches as we frantically tried to reach him.

'Darkie! Darkie!'

He was gone.

The rest of us stared, shaking and plainly terrified. We began to shout at each other, panicking, unable to believe what had happened thanks to a stupid game.

Our best pal drowned in front of our eyes.

In bed that night, I cried for Darkie, my next-door neighbour on the Stoneygate estate. I'm not afraid to admit that I cried for myself, too.

I became devoted to football. On the field, I could at least wipe away the memory of seeing Darkie die.

Each Saturday morning, I ran out for the school, or the town team when I was picked. In my teens, I played for St Mary's Boys Club in Newcastle, one of the best young sides in the area.

On Sundays, we were up early so Dad, a devout Catholic, could go to church at St Patrick's. Then we jumped on a bus so I could turn out for teams at either Bluebell or the Catholic club, Knights of Saint Columba.

We were home by 1.00pm – via Dragonni's ice cream parlour – when Mam was expected to have dinner on the table. After the grub, everyone else would go to the pub while Dad insisted on a two-hour afternoon kip.

I was an uncompromising player, physically strong, even at 15. I forced myself to be fierce in the tackle. Bravery is an underrated quality on a football pitch. I would never back off in a challenge, and if someone came looking for me during those 90 minutes, I tracked them. I was merciless. I learned to bear grudges on those Saturday mornings. I also made my reputation.

Newcastle watched me on half-a-dozen occasions. They took me on trial to St James's Park and manager Joe Harvey begged me to sign a contract. I had offers from Preston, West Bromwich Albion and Middlesbrough.

As I considered my future, a railway clerk at Newcastle Central Station knocked on our front door and changed my life for ever.

'Hello, Mr Ternent,' he said to my dad, 'I'm Jack Hixon.'

He sat down in our front room, adjusted his crumpled raincoat and opened a dossier on me that he had been collecting for months.

'I've been watching your lad,' he said. 'What I see is sheer footballing intelligence. He has the ability of someone twice his age to understand the game. He seems to have lots of heart.

'I like the way the opposition are afraid to get on the wrong side of him, physically or mentally. I like his aggression. He's a winner, a competitor. He lets people know about their faults and, if they disagree, he's after them. He lacks one thing – pace, but we can cope with that.'

My dad shuffled his feet, full of pride, but taken aback.

He asked Jack, 'Where are you from?'

'Me?' answered Jack. 'I'm chief scout at Burnley.'

So that was it.

Burnley had just missed out on winning the double, beaten in the Cup Final by Spurs, and pipped to the title by Ipswich on the last day of the season.

They were winners of the old First Division Championship just two years earlier and quarter-finalists in the European Cup. Their captain Jimmy Adamson was the current Footballer of the Year and Jimmy McIlroy, their Northern Irish star, was runner-up in the same competition.

Burnley were a huge club in the early 1960s and Jack was their favourite and most trusted spy in the North-East. Hixon scoured the region on Burnley's behalf, spotting schoolboys and packing them off to the North-West to embarrass the bigger clubs from his own area who had missed them. Brian O'Neil, Dave Thomas, Les Latcham, Arthur Bellamy and Dave Merrington all got their breaks at Turf Moor through Jack. At one stage in 1963, the Burnley reserve team sent to play a league match at Newcastle contained 11 Geordies.

Later, Jack would become a modern-day legend after signing up another Geordie, a 12-year-old called Alan Shearer, for Southampton. As a sign of his thanks, Shearer later presented him with his first England shirt, and his last.

In my dad's front room, Jack had to be content with a mug of tea before he made his offer. 'We'd like your Stan to join the groundstaff at Burnley.'

I knew immediately I would listen to no future offers from other clubs. Even at such a young age, once I'd made a decision, I stuck to it. I was going to join the Cup finalists.

Weeks later, soon after my sixteenth birthday, I sat alongside Mam and Dad on the train, journeying south to become Jack's twenty-fifth recruit for Burnley. Before we left, he spoke to me privately at the station as he saw us off.

'Listen, lad, work hard. You can be a good player. In my opinion, one day, you'll make an even better manager.'

The boss at Burnley, Harry Potts, shook my hand later that morning as we completed the forms to designate me as an 'apprentice professional'.

Potts was a curious character. He was a balding man who more resembled a dapper middle-aged geography teacher than one of Britain's top soccer bosses.

'Right, lad,' he said. 'Have you brought your kit? You're playing this afternoon.'

Mam and Dad left before kick-off. There was no time to

consider missing them before I faced a Tranmere XI at the club's country park training ground at Gawthorpe.

Afterwards, shuttled to our landlady's depressing house, I felt like a school boarder abandoned at the start of term. I knew I had to become independent if I was to cope with life away from the North-East and soon became pals with my fellow boarders Coates, Morgan and Todd.

During our first night, we passed around the tattered remnants of a souvenir issue of the *Burnley Express*, packed with photos of the day, a month earlier, when the first team arrived home after their 3–1 Cup Final defeat against Spurs. An open-top coach toured the town centre as half of Burnley's 80,000 population turned out to cheer their heroes.

Waving to the crowd from the roof were internationals Ray Pointer, Jimmy Adamson, John Connelly, Jimmy McIlroy and Andy Lochhead. All of them genuine football stars. Standing at the rear was the unassuming Potts, a player when Burnley had last reached Wembley in 1947, and now their boss.

As we gazed at the photographs, the four of us reflected on our futures. Burnley were renowned for developing young talent. Of the team which won the championship in 1960 and then reached the Wembley final in 1962, only two players – Alex Elder and McIlroy – actually cost money. £13,000 for the pair.

We were the first intake since the Wembley appearance and were determined to become as famous as the bunch who had paraded through the streets in their club blazers but the closest we got to these legends over the coming weeks was cleaning their boots.

Half-a-dozen of us worked on the kit of 50 professional players. Nowadays, clubs are fined for making kids do such menial work. In their spare time, modern-day apprentices are sent to college to study the migration patterns of Egyptian geese or whatever bloody else takes their fancy.

After scrubbing studs all morning ... I had to go to work! As part of the deal to take me to Burnley, Dad insisted they find me employment as a cabinet-maker. I had begun an apprenticeship back home and he was adamant it should not lapse.

The club agreed an unprecedented schedule. Each morning, I left my mates in bed to make my way to Earnshaw and Booths for a 6.30am start. I made my furniture before returning in the early evening to train as a pro footballer.

It was impractical. I was constantly knackered and, more importantly, I missed vital drinking, er, bonding sessions with the lads. I quit.

A few nights later, during one impromptu 'bonding' session at the bar of the cricket club in the shadow of Turf Moor, I spotted a shy brunette with a smile that could stop conversations. Looking the dog's doo-dahs in my club blazer, I walked over and introduced myself to Kath, my future wife.

What impressed her most was my instant use of a nickname for her ... 'pet'. She wasn't well travelled and remained thrilled until she came home to meet my parents two years later and realised all Geordies call everyone 'pet'.

I arranged to meet her at the Locarno Club, the local Mecca, and offered to buy her a drink, not realising she was under age until she ordered a glass of milk. Our first 'proper' date was at the town centre Odeon cinema where Shirley McLean was starring in some bollocks called *What a Way to Go*. We settled down in the back row and my arm had just found its way around her shoulders when a familiar naff hairstyle sprouted from the seat in front.

Ralph Coates – who occasionally huddled together with me in our bedsit room as we sought warmth from snow falling through holes in the roof – had brought the other lads to take the piss.

I worked hard to impress Kath, not least on the pitch, and battled my way through the C-, B- and A-teams into Burnley Reserves. I played alongside Coates at an international under-21 tournament in Germany against Ajax and Juventus and then in

Switzerland where Burnley were invited to represent England.

Our reserves regularly played in front of crowds of 10,000 or more. We won the Central League, the reserves' championship. I scored my fair share of goals. We stuffed Leeds with their young stars Peter Lorimer and Paul Madeley. I scored one penalty and missed another as we drew 1–1 with Manchester United at Turf Moor in front of 12,000 fans.

While I shone for the second team, Burnley's first team finished third in the old Division One in 1963, but slipped to ninth the following season. In 1965, they dropped to twelfth.

Despite these disappointments and the years I spent trying to develop my Turf Moor reputation, I saw too many other youngsters bypass me on their way to the first team. What did I have to do to impress the management? My desire to succeed became a physical pain.

In a night match for the reserves at Old Trafford, frustration at my failure to achieve a first team shirt erupted. I played alongside Doc who was recruited to Burnley in 1966, and we were drawing 0–0. With the help of a youngster called Brian Kidd, they were passing us to death.

Minutes into the second half, I stopped near the centre circle and roared at the team, 'Are we going to fucking sort these twats out or are we going to sort these twats out?'

Our lads knew what I meant. United had four or five internationals in their team and, while Burnley were not able to match their skill levels, I was determined we would fight them to the final whistle. I had worked my arse off and when we won 1–0, I headed back to my rented room convinced Potts was bound to give me my senior début.

I trained full-time with the first team at this point. Jack Hixon's warning that my lack of pace would be a problem – 'Your hips are too broad, lad!' – began to haunt my preparations.

I knew Potts was a fitness freak so I employed professional sprinter Dougie Hutchinson to put me through my paces. He tortured me during close-seasons as he trailed me over hills around Heaton in the North-East.

Jack came to watch as Hutchinson bullied me, 'Get your effing knees up. Pump them, man!'

As I completed lap after lap of The Oozeburn, a stadium carved out of an old refuse tip, I accepted that my crucial shortage of pace was going to prevent me from becoming a world-class player. But I was prepared to work myself close to death to make it at Burnley.

I had an instinctive ability to read a game and I could find another yard of pace by improving my technique. Surely Potts, who started to rebuild his side after the successes of the early '60s, would have to pick me soon.

His coaching methods took some beating. During sessions on the Turf Moor pitch, he pulled wingers to one side, pointed at advertising billboards and shouted, 'You're knocking it over too early. You're crossing at Woolworth's, wait until you get to Tesco's!'

He spent weeks planning five-mile cross-country runs and effortlessly completed each one himself days before he forced us to try it. He was always at the head of the straggling squad as we gasped our way along. Exhausted, we'd reach the remote Fighting Cocks pub on the edge of the moors around Burnley to find Potts doing push-ups as he shouted, 'Right, lads! Now for the warm-up.'

I persevered and towards the end of 1966–67 finally impressed enough to earn a first team shirt at centre-half. I was a kid of 20. Coates was already a regular.

Along with Willie Morgan, Willie Irvine and Andy Lochhead, I was given a chance to compete with Burnley's proven veterans ... Connelly, Pointer, Adamson and Elder.

The 7–0 mauling on my début by Sam and his mates at Sheffield Wednesday was traumatic for us all but I already knew teams are at their best when they pull together in a crisis. If you lose, the most important thing is how you react in the next match. When Potts denied me a chance to recover – I was the only player dropped the following Saturday – I resented it. And I resented him. I knew I merited a run in the team.

Potts did look to me again, for a game at Wolves when Derek Dougan gave me a good going over as we lost 3–2.

I played against Fulham and was then picked to play at Southampton in 1968 against their emerging talent, Mick Channon and Martin Chivers. We drew 2–2 and, on the journey home, I wondered if Potts finally regarded me as a permanent option.

That was the last time I ever wore a first team shirt.

Reality dawned. Potts had never done me any favours and he was never likely to. He even took advantage of the day of his best mate's funeral to try to bury my career at the age of 22.

* * *

Balding Ray Bennion had a pudgy nose and a wrinkled mush that would have made a boxer dog jealous. With his flat cap and woolly cardigans, he had been a fixture around the Burnley dressing rooms since 1932. He joined after a successful playing career at Manchester United where he won 10 international caps. Not one of them flat.

He had been Burnley's A-team trainer, reserve team coach and first team trainer since 1957. Potts trusted him completely. Together they plotted Burnley's most glorious successes along with physio Billy Dougall, a bloke who looked like Harry Worth and often operated like him, too.

In the days when there were no playboy players with ponytails, Billy trucked no nonsense. Nowadays, clubs have nutritionists and develop individual training and recovery programmes using the highest science. You could be wheeled into Billy's room with two broken legs and he'd say, 'Young lad? Injured? Bloody run it off.'

This unlikely threesome ran Burnley's bootroom and, when Bennion died aged 71 at the end of the 1967–68 season, the whole club attended his funeral at a hillside cemetery a mile from Turf Moor.

After prayers, my thoughts turned towards my tedious 10-hour bus journey home to the North-East and Mam and Dad. As the mourners dispersed, we players shook hands and shouted farewells. An assistant coach at the club, Joe Brown, wandered casually over as he buttoned his overcoat. He looked more like John F Kennedy than ever.

He also looked sheepish.

'Er, Stan, lad. Mr Potts would like to see you.'

I returned to the ground. Potts saw me in his office. 'Good news, Stan, Carlisle want you.'

So that was it. Condemned to the Second Division.

Burnley were reshaping their future. The previous season they had finished in the bottom half of the table and were the last of the famous Lancashire mill town clubs of Bolton, Blackburn, Blackpool and Preston still left in Division One. The minimum wage had been abolished. The club had peaked yet I still wasn't part of its future.

'Listen, Stan, Carlisle is only an hour away up the road.'

The next day, four hours into the journey with Sammy Todd in his car, we were still nowhere near the place, stuck on the M6.

As each mile passed, the energy I wasted feeling pain and anger from injured pride developed into something more fulfilling. For the first time since Jack Hixon told me I was heading to Burnley, I actually felt wanted.

Carlisle was close to my family home, and Kath approved, so I agreed a deal.

A week before I was due to leave Burnley, Jimmy Adamson contacted me. He had been told Potts was 'moving upstairs' and he would soon be manager. Naturally, he wanted young talent to stay at the club. Ammo even posted a contract to my house, but I was insulted. It was too late to reconsider, so I returned it unopened.

There were lots of lads like me at Burnley, desperate to make an impact. The youth scheme was so prolific, when they signed Frank Casper from Rotherham for £30,000 in 1967 he became the club's first paid-for recruit since 1959. When he made his début, Casper was the first Burnley player to appear in League football having had previous League experience elsewhere since 1955.

Life at Turf Moor had become a scrap for survival among England's best young players. The team was regularly in Europe and packed with home-grown superstars. They could still afford to carry up to 50 professionals and we all recognised we had to be exceptional to make our mark.

I was ambitious and prepared to make sacrifices to reach the First Division as a *bona fide* first team regular. Public rejection, I supposed, was part of a footballer's lot. However, it took me months to get Potts's decision out of my system.

As I skulked away from Burnley, I never imagined things could be worse. Mind you, I never imagined in 1968 that, 23 years later, I would join Chelsea.

4

'I Dreamed of Killing Him ...'

CHELSEA, 1991–92

E ven Dennis Wise shut up for a minute.

I cursed for months that Chelsea's training pitch was directly under the flight path for Heathrow Airport. But when Concorde's engines roared over us once a week, I could at least relish a moment of relief when Wisey's voice would be drowned out completely.

With his mates Vinnie Jones and 'The Beak' – big-nosed Andy Townsend – sessions with Wisey and his gang were always a handful. They worked hard at their game but were easily distracted.

The club's Harlington training ground, owned by London University, is surrounded by greenery and one morning, when Concorde had passed, I found the players still disturbed, rubbernecking towards the next field. A group of men dressed in camouflage jackets unloaded sinister-looking packages from a collection of four-wheel-drive vehicles.

I had to restrain the lads from wandering over to have a nosey and barked instructions to get the training session back on track.

'Wisey, for fuck's sake!'

'Sorry, Stan.'

We did well for five minutes until an aerial dogfight broke out between two planes 30ft above us. The players stopped in their tracks and craned their necks upwards to trace the movement of a Spitfire and a Junkers as they weaved around with deadly menace.

My gaze returned to the men we'd seen earlier. They now looked less like an SAS hit squad and more like the nerds they were, model plane enthusiasts, each cradling a small control unit. They excitedly cheered every near miss.

Chelsea were wobbling in the bottom half of the old First Division in the final season before the launch of the Premiership. The Old Man, Chairman Ken Bates, left me in no doubt of my responsibilities as first team coach. Now I had to compete for players' attention with a collection of Douglas Bader dickheads.

The training stint petered out into a useless five-a-side knockabout. We'd try again tomorrow.

The next morning we were back, fighting fit and ready to prepare for Saturday's trip to Arsenal. So were the nerds.

It couldn't go on. We officially complained, but the land belonged to a private individual who didn't give a toss about Chelsea. After three weeks of loop-the-loops and assorted fly pasts, I lost it. They had driven me round the bend.

One slovenly fella in a bobble hat seemed to be pushing his luck. He was the controller of a First World War bi-plane and I clocked him for a few days. He repeatedly dive-bombed my multi-million-pound squad. It was quite deliberate. Maybe he supported Spurs.

One day, as I mouthed obscenities in his general direction, Vinnie Jones appeared alongside me. 'Listen,' he whispered. 'Leave it to me, Stan.'

A week later, the bi-plane was back. It climbed to 50ft before hurtling towards the ground. The grinning fool behind the controls happily waved in response to our two-fingered salutes.

Then, without warning, his plane exploded in mid-air. The guy was left holding an impotent control panel as bits of wing, wheels and a section of the tail plummeted to earth, accompanied by an ominous whiff of petrol.

Players and the controller stared in shock at the wreckage site.

Out of the corner of my eye, I caught sight of Vinnie, hidden amongst some trees. He crouched down but, as he met my gaze, he stood and triumphantly held aloft his double-barrelled gun. He'd shot the fucker down.

Vinnie's a country-loving lad ... and he's a crack shot.

I wasn't to know it but, within weeks of his attack on the plane, I'd be seriously considering borrowing his shotgun to shoot our own manager.

* * *

Ian Porterfield was practically in a coma. Only 12 months after becoming Sunderland's goal-scoring hero in the 1973 FA Cup Final giant-killing over Leeds, he was unconscious in a hospital bed with a fractured skull.

Ports was a big, bluff Scotsman with a lop-sided smile and a readiness to live life to the full. As commanding as he was on the pitch, he was wilder off it. I'd joined Sunderland as a player in 1974 and Ports was an ebullient character who dominated the dressing room.

As I arrived at our Washington training complex on a freezing December morning, and sat with other players as we digested the latest news of his crash in the *Newcastle Evening Chronicle*, the club was in crisis.

We were fighting to get out of the Second Division but Porterfield had written off his sponsored Toyota Corolla, ploughing into a field close to Sunderland Airport late the previous Saturday night after our 4–1 win over Portsmouth. He hit a fence near the Three Horseshoes Inn and was thrown forward, pulverising his head on the windscreen.

He wasn't wearing a seatbelt. If he had, Ports would have been immobilised and speared through the heart by a wooden fencepost.

Doctors who rushed him to the nearest hospital feared for his life. Our boss, Bob Stokoe, visited, but Ports deteriorated rapidly and was transferred to Newcastle General Hospital.

My knee ligaments were knackered so I had time on my hands and offered to go and see him. He was a good friend. But the doctors refused to let me or any other player in for ten days. Gradually, after a major operation on his skull, he began to recover.

Neurologists in the hospital's special brain unit worked hard to save his life. I'm not sure he would have lived if he had been a humble window cleaner. There's no doubt Ports received the very best treatment because he was a famous footballer.

When he began to reappear at training, I helped him recover from his injuries and resume playing. We were grateful he was alive. There was no false sentiment. Once we shook his hand, we took the piss mercilessly about his shaven head, calling him Kung Fu after the hit TV show.

I worked with Ports for four more years as I moved into coaching at Roker Park until we lost contact. Out of work, years later in 1991, I was scouting for John Lyall at Ipswich when my phone rang at home.

'Hi, Stan, it's Ports.'

Quite an honour to get a call from the new Chelsea boss. Especially when you are on the dole.

'I want you to come down and see me. I've got something you might be interested in.'

Porterfield had already managed Rotherham, Sheffield United, Aberdeen and Reading when Ken Bates invited him to Stamford

Bridge. He was the Chairman's fourth choice in 11 years, following John Neal, John Hollins and Bobby Campbell.

I wondered what had led Chelsea to believe that their ex-coach was the answer to their present predicament as a spent force in the First Division.

After I drove hundreds of miles to Ports's home in Bagshot, Surrey, I had my answer. He came cheap. Bloody cheap.

'Have a beer,' said Ports as I sat in his lounge.

'No thanks, mate. What's going on?'

'Well, Stan,' he said, 'I'm going to give you the job of coach at Chelsea.'

Interesting, I thought. 'Fine,' I said.

We talked players. We talked facilities. We talked prospects. Still fine.

Then we talked money. That's when I needed a beer.

'*How much*?'

'Listen, Stan,' said Ports. 'Blah, blah, blah, blah, blah, blah ...'

I didn't hear another word he was saying. I was still stuck at the point when he mentioned my salary – £25,000 a year. Was he joking? Apparently not.

George Graham was on £265,000 a year at Arsenal. Alex Ferguson was on £300,000 a year at Manchester United and Brian Clough earned £175,000 at Nottingham Forest.

I reckon Porterfield took the job as manager of Chelsea, one of the world's most glamorous clubs, for around £50,000 a year – less than his last job in the Third Division. He had become one of the lowest-paid managers in the top league on a rate that wouldn't even attract a Fourth Division full-back, and he wanted me as his assistant for half that amount.

I had a dilemma. Bloody hell, it wasn't enough money. It would *cost* me to take the job. I would have to leave Kath and the lads up north and move away from home. My rent would be over £800 and I would still have to pay my mortgage in Burnley.

But I needed the work. I lived for football. Scouting for Ipswich was piecemeal. I did it to make sure my face was still seen at matches. I needed to persuade myself I still had a meaningful future in football.

Chelsea was glamour. Chelsea was top flight. Chelsea was possibly the last chance to make my name and ultimately have a crack at managing in the First Division in my own right. A job I was born for.

But it was also a joke. I had to reduce myself to accepting a pittance to be number two at such a big club.

Bates and his Board were obviously wary. I should have recognised the omens. Managing Director Colin Hutchinson, who signed most of Chelsea's cheques and therefore their players, admitted Porterfield was forced to sign his three-year deal subject to bonuses.

He said, 'If Ian does well, he could earn £150,000 and be up there with the likes of George Graham. There is a tendency these days for people to sit on fat contracts but Ian has joined us on a fairly realistic wage ...'

Fairly realistic? Not for football.

'... a fairly realistic wage,' added Hutchinson, 'and all his rewards will be geared to results.'

In effect, Chelsea took a gamble on Ports. Now he asked me to be part of his winning hand.

I was flattered, yet my instincts screamed at me to walk away. Instead, I ignored my gut, my heart, even my head, and shook Ports's hand to become Chelsea's new coach.

I drove home to break the news to my family that I was moving out. Kath is a realist. She helped me pack my suitcase and ordered me to 'take care'. We hugged and I left for London.

The big gamble for Ports was about to become a game of Russian roulette for me.

As I strode on to the Chelsea training pitch in my pristine white trainers for the first time, I knew the calibre of players lining up in one of the goalmouths would suss within five minutes whether I was up to the job. I was the ex-manager of lowly Hull City. Maybe they would fancy their chances.

Wisey, Townsend, Clive Allen and Dave Beasant were all established stars – self-confident, judgemental and thick as thieves. Intimidation was not an unknown ploy. Predictably, during a five-a-side match I refereed they tried it on. Dennis Wise committed a foul and I blew for a free-kick. He didn't like it and booted the ball away. A long way away. A small test for Stanley on his first day.

We had a delicate discussion.

'Go get it,' I said.

'Fuck it,' he replied.

There are three ways to react in this sort of situation: (a) apologise for upsetting the player and run after the ball yourself; (b) ask one of the other lads to go and get the ball, thus defusing the situation; (c) knock him clean out.

As it was my first day I felt option (c) would be a touch excessive. Not on day two, mind. I had to be strong, or my disciplinary hold over the squad would be worthless.

I strode up to Dennis, bent down and looked him in the face. 'You're taking the piss,' I suggested. 'Move your arse!'

He stood his ground.

So I sodded off. Walked away. It was time for Ports, the gaffer, to trot over and get a grip on his players.

As I left the training pitch, I turned, expecting to see Porterfield tearing Wisey a new arsehole. Instead, they were having a right old laugh. All pals together.

I was horrified. I felt that Porterfield had undermined my authority with one crass pat on the back for a player who, in my judgement, he should have fined or sent home.

I carried on walking. I had no stomach for Porterfield's display. I believed it was a massive misjudgement. Did he not understand? If I was weak, he was weak, too. I wasn't surprised to hear, ten minutes after the two cosied up, they had a barney. It occurred to me that the players didn't show the respect for Porterfield that was due to a manager. They tried to run the gaff.

I always demand loyalty from my senior staff. Now, thanks to Porterfield's apparent refusal to show any to me, the team thought they could take the piss out of his new coach.

As we lost 3–0 to Oldham in our second match of the season and then drew with Notts County, I felt he would live to regret giving the impression of being spineless. There are some occasions and some clubs where a softly softly attitude is effective: this was not such an occasion or such a club.

I was sure of one more thing. After only a week, I regretted ever setting eyes on Porterfield. He'd come to Chelsea a month before me, soon after getting the sack as manager of Reading for a drink-driving offence. Police found him with twice the legal amount of alcohol in his system. The court was told that he'd 'drowned his sorrows in booze' after Reading were whupped once too often.

Reading Managing Director Mike Lewis said, 'The Board took the incident very seriously as a breach of club discipline.'

Ports was fined £500 and banned from driving for four years.

When he signed his Chelsea contract, he swapped jokes with Hutchinson about hiring a chauffeur. Except, as far as Porterfield was concerned, it was no joke. *I* was his chauffeur. And that was all. I was just short of a cap.

He expected me to drive him to work in the morning and take him home at night, a round trip that put 90 minutes on the journey back to my flat. It wasn't quality time either. Porterfield had little to say on most journeys.

He had the choice of four different coaches before he offered me the job. Previously, I'd worked under Steve Coppell and was allowed free reign to improve his Crystal Palace team which included Mark Bright and Ian Wright.

I assumed, stupidly, that, because Porterfield had hand-picked me, he wanted more of the same. Instead, I felt I was being used as a skivvy and he seldom discussed tactics, selections or even coaching with me. He preferred to telephone some of his part-time scouts for advice instead of listening to me. I couldn't understand his neglect.

But that was the least of my worries. After he repeatedly blanked me in training during five-a-side matches, and constantly overruled me, it didn't take long for the cockiest players to grasp the situation and take advantage. Each time I tried to lay down my authority, they joked, 'Fucking hell, Stan, just go and get the fucking balls.'

I tackled them head-on and confronted the strongest characters first. After one session, I cornered Kerry Dixon. 'I've sussed you. You need to provide more physical contact. Get stuck in!'

He looked at me with scant respect. I couldn't blame him. He knew how his gaffer treated me. Why should he be any different?

Partially as a result of Porterfield's reluctance to show balls, the season began to fall apart.

In training, he'd suggest, 'Right, lads, a few sprints.'

They'd say, 'Nah, gaffer, get the balls out. It's five-a-side. Get the goals.'

To his shame, Porterfield let it continue. I felt he couldn't handle big-time players. As a consequence, the most forceful stars felt they could pick the team by committee. Big mistake.

I was ostracised so successfully at this stage, it took chief scout Gwyn Williams – who is now assistant manager to Claudio Ranieri at Chelsea – to let me know the full extent of Porterfield's acquiescence.

Gwyn told me, 'Porterfield had four players who would pick a team. There was a young player at the time – Graeme Le Saux. Before an official team meeting even took place, this gang of four approached Le Saux and told him, "Unlucky, son, you're not playing today because we're not picking you. Don't bother getting changed."'

The situation depressed Le Saux as much as it angered me.

Gwyn told me when Porterfield once substituted Le Saux, he

threw his shirt down in disgust. Le Saux apologised to the club and fans, but refused to say sorry to his manager.

Porterfield was in deep trouble. He was Chelsea's former coach but it soon dawned on me he was never cut out to be their manager. He lacked strength and character. If running Chelsea had been a military operation, it would have been classified as a 'clusterfuck'.

We lost at Leeds. We drew disappointingly with QPR. Four days later, we faced Tranmere Rovers in the League Cup. We scraped a draw at Stamford Bridge and lost the away leg 3–1.

John Aldridge scored one of his famous dodgy penalties when he almost stopped during his run-up to make the keeper dive too early. The ref told our lot he would make Aldo re-take it if he stuttered. But he gave the goal. Predictably, Wisey and the rest went potty and it went off big style. I reacted to one awful decision by a dictatorial linesman by repeatedly goose-stepping behind him along the touchline with one finger under my nose and my other arm pointing stiffly in the air.

Back in the dressing room, the farce continued with a huge row, as usual. And, as usual, every player had a point of view. Porterfield would show up, Vinnie would argue his points and too often the gaffer would give in and say, 'OK, you're right.'

In the early days, I tried to intervene to restore order, but the lads knew my position was fatally weakened because Porterfield had made it clear to me he wouldn't piss in my mouth if my teeth were on fire.

Tony Cascarino admitted to me that even the squad believed it wasn't the right way to run things, but their manager seemed to be afraid of player power and they took advantage.

I regarded Porterfield as a waste of space. Before the Tranmere match, I asked him for permission to drive the 30 miles from Merseyside to Burnley after the game to spend a night with my family. After the final whistle, Kath, Chris and Dan waited for me outside the players' entrance in the pissing rain for over an hour.

Then Porterfield made me walk out to them like a naughty little boy with the message, 'Sorry, I've got to get on the coach back to London.' He refused me the chance to see my own wife.

I gave Kath a quick kiss on the cheek, smiled at the boys and, after a 30-second reunion, jumped on the bus. Kath wanted to hit him.

As we pulled away from the ground, I sat at a window seat and seethed, remembering a similar snub three days earlier.

I brought my younger son Dan to watch us play at Arsenal. I'd organised a lift to get him to their ground, but Porterfield surprised me and offered Dan the chance to sit on the team bus for the short journey to Highbury. He even joined us for the pre-match meal.

After we lost 3–2, we went to get on the bus for the trip back to our ground when Porterfield pulled me to one side. 'Look,' he said, 'I don't want your son on the bus.'

On a whim, he had banned Dan. Was he trying to provoke me into assaulting him? I couldn't believe it. I was convinced he was trying to humiliate me. The process was complete when the players invented a nickname for me – BBC. Bibs, Balls and Cones.

'How's it doing, BBC? All right?'

The main responsibility Porterfield ever gave me was to set up the training equipment. The squad recognised I was not being given a chance, but football is a cruel game and they piled on the ridicule.

A chance of escape emerged when I was placed on a shortlist with Bruce Rioch for the manager's job at Bolton Wanderers, but I was not their final choice.

I became depressed. My home life was in tatters. The first 12 weeks of my Chelsea hell were spent in a poky flat above the Fighting Cocks bed and breakfast pub in Bagshot. I was only a 15-minute run from Porterfield's house and he used me as his gofer.

I had never felt so lonely. My only relief was an odd round of golf with the landlord. I had too many afternoons with nothing to do and an eternity to think. I became terminally homesick.

My family sensed I was in trouble and drove down to Bagshot

in relays to comfort me. Often, Kath would return up the M6 to be passed by my elder lad Chris coming down the other side to take over as my baby-sitter. They brought huge piles of Tupperware containers labelled with days of the week, so Kath could reassure herself that I wasn't starving.

A salesman pal of mine, John Evans, stayed the night whenever he was in the area. We would scoff a Chinese meal, demolish a couple of bottles of Chablis ... and it would solve nothing.

I refused to become a case for the Samaritans. A problem shared is not a problem halved. A problem shared is an embarrassment. Too proud to go to Old Man Bates or Hutchinson, I obeyed some kind of twisted logic which dictated that since Porterfield gave me a job I could not betray him, however harshly he treated me. That is not how I normally handle such situations.

If a man felt he had the power nowadays to ridicule me and subject me to a form of humiliation in front of my own wife and kids, I would happily nut him. At Chelsea, only 12 weeks into my job, I had to persuade myself constantly to persevere. I faced daily battles merely to retain my dignity.

On occasions, very privately, I was in tears. I forced myself to stay for the paltry money Chelsea paid. I hated it. I began to hate myself for tolerating it, too. I was afraid my enforced loyalty to this manager was taking me close to a nervous breakdown. I felt Porterfield clearly had no trust in me whatsoever.

We travelled together to a Trust House Forte hotel alongside Heathrow Airport for transfer talks with Vinnie Jones. Jonah, who at the time played for Sheffield United, was a character we needed at Chelsea to help the club progress. I was sure of it. I assumed Porterfield agreed. He never discussed it.

Jonah bustled into the room, shook hands with us both and told us how relieved he was to get the chance to move back to London. We told him about Chelsea ... the good, the bad, the indifferent.

He told us he thought it was time Chelsea started battling to win something. Music to my ears.

Then, astonishingly, Porterfield looked over towards me and said, 'Right, Stan, can you leave the room while we talk terms?'

I sat, immobile with embarrassment. Vinnie looked quickly from one of us to the other. I could imagine his brain shouting, 'Does not compute. Does not compute. Does not fucking compute!'

This sort of public slapdown just didn't happen among management teams.

'Stan?' Porterfield looked to me, then shifted in his chair to talk money with Vinnie.

I had no option. I had to leave. I found a chair in the hallway outside the room and sat impatiently to await the completion of their negotiations.

After 20 minutes, the door opened and Jonah, looking sheepish, emerged. Beneath his bluff exterior, Jonah is a sensitive kid and he recognised the snub he had witnessed, and exactly what it stood for.

As he passed he said, 'See you later. Oh, it's a £575,000 fee and I'm on £160,000 a year, son.'

Vinnie was as uncomfortable as me with Porterfield's rudeness and took it upon himself to apologise in typical fashion as he willingly spilled the beans about everything they had discussed. Vinnie is a true gentleman, a man of honour.

Days later, Porterfield had enjoyed a beer and I was driving him home. On rare occasions when I tried to talk about the playing staff or our tactics, Porterfield could react with abuse. As we headed back to Bagshot that night, I made the mistake of defending goalkeeper Dave Beasant. I was Bez's biggest fan but Porterfield ranted at the smallest mistake he made.

'Bez? Bez ...' he screamed in my earhole, 'is hopeless!'

He stuck his feet on the dashboard and verbally slaughtered me. As we made our way slowly through built-up traffic on the outskirts of London, he used Beasant as a huge stick to beat me with.

What made this attack worse than any stunt Porterfield had pulled before was that, as he abused me, ridiculed me, insulted me and poured scorn on my judgement as his assistant, my wife Kath sat in the back seat.

That night, for the first time, I dreamed of killing him.

I couldn't forgive Porterfield. Kath hated him passionately. She urged me to leave and return home but it was not my style to run away.

A short bout of physical violence between him and me armed with a corner flag was a distinct possibility, but I pushed even that thought from my mind when he appeared at my flat the next day to apologise. He appeared pathetically repentant.

After he left for home, wobbling away on his bicycle complete with a shopping basket over the handlebars, I reached a decision. Just three months into the job, and two days after we had struggled for a point at Crystal Palace, I got into my car, put my foot down and headed north.

I was going home to Burnley. And I wasn't coming back.

I stopped for fuel at a petrol station on the A40 near Chalfont. Minutes earlier, I'd taken a phone call from Kath. She had already returned north, was missing me and became upset. I found it difficult to communicate, constantly trying to disguise my vulnerability. I had allowed pride to fog my judgement.

As I filled the car with four-star, I realised I'd had enough. I was supposed to be heading for the training ground but I dreaded it. I knew I faced the real risk that Porterfield would spend another morning ignoring me.

I imagined how he would have felt if Bobby Campbell, the Chelsea manager when Porterfield was coach, had treated him in such a way, but I doubted Campbell could be capable of such behaviour.

I paid my petrol bill and prepared to leave, when our chief scout Gwyn pulled on to the forecourt by coincidence. He tooted his horn and signalled me over for a chat. Gwyn spent most of his time on the road, trying to spot players who could pull Porterfield out of the mire. 'How're you doing?' he asked me.

The dam burst. I told him, 'The set-up's knackered. Players are taking the piss. Ports is a walkover. The club's future is threatened. There's no discipline. What's more ... I'm off.'

To his credit, Gwyn didn't try to pretend he was surprised. My humiliation was common knowledge throughout the club. He persuaded me to get into his car and together we drove a mile down the road and sat with a view of local playing fields, watching kids have a kickabout.

'Don't let him win, Stan,' he said. 'You've come down here as his assistant and he's fucked you off. I've no idea why. But why walk out? Sit tight and take the money.

'The first thing you need to do is leave that poxy flat. You don't want to be steaming round Porterfield's house every ten minutes at his beck and call. You're living every moment with him. Don't stand for it. Come and live in my village.

'Don't kill yourself over it. Get on with your job. You are here to coach. If he wants you to do as little as possible, that's the way it is. If he decides he wants you to do more, fine. You have to accept that, good or bad, he's making the decisions, but we've got to be solid as a staff to get results.'

I complained to Gwyn that I couldn't understand Porterfield's reluctance to engage me at what I did best – motivating footballers and finding ways for them to win. I wanted the best for Chelsea. Hutchinson had already given Porterfield a public warning after our humiliation at Tranmere. Did he not need my help? I wanted players who would work hard. I was prepared to stand up to them.

Gwyn listened patiently as I spewed out my frustration. I shrugged and said, 'I don't think that Ports can handle big players. They handle themselves. Each has to be right to play football. A gaffer has to be strong but being strong isn't about threatening them all the time. You've got to get into their heads.'

Striker Tony Cascarino admitted to me that, after his transfer from Celtic, life at Stamford Bridge was so lax he thought he'd arrived at a Christmas Club. Andy Townsend lived miles away from training around the M25 and, though he was thoroughly professional, would occasionally turn up late. Porterfield laughed it off and said, 'OK, Andy ... join in with the yellows.'

Join in with the yellows? Gwyn nodded in recognition. We all felt we knew what was wrong at Chelsea. I had the strength to put it right, but not the access.

Thanks to Gwyn, I didn't drive home to Burnley. Instead, I went into training and treated Porterfield with utter contempt. The following week, I moved to a flat above a ladies' dress shop in Chalfont St Peter, close to Gwyn and closer to the M40, which meant closer to home. I resolved to take life easier.

As soon as I accepted my role of 'BBC to the stars', I settled down at the club. I stopped fighting my own instincts and allowed Porterfield to cock it up on his own.

Over the next few weeks, I enjoyed Sunday lunches with Gwyn and his wife Alison at their home. I also played golf with fellow northerner Bob Ward, the club physio. Most of all, as I relaxed, I finally developed bonds of mutual respect with many of the players, which are as strong as ever today.

That's why I found it difficult to understand when they tried to assassinate me.

* * *

As we approached Christmas, our form nose-dived and results reflected it. We lost 3–0 at home to Norwich City, 1–0 away to Southampton, 3–0 away to Sheffield Wednesday, 3–1 at home to Manchester United, 2–0 to Notts County and 2–0 to Luton. All within 42 days.

At the time, Ken Bates was consumed with worry about the club being evicted from Stamford Bridge. His eight-year fight to win the freehold of the ground reached its climax just as his team went down the toilet. He is a great chairman, 200 per cent Chelsea; my predicament would barely have registered on his radar.

Bates eventually won in the High Court and had to pay around £13m to secure Chelsea's long-term future. I hoped he agreed with me that, in the short term, Porterfield was bankrupt of ideas.

Even our Christmas party was cursed. We all enjoyed a knees-up at the Lakeside Club in Essex. As we waited for The Drifters to appear on stage, the lights fused. The only way we would see The Drifters now was if they wore miners' helmets.

Without power, the lager pumps dried up and the cash tills wouldn't work. Punters resorted to drinking bottled beers while our ex-Wimbledon lads – Beasant, Wisey and Jonah climbed on stage to sing a medley of Madness hits to keep the crowd from getting too restless.

Despite everything, team spirit among the players was good. Now that I had taken a vow of sorting myself out first, I enjoyed their company, too.

Just before a crucial fourth round FA Cup tie at home to Everton, the club announced a five-day, all-expenses-paid golfing trip to Spain. Best of all, the manager was staying at home.

Cue holiday spirit. We arrived at the sumptuous five-star Torrequebrada Hotel in Malaga determined to chill out, play some golf and try to forget the flawed first half of the season.

Frustratingly, as I tucked into my first coffee and brandy of our first night, the morons behind the hotel reception desk lost my passport.

'Get me the manager.'

A little fella with a thick moustache, short arms and hair as neat as Dale Winton's armpits appeared and tried to explain something in Spanish. I don't do much Spanish. Neither do I do incompetence.

I monstered him. 'We're a professional football team, not some friggin' package tour. Get your finger out. I want my passport.'

I spotted Gwyn tucking into another brandy as I stood around in the marbled reception area arguing with a dimwit in pidgin English. I upped the stakes.

'Also, I want compensation.'

The apologetic manager plied me with free drinks and gave me chips to spend in the hotel casino. After two hours of brandy and blackjack, I was suitably relaxed.

'Would Mr Francis Ternent please return to his room?' The deafening tannoy message shattered the contemplative atmosphere around the card tables.

'Would Mr Francis Ternent please return to his room? Immediately!'

I scrambled to my feet alongside Gwyn. He reacted to hearing my name echo around the card room. I was more alarmed by the use of 'Francis', which is my secret Christian name, contained only in my passport. Whoever had nicked it had left the message. Something was up.

Gwyn shouted, 'Quick, up to the rooms,' and I raced with him to the lift. Moments later, we spilled out into the hallway on floor six to be met by the same manager I had slaughtered earlier. He was surrounded by the contents of Gwyn's room, laid out impeccably in the corridor, including pictures which had been rehung above a wall-mounted fire extinguisher.

The players had spent the night working an elaborate trick. I feared there was more to come.

Oh-oh. Gwyn spotted something on the floor and I knelt down alongside him to take a look. It was a tooth. There was another tooth. It was a trail of teeth. To be precise, it was a trail of Gwyn's dentures, crushed beyond recognition.

As the hotel manager began to pester us, we followed it. The false teeth led directly to my door. Once inside, Gwyn and I looked at each other with trepidation as we spotted it. Well, spotted absolutely nothing to be precise.

There was nothing in the living room. Nothing in the bedroom. Nothing on the walls. Nothing, even, on the floor.

Eventually, the manager found everything piled on to the balcony, including the carpet, completely obscuring the sea view.

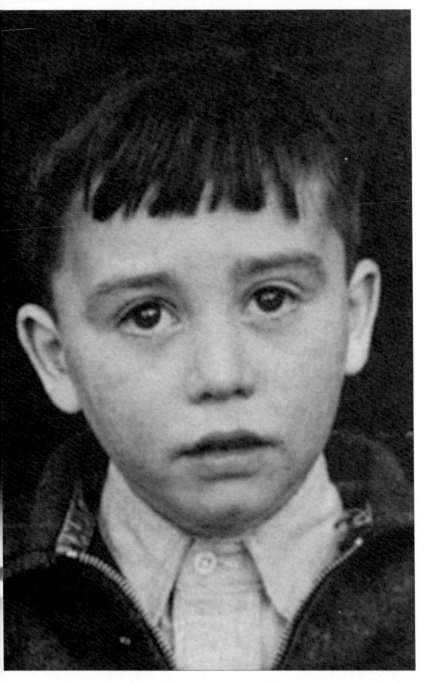

Dad would carry me, aged five, on his shoulders the whole nine miles to Roker park.

Top: Starring for the St John's school team aged 12. I'm second boy from the left in the front row.

Bottom: My final first team appearance for Burnley, away at Southampton, before manager Harry Potts sold me.

Carlisle manager Tim Ward signed me for £5,000 aged 21 in 1968.

Pin-up star of *Shoot* magazine.

Top left: Sent off in disgrace after I nutted Birmingham's Bob Latchford. *Top right*: Gazza's inspiration for the dentist's chair. *Bottom*: Contemplating weighty matters.

Top: I do … (*from left*) my dad Mick, mam Peggy, me, Kath, her mum Amy and her dad Bill.

Bottom left: Proud of my son Chris, who at least had a club car.

Bottom right: Skinning Chopper Harris at Stamford Bridge.

Top: The assistant boss at Blackpool … one of the few days I raised a smile.

Bottom: Mrs T and me at Bradford.

Top: Butch and Sundance! Steve Coppell about to be beaten at golf.

Bottom: Where the f*** is everybody? Bury's unseen victory parade.

'Stan, in here!'

Gwyn called from the bathroom where a message was sprayed on the mirror in shaving foam. It dripped slightly but there was little doubt. It read, 'You fat bastard!'

Hours later, I was still sucking up to the hotel manager, desperate to stop him from throwing out my squad.

I had my suspects but there was no way of proving which of the players had taken the piss. The only surefire way to punish the offender was to punish the lot of them. I arranged a training run for 6.00am the following morning.

The squad lined up in the baking heat outside the hotel's main door, unshaven, unkempt and unhappy.

Good. Most of them had had nothing to do with the whirlwind that had hit our rooms. Perhaps they'd take revenge for me privately on the guilty parties.

'Right, we're running along the front. Whatever happens, no one passes me. Got it?'

We set off and I took it slowly. An hour later, we were still pounding the streets. Satisfyingly, some of the players began to spew. We reached a beach-front café, the halfway point for our run. I turned towards the hotel and started to jog back.

The players stuck rigidly to my rule not to overtake me. I picked up the pace. I wanted to see them throw up again.

Beep. Beep. Beep. Beeeeeeep! A taxi raced past me, an inch from my elbow. And another. Then a third.

The players filled every window, some with their faces, some with their arses. All of them flicking V-signs. They had sussed out my route and booked taxis in advance to make their escape.

I slowed to walking pace as I watched their getaway cars disappear in a cloud of dust round a bend ahead of me. My revenge would have to come on the golf course instead.

I teamed up with Gwyn to play Vinnie Jones and the club skipper Andy Townsend. I'm a good golfer, Gwyn was practically a novice, while Jonah and Skip played off a handicap of six. It meant I would have to take them on almost single-handedly, but I was prepared to work hard. They had it coming.

Before the first round, Jonah asked, 'What stakes, Stan?'

We settled on a tenner on the first nine and a tenner on the second.

Me and Gwyn won.

The next day, we doubled the stakes. We won again.

The next day, the bet was tripled. We won again!

Day four. Vinnie and the Skip faced a hefty payout.

Our round began well. We were three shots up and motored to the eighth tee on a magnificent hole carved into the side of a hill. It was a short par four leading down to a lake.

The tee-shots were average, mine was just a little left but safely on the fairway. We drove slowly down the slope and putted out.

Gwyn and I notched another victory and jumped aboard our buggy. I confidently floored the accelerator to take us to the next tee.

Slam!

For a brief second, my brain refused to register what was happening. Instead of nudging forward, the buggy shuddered backwards over a cliff.

While I struggled to comprehend that death was a moment away, Gwyn responded quicker and leaped for his life. Along with the wildly revving buggy, I plunged into a ravine, clutching the steering wheel with a look of puzzled horror fixed on my face. While I'd been holing the ball, one of the bastards we were playing had fucked about with the gears and switched them from forward to reverse. I landed neck-deep in clumps of razor-sharp brambles. My shorts and T-shirt offered no protection to their spikes and my body was torn to pieces. Livid welts appeared all over my legs. My shirt rode up and my torso was pierced, scraped and ripped. Blood oozed from every cut. I screamed for help. 'Get me out! I'm trapped!'

No response from above.

'Lads! Get me the fuck out of here!'

I laboured to breathe. I was in agony. I had a vision of my accident being screened on TV as an air ambulance hovered precariously above the flag on the eighth green.

'Lads!'

My voice began to waver. Then, as the buggy's engine cut out and was silenced, I heard a sound from high above, at the top of the cliff.

There it was again ... if I could just make it out ... it was ... it was ... laughter. Huge gales of the stuff washing over the edge down to me, still encased in 6in barbs.

Gwyn's head appeared over the rim of the ravine. 'Stan? Stan? Are you OK?'

'Fucking OK? Get them to pull me out.'

'I can't,' he said. 'They are rolling around on their backs, pissing themselves. I think Vinnie is going to be sick.'

I heard Townsend's voice. 'Unlucky, Stan, we've done you.'

Thankfully, four other players enjoying a round behind us turned up in their carts. They found a rope, hauled me out and then went back for my buggy.

I was escorted back to the hotel dripping blood.

I ached to get my own back. Perhaps it was the effects of the assassination attempt on my nervous system. Perhaps I took too many shots to the head as I somersaulted inside the buggy. Perhaps I completely lost my mind. I still cannot explain what made me think that going out golfing the next day to play a foursome with Vinnie, Skip and Dennis Wise would ever provide me with a chance of revenge.

It started at the fourth hole. Wisey is a nightmare golf partner. Chaos follows him around. After three holes he is bored and scoots around in his golf cart looking for trouble.

We played slowly, due to the others pissing around. A middle-aged English couple behind us began to get impatient. Wisey spotted this.

'Overtake us, mate,' he offered.

The greying husband and his wife thanked us. They were delighted when Wisey suddenly made another offer. 'Have this ball as an apology for us being so slow.'

The man was so chuffed to receive a gift from a soccer star that he decided to use it straight away. As he placed it on his tee, I noticed Wisey take a few steps backwards.

I had little time to register anything else before the man swung his club and the joke ball exploded in a cloud of powder and smoke. Wisey was off. He raced away in his buggy and left us to bung the couple cash to keep them quiet.

A few holes later, one of our group excelled themselves. The round was drawing to a close when I triumphantly holed a 12ft putt. As I reached in to reclaim the ball, I reclaimed something else instead. A turd.

One of the lads had squatted over the hole on the sixteenth green and taken a dump. My hand was caked.

It's a real shame none of the other lads saw it. Because as each and every Chelsea player following us finished their round, I shook hands with the lot of them.

As an exercise in hygiene, the tour was a failure. As a bonding session, it worked a treat. We arrived back and won our next three matches, beating Wimbledon and Liverpool away.

Crucially, we also won the fourth round FA Cup tie against Everton, a game Porterfield classed as a 'must-win' and a result which, ironically, kept him in work for another season.

Once again, I settled into my role as Porterfield's personal leper.

Since Torrequebrada, my relationship with the squad became based on trust and mutual respect. They each recognised my talents as a coach, even if their manager appeared to differ. We had many one-to-one sessions where, away from Porterfield's gaze, I could work unhindered. Meanwhile, he continued to suffer at their hands.

They rushed to take advantage. After some matches, Porterfield went into the players' bar where the lads would set on him. They felt brave enough to question his tactics, his judgement and his ability. They even argued with his substitutions.

My code of loyalty precluded me from running off to Bates to complain about him, but the players had no qualms. They bypassed the manager's office to go over his head to the Old Man to pass comments or have a whinge.

His aloofness towards me and his over-indulgent chumminess to the lads left Porterfield isolated. I saw the players laugh at him behind his back and call him Rab C Nesbitt.

Even supporters began to lose faith. First they urged the club to ban celebrity fan John Major from the ground. Every time the Prime Minister turned up, we lost. Then their protests became more direct.

A 1–1 home draw against Southampton in February attracted a paltry crowd of 7,148 – the lowest attendance for a First Division match at Stamford Bridge since the Second World War.

Despite this, I worked hard to pull the lads together and forge them into a fighting unit. We had decent players – Vinnie, Wisey, Skip, Cascarino, Bez and Clive Allen – who ought to have inspired others on the teamsheet, such as Jason Cundy, Ken Monkou, Paul Elliott and Tommy Boyd. On occasions, they did.

We travelled to league leaders Manchester United and were 1–0 up through a Mal Donaghy own goal until a minute to go when Mark Hughes hit a volley to equalise. Alex Ferguson was the perfect host to us after the game as he chatted and offered us a drink. I walked away from Old Trafford having seen a gentleman manager operate, in contrast to the way I felt I was treated at the Bridge.

As the weeks wore on, I relied on the players to help me through turbulent times. Surprisingly, Vinnie Jones identified my problems and showed his caring nature. He invited me round to his dad's house for barbecues and often asked me, 'Can I stay at your place tonight?'

When he popped round to my flat, we demolished Chinese meals and the odd glass of wine before he'd stop the night, kipping on the floor surrounded by discarded chow mein cartons.

Dennis Wise invited me round to the Bridport Arms, a pub owned by his family, and, occasionally, Jonah hijacked me for a night out.

He'd ring Kath from his mobile phone as we bombed around in a black cab shouting, 'Don't worry, love, we're up the West End. He's all right with me.'

However close I got to Vinnie, I couldn't reveal the true extent of my living hell in London. It was enough that he recognised something was wrong at all.

With the rest of the lads, we sometimes headed for a pint at the Ferret and Firkin in Chelsea Harbour. More than once, I emerged to find they'd let down every tyre on my car or moved it three streets away.

We tried to repeat the success of Torrequebrada by flying out to Ireland on a promotional tour. As soon as we landed at Dublin Airport, our two Irish internationals – Townsend and Cascarino – were treated like gods ... Guinness gods.

'Will you come and have a drink, lads?'

During a round of golf in Mallahide, a local butcher offered to caddie for Vinnie. After the first nine holes, the fella stopped and asked, 'Would it be all right if I just popped away for a pint?' The players looked at each other, downed clubs and went with him. They were still in the pub at 6.00am the following morning when passing supporters stopped off to share a drink on their way to work.

On the journey home, it became rowdy on the plane. A businessman who complained about the noise lowered his *Financial Times* to have a word with one of the players when a fried tomato hit him square in the forehead, before it dripped in huge gobbets down his shirt.

It was Wisey's unique way of adding a full-stop to a conversation he wasn't enjoying.

Back in the real world of the First Division, others began to throw rotten fruit at us. Chelsea legend Ron 'Chopper' Harris launched a systematic assault on his former club in a newspaper.

Normally, I don't take any notice of veteran gobshites who run to the tabloids for 30 pieces of silver once their playing days are over. But Harris only said out loud what many Chelsea fans already thought. Home defeats to Sheffield Wednesday, Coventry City and Sheffield United forced us to accept we were struggling. I worked hard with the squad on their individual strengths, but Harris's article spared nobody, not even those I personally respected as good players.

Under the headline FLOG THE LOT KEN, he wrote, 'I can't see loyal Chelsea fans putting up with it much longer. Vinnie Jones should be the first to go. He wouldn't have got in our youth team. I wasn't the fastest of players but, compared with him, I look like a greyhound.

'Kerry Dixon couldn't lace Peter Osgood's boots. Dennis Wise is the luckiest player ever to get an England call. Clive Allen's been sold too cheap for £300,000. As for Ian Porterfield, it would take him a lifetime as a football manager to learn what I have.'

Dodging abuse as we limped from one match to the next, our season was effectively over in March when we lost to Sunderland in the quarter-final of the FA Cup.

They won 2–1 in a replay at Roker Park with Gordon Armstrong – a player I later signed at Bury and Burnley – getting their winner. After the game, Ken Bates ordered me and Porterfield to travel back to London on the directors' executive coach instead of the team bus. We were subjected to rigorous questioning about our plans for the future before being severely bollocked. From our body language, the Old Man must have sussed the depths to which our relationship had sunk.

The season petered out. We won three of our last eleven games, finishing fourteenth with a goal difference of -10.

When the end came, it was as swift as it was expected. After a training session before the final defeat of the season at Everton, Porterfield asked to see me at the same hotel where he had snubbed me during the Vinnie Jones transfer. 'I'm not going to renew your contract.'

I had barely sat down. 'You don't have to explain,' I said.

Relief was my main emotion. Instead of going to Vancouver the following week on tour with the lads, I'd have my feet up in Burnley with a nice glass of dry white wine. I shook hands. To my amazement, I even wished him well. I suppose the alternative would have landed me with ten years in jail.

The players were more shocked than I had expected. They all telephoned me and promised to keep in touch.

Don Howe joined Chelsea in July 1992 and their form improved. By November, they were top of the league. Tragically, suddenly, Don had a stroke and never went back to work. Two months later, after Chelsea had gone 12 games without a win, Porterfield was fired.

Gwyn told me, 'It went from having everything to a shambles.'

Once Porterfield had left, the whole saga degenerated into bitter recrimination. Bobby Campbell, the manager who had employed Porterfield as a coach during the Division Two promotion-winning season of 1998–99, was rueful. He said, 'I took Porterfield on and soon realised that he had problems at home and I would let him go straight there after training.

'It was his job to warm up players and I would then go out and work with them. But we all think we are better than we are and he went round telling people that he did all the training, especially when we were having success.

'It's called brainwashing. I should have told Batesy that Porterfield was not the right man for the job.'

Bates announced, 'I decided over the weekend that it is time to make a change. The fact is that we lost as many games as we won over the last two seasons and that's not in keeping with our aspirations.'

He has revealed since, 'The only manager I didn't enjoy working with, the only real mistake I made, was Ian Porterfield. He was a disaster. He used to make long rambling speeches in his thick Scottish accent that I couldn't understand. There were times, especially in his last six months, when I couldn't bear to talk to him.

'I would say to Colin Hutchinson, "Colin, you take over, I can't stand him." We had to get rid of him quickly. The team was sliding. 'People come to Stamford Bridge to be entertained. Our fans only turned on the team once, in the days of Porterfield.'

The man himself reacted dramatically to his sacking. 'It feels as if a knife has been plunged into me and I'm left asking myself if football is really worth it. Football is a very cruel game. I'm the kind of guy who takes it so seriously it could ruin my life. I've had a long shot at being a manager. But I came to Chelsea at first as a coach and I seemed to enjoy that much more. Perhaps I would be better off as an assistant manager or a coach instead of being a boss.'

I've never seen him since. The players are still some of my closest friends. Vinnie pops around to my house occasionally. He rang me the other night to take the piss out of Townsend. I had nicknames for most of the players. Le Saux was always Le Socks, or Bergerac, because he's from Jersey, and I called Townsend The Mole or Adrian because he had a humdinger of a growth on his face. After watching *The Premiership* on ITV one Saturday night, the phone rang in my living room. It was Jonah.

'Look at The Mole's mole, Stan. It's gone!'

It had as well.

I called Townsend and he admitted he'd had it chopped off.

Vinnie invited me to his wedding, saying, 'All the glitterati will be there.' But I'm not into all that swanky stuff. He knows it, too.

I did miss Chelsea. We'd be having our pre-match meal of beans on toast and suddenly be surrounded by John Major, Phil Collins and Richard Attenborough. I wasn't too impressed. The car parks were full of Rolls-Royces and shining Maseratis. I drove a Cavalier.

Instead of all the glamour, my abiding memory of Chelsea is Porterfield's nonsensical attitude. Working with him, for me, was one of the worst experiences imaginable in football.

Four years after leaving Chelsea, he became number two to Colin Todd at Bolton Wanderers. After only four months, Bolton were relegated from the Premiership and Porterfield was found drunk in his car, three times over the limit. Coming so soon after his ban while we were at Chelsea, he was barred from driving for eight years. As a result, he quit.

I found it hard to sympathise. His final act of betrayal on my last day at Chelsea saw to that.

After he had sacked me, I made my way out of the hotel near Heathrow Airport and bumped into one of his assistants, Eddie Niedzwiecki, whom I believed Porterfield recruited from Reading when he'd decided I was not to be relied upon.

Eddie saw me walking through reception and offered his hand. 'Listen, Stan,' he said, 'sorry to hear about your news.'

What? My sacking? Bloody hell, my execution had been public. Porterfield had not even been prepared to offer me the courtesy of letting me be the first to know that I was doomed.

5

'He's the Yorkshire Ripper ...'

CARLISLE, 1968–74;
SUNDERLAND, 1974–78;
BLACKPOOL, 1978–80; LEEDS, 1980–81;
BRADFORD CITY, 1986–89

Seconds before I headbutted my own centre-forward, I paused to review the situation.

Ron Futcher had naffed me off completely. As assistant manager at Bradford City, I expected players to respond positively to my coaching sessions. No slackers. No taking the piss. I like a laugh but work is work.

Yet runouts at our Harvesters training ground were occasionally disrupted by players who expected to be paid small fortunes to play football but who would do anything to avoid practising.

Time on the training ground is invaluable. It was time for a show of strength. My strength.

A sense of discipline was crucial for Bradford at a time when morale was low and the club was forced into a nomadic existence. Dismally, we had to play our league matches at the city's decrepit former speedway track, Odsall Stadium. An enforced exile from our normal ground at Valley Parade would last until it was rebuilt after the horrific fire which had killed 56 supporters 20 months earlier. Yet, along with manager Terry Dolan, I was convinced we could outplay Sunderland, Leeds, Ipswich, Blackburn and others in the old Division Two in 1987, if only I could get their full attention in training.

It wasn't always Futcher's fault, but he was not a first-time offender. He acted the goat. Every time he messed up and the lads decided to cop out of an exercise, I shouted, 'Right, put the balls down and get running over the hill.'

The whole squad moaned, 'Fucking hell, Stan!' But they had to learn to bollock him, not me!

I once accused Futch of skiving at his house up in the hills of Yorkshire at Holmfirth. A huge public row erupted. 'Look,' I told him, 'if you want a day off, have one. Don't come here telling me you're snowed in somewhere up in *Last of the Summer Wine* country.'

But he walked away laughing once too often and, after yet another session, I pulled club skipper Stuart McCall to one side. Judging from the look of apprehension on his face, I knew he and the other lads expected something to happen. I told him straight. 'In 30 seconds, it's going to kick off. Don't jump in. Tell the lads to stay out of it, too. I want to sort it once and for all.'

McCall got the message and I watched the squad play Chinese Whispers, passing my threat from man to man. The moment Futch messed up, I called him over. Christ Almighty, for a balding 30-year-old he was a big lad. Too big for me, I thought.

Sod it. Now I'd told the others players I was going ten rounds with him, there was no turning back. I settled for a surprise attack, launched myself forward and butted him square on the nose.

He didn't go down. He swayed backwards. He even looked stunned and in pain. But he didn't go down.

Out of the corner of my eye, I spotted Terry watching. At that stage, I thought better of continuing such a one-sided attack. It would be difficult to justify.

To avoid any complaints, I needed Futch to hit me back. It was my turn to take his medicine. He swung a right hook. I could have ducked, but I took the punch flush on the face and rolled with it. There. Enough was enough.

We were about to shake hands when I looked down at my chest and noticed that, in the mêlée, he had ripped off my Anglo-Italian Cup souvenir gold chain I won at Carlisle.

Aaaaaaaaagh! I jumped on him and we rolled around on the grass, trying to dig each other in the ribs or get another clear face shot. As instructed, the players didn't try to split us up. Instead, they looked in amazement as I scrapped with Futch amongst the cones and balls we had humped out to the centre of the pitch.

With the fight at deadlock, we broke it up ourselves and got to our feet. Terry wandered over and beckoned me to his side. 'What were you doing with Ron, playing crab football?' he asked. 'Let's put it down to high spirits, eh?' Then he shouted over to Futch. 'Ron. You can't do that to a member of staff. You're fined two hundred quid.'

Justice at last.

Short bursts of violence followed by intense sessions of camaraderie are common in football. Futch understood that. We shook hands after our fight and he went on to score plenty of goals for me. But like every other mug in the game, from my earliest days as a player, in order to survive such hassle you need to develop a hide thicker than Judy Finnigan's. If you are daft enough to indulge in sentiment you are knackered.

It's hardly a slave market, but men you consider to be good friends are sold like cattle. Contracts are ripped up at the whim of management. Rejection is par for the course.

When Burnley had kicked me out as a young player and exiled me to Carlisle, I was forced to abandon any pals I had in the game and make my way to football's furthest-flung outpost.

Whatever positive spin I put on the transfer, there was no doubt in 1968 that my new home, Brunton Park, was the Second Division's equivalent of the Khyber Pass.

Manchester United bathed in the glory of their first European Cup victory; Chelsea's stylish stars paraded down the King's Road wearing the latest, glamorous fashions. Even Burnley held their own in the First Division.

At Carlisle, a beautifully scenic town, the pace was slow to semi-conscious. Wednesday night was darts night when local pub teams would challenge the players to tournaments over bottles of beer. That was it.

The fact that every player lived and socialised in the town helped the squad bond together but we became insular. We all trawled a familiar circuit of parties at each other's houses and it became oppressive. Light relief was catching our hosts rowing with each other over a baby listener they had forgotten to turn off. We were a million miles from anywhere and a million years behind the rest of the country.

One afternoon, we arrived at the Hawthorns to play West Bromwich Albion and stood in awe as their players' wives slunk into the ground wearing skintight all-in-one leopard-skin catsuits. We turned to see our wives arrive looking like the Dingles, wearing duffel coats.

On the way home, the coach driver hit the motorway heading north then wedged the accelerator down with a block of wood to save his weary foot. We only ever stopped if our trainer Dick Young wanted to release some of his racing pigeons.

Manager Tim Ward paid £5,000 for my services. I was 21 and he hurled me straight into the thick of a dogfight to survive in the Second Division. Carlisle were on a charge from the lower leagues. Two consecutive promotions in 1964 and 1965 catapulted them from the Fourth Division to the Second.

Fans imagined they could pull off the impossible and take this unfashionable, country hick side into the First Division and they narrowly missed out on rising from the Fourth to the First in four years when they finished third in 1966–67. Now the campaign had stalled and Carlisle were becalmed in the Second.

I was determined to make the most of my first team opportunities and lost a stone in weight during a strict training regime within the first three weeks. My weekly wage of £3 was poor, so I took building jobs in the summer – I even helped to construct mountaineer Chris Bonnington's house – to ensure Kath and I could make our way after we married.

The wedding took place in Kath's home town of Burnley after the Football League's fixture compiler chose the date. We waited until Carlisle were scheduled to play away at Blackburn Rovers in order to plan the ceremony just down the road for the following day.

Our honeymoon was at the Queen's Hotel, four miles from Burnley centre in Todmorden, a rain-drenched hamlet in the depths of a gloomy, narrow valley. It was run by a bloke who looked like Arthur Askey.

Throughout the night, a huge clock on the wall outside our room struck deafeningly every hour. We hardly slept and, as we prepared to head off back to Carlisle the following morning, I saw other guests nudge and point at the knackered honeymooners.

I became the only player to turn down the club's offer of a rented house and stretched our finances to the limit to buy our own property. Harry Potts had shown me how football was cruelly fickle. I wanted the security of my own roof over my head to prove I was achieving. It was just as well.

After five points from our first 12 games and without a win, we were rock bottom of the table, two points behind Aston Villa, and manager Ward had quit. It was a tough league.

Ward walked away after suffering horrendous abuse from fans. We were beaten 5–0 by Crystal Palace and 4–0 at home by Norwich a week later. Angry supporters daubed offensive messages in creosote on fences around the ground.

After Leicester City – with their £150,000-rated striker Allan Clarke on form – beat us 3–0 at home in the League Cup, Ward had suffered enough. He said, 'I don't think I would ever have the public behind me, however long I stayed.'

Too many other teams ranged against us spent big money; Birmingham had £70,000 Jimmy Greenhoff, and Fulham paid £75,000 for Cardiff's John Toshack.

Then in walked our saviour. Bob Stokoe, one of the most charismatic men in football, was employed to turn Carlisle's fortunes around. Within weeks, with essentially the same players as Ward, we went 13 games unbeaten, 11 hours without conceding a goal and climbed to twelfth in the table, just five points behind leaders Derby County. It was a remarkable feat.

My first encounter with this gruff, tough fella with a Geordie accent as impenetrable as mine was to change the way I viewed football for ever.

His training sessions at Sheepmounts were extraordinarily refreshing and cavalier. Stokoe's motto was 'Avoid Boredom'. He told us, 'We're not practising offsides, corners, free-kicks or throw-ins. This is a game for individual flair and we will play to our strengths. Too much method ruins free thinking. I don't go for intricate plans, lads.' It was revolutionary.

We played 90-minute five-a-side matches in training. Stokoe captained one side against another skippered by Dick Young. Everyone was encouraged to take the piss. As the game progressed, Stokoe instructed, 'If you can't score, sod off and get in the bath.'

We were stimulated, emboldened, unafraid. The season ended with us in twelfth, a remarkable rescue act. At one point, Stokoe took 34 points from a possible 48. Without our dreadful start, we could have been promoted along with Brian Clough's Derby.

Over the next five seasons, I became slightly too emboldened. After I headbutted great hairy mountain Bob Latchford during a match against Birmingham, it was a toss-up over who gave me my biggest bollocking, my manager or my missus.

* * *

As we struggled to maintain our mid-table status the following season, I fought a battle to control my temper and win over the crowd. Whether I played at sweeper covering for Tot Winstanley, as a specialist man-marker or as a straightforward half-back, I continually compensated for my lack of pace. Usually, I picked opponents' brains and used my positional sense to outdo them. If that failed, Plan B was to hammer them into the ground.

Graeme Souness claims I was the hardest player he ever faced. He's right. I fought for my livelihood.

Kath gave birth to our first son Chris at Carlisle and I became doubly determined to succeed to provide him with luxuries I missed as a child. There was a long way to go. We were so skint in the early '70s that Kath could do 50 things with a pound of mince. Two friends once took Chris out for the day and brought him home wearing a new pair of winter boots. They recognised we were struggling and were too sensitive to say anything. I was grateful and too proud to say thank you.

So if Souey shuddered when I rolled him over, it was hardly surprising. I flew into tackles, even in training. Each practice match was like a Cup Final to me. I'd go crunching in. I knew it narked some of the lads but it added needle, a sensation I thrived on.

If I lost a match, I despised myself and moped around the house all weekend. I could hardly bear the wait until the next game so I could be a winner again. It was and *is* the only way. Losers were rejected and I'd had my share of that. This attitude got me booked too often, but having bollocks was a good thing, wasn't it?

Stokoe pulled me to one side and said, 'Stan, you are a powerhouse of a player but get that discipline under control.'

That was rich! Stokoe boosted my confidence when he declared publicly, 'I wouldn't swap Stan for Colin Todd,' but he also bred my competitiveness. He was a terrible loser. I saw him get worked up on the golf course and start screaming and shouting during supposedly friendly foursomes.

My shaky disciplinary record finally exploded in controversy during our first home game of the 1970–71 season. Pele's Brazil had just walked away with the World Cup, dazzling us all with his beautiful football. More mundanely, we played Birmingham City, whose centre-forward Bob Latchford had just become an England youth international. He obviously didn't subscribe to the South American method.

Bulky, ugly and arrogant, he was everything needed in a typically English centre-forward.

I was Vice-Captain and, with the score 0–0, we battered each other like Tom hitting Jerry with an anvil. I ought to have steered clear of the big lump but, as we crashed into yet another challenge close to our penalty box, we clashed heads, and he collapsed as though he'd been shot.

I may have butted him. He may have butted me. I was man enough to walk away. Latchford rolled around like Lassie begging for a biscuit.

Ref Bob Darlington didn't seem too interested in me until the Birmingham players surrounded him and howled for my head.

'Off you go, lad,' he said, and jostled me towards the tunnel while their team tried to tear me apart. As I traipsed away, I saw Latchford spring to his feet and dust himself down. I was furious and booted a chair all around the dressing room. While I showered, I heard the muffled cheers from Birmingham's fans as they hit one, then two, then three. Latchford even got a couple himself.

Stokoe went potty. 'Stan and I are tarred with the same brush,' he said. 'He hates to lose and he gives his all. Sometimes he gives too much. He realises he has let the club, his team and himself down badly. Through him we lost the match. It will cost him wages.'

Kath continued the bollocking when I got home.

We were practically potless as we scraped to afford the monthly mortgage payments. Every time I took someone off at the knees, my wallet was emptied by levies set by the club and the Football League. When my £100 fine for the Latchford farce arrived, Kath made me spread the money out in cash on our kitchen table. Bloody hell, I realised, there's a lot there. Kath made me count every penny and even lick the envelope before she popped it in the post.

I felt victimised. I was a hard player but I was not dirty. I'd marked players like Johnny Haynes and Willie Carlin completely out of matches and they'd shaken my hand at the final whistle.

Stokoe quit to manage Blackpool halfway through the season and giant Scot Ian MacFarlane took his place. At the time, the Carlisle Board was packed with sober country gents who were over-precious. They once sacked a player for miming a gag about arse-wiping at a club dinner. In contrast, man-mountain MacFarlane was a walking air-raid siren.

When he heard I was attending a League disciplinary hearing in Sheffield, he decided to defend me himself. 'Let me handle it, wee man,' he said.

I was only in the dock for five bookings but, by the time Mac bawled out the committee, they were on the verge of giving me three years in jail.

On a team trip to watch The Open Golf Championship at Lytham St Anne's, we watched in hushed awe as Lee Trevino settled to attempt a putt from 20ft, observed by his playing partner Jack Nicklaus.

Just as the legendary Mexican lifted his club on the backstroke, Mac stood on a discarded soft drink can. In the silence surrounding the fifteenth green, the crunch reverberated like a cannon shot.

Trevino stuttered and stopped. Nicklaus scowled. Irked officials craned their necks to see which buffoon had disrupted the master at work.

Mac chirped cheerily, strode towards the green with his hand outstretched and said, 'Sorry, pal, never saw it. Sorry, Jack. Hello, Lee. Ian MacFarlane, manager of Carlisle United.'

Mac took us to fourth in his first season, advocating flowing, comfortable, free-passing football. Only a poor record of four away wins all season stopped us winning promotion. As we progressed, I began to attract my own fan club.

Scouts from First Division sides West Bromwich Albion and

Nottingham Forest watched me regularly. I also became a pin-up. In an edition bearing the front-page headline THE DAY ENGELBERT HUMPERDINCK LOST HIS VOICE, the *Weekly News* listed me as one of the top ten most handsome footballers in Britain. Despite my dodgy '70s-style Richard III haircut, I was offered modelling work. Reader Brenda Wheadon from Brampton in Cumberland even wrote to the editor begging him to print a poster.

Other writers were not so kind as I tried to establish myself as a household name. A poster of the Carlisle team in *Shoot!* magazine listed me as *Frank* Ternent. The *Sunday Mirror* printed a lovely picture of my ferocious tackle on Aston Villa's Willie Anderson but referred to me as *Jimmy*. And a biography in the programme as we travelled to play Cardiff City said I was *Steve* Ternent.

To avoid confusion, Carlisle fans knew me as Tiger Feet. I was made captain and quickly grasped another discipline. Skippers have to possess the balls to bollock the rest of the lads, even when you're having a bad game yourself. I was supposed to lead by example but often found myself fighting battles for other players.

On a club trip to Benidorm, we all got pissed in the notorious 007 Club. Joe Davis was on the dance floor drunkenly strutting his stuff.

Seconds later, a huge brawl erupted and I was into it big style. In true Musketeer fashion, it was 'all for one and one for all' at Carlisle. Usually.

That night, it was 'all for one and all for the fire exit'.

I piled into the punch-up, swinging wildly. As I paused to see exactly who I was hitting, I noticed that the rest of the lads had retreated. Suddenly, I was on my own fighting the Spanish Eighth Army. They booted me down a spiral staircase and bottled me. My white shirt was covered in blood.

The next morning, Mac saw me at breakfast as I dabbed at my bloody wounds with a napkin. 'What happened, Skipper?'

I owned up. 'I could tell you I've fallen down some stairs but ...'

He sent me home. I couldn't get the stitches I needed in the resort because a local newspaper reporter was with us on the trip and Mac was terrified my punch-up would become front-page news. I flew to Manchester and was warned to avoid Carlisle until my face healed.

Kath picked me up and bollocked me, too, for good measure.

Mac soon forgave me. He said, 'Money can't buy players like Stan. He has a will to win and plays on occasions when he is injured or unwell, perhaps even when he should not do.' No one was getting my shirt.

I still walked determinedly out of the tunnel, even when I was crippled and my playing career was effectively over at the age of 27.

* * *

Mac was sacked at the end of 1971–72 and Carlisle turned to their ultimate hero, softly spoken, suited Yorkshireman Alan Ashman. He was the genial figure who had inspired the team to successive promotions from the Fourth Division to the Second in the early Sixties and subsequently took them to within one place of the First in 1967.

He was rewarded elsewhere, with a contract as boss of West Bromwich where he won the FA Cup. Now, after being sacked, he was back.

Ashman was a gentleman. Whenever he dropped a player, he would hand over a Polo mint first to sweeten the blow. In his first season after his return to Brunton Park, we struggled to stave off relegation, but in the summer of 1973 he rallied his troops for a final push for that elusive, historic promotion. He inherited a decent team and part of his strategy was to take the lads to the Harraby Inn every Wednesday for a pint.

When Mac was in charge, he'd been forced to sell our top striker Bob Hatton to rivals Birmingham City for £80,000. As a replacement, he bought Stan Bowles from Crewe Alexandra.

Bowles, all big collars and sideburns, used me as his bank. Each Monday he borrowed a lump of cash, paid it back the following Sunday and then asked to have it again a day later. Kath complained.

'He has nowt,' I explained.

'Neither have we,' she said.

We had just had our second child, Dan. I drove Kath to hospital and, conveniently, he didn't pop out until I'd seen the whole of the England v Poland World Cup match on the ward's TV.

She hated the thought of having Bowles as another mouth to feed. Stan is regarded by those who don't know him as a luxury player who would either perform for 90 minutes or go missing soon after kick-off, but he was a steely, determined individual. We constantly challenged each other to head tennis duels, spending hours waiting for the other to weaken for a stake of 50p.

Our team also boasted Ray Train and Chris Balderstone, a sublimely skilful footballer who played cricket for England, too. When I was busy falling through ceilings on building sites during the summer to boost my wage, I'd telephone Balderstone as he prepared to walk out at Lords and call him a lazy bastard. Together, we began the season disastrously, smashed 6–1 at Luton. We were 6–0 down at half-time.

Ashman skulked into their Boardroom after the match to find their famous director Eric Morecambe serving behind the bar. Other VIPs maintained a diplomatic silence about the result as Eric handed over a glass of beer.

'You know,' Ashman said to the comedian, 'to get to this match today I had to leave Carlisle at 6 o'clock this morning.'

Morecambe leaned over the bar, slapped Ashman playfully on both cheeks and said, 'I don't blame you, Sunshine.'

My parents decided to travel to watch us play away against our nearest rivals Middlesbrough. I arranged for complimentary tickets to be left at the Ayresome Park reception desk. After our 2–0 victory, an official told me that the passes had not been collected. I telephoned their house later that night but there was no answer. Frantic with worry, I was on the verge of calling the police when Mam rang. 'Would you believe it, Stan,' she said. 'Me and your dad got on the train at Newcastle but it didn't go to Middlesbrough. It was a non-stop express to King's Cross in London. And I didn't even have my knitting.' Mam didn't come to see me play too often.

During one game, she pointed to the referee and asked, 'Who's that little man in black? He's done nowt.'

My dad finally managed to see me in action in the FA Cup against his heroes Sunderland. We had drawn 0–0 at Carlisle and there was a huge crowd for the replay at Roker Park. Dad stood in his usual spot on the terraces with his pals Corny O'Donnell, Franky Scullion and a Catholic priest, Father Strong. I'd got them free tickets and I'd shook on a bet. I staked a quid that we would win and the four of them watched in horror as I headed the winner. Bang. Pick that one out.

After the game, only Corny had the guts to come and see me. 'Where's Dad?' I asked.

'Gone,' said Corny. 'He's left your money.'

The next day in church, Father Strong mentioned me in his sermon.

'One of our parishioners scored a goal yesterday that sent Sunderland to defeat. May God forgive him.'

Playing elegant football, we worked hard to retrieve our pride after the mauling at Luton, and took revenge by beating them 2–0 at Brunton Park.

A week later, we played Sheffield Wednesday and my world exploded in pain as I tore my cruciate ligament in a mistimed tackle. Our physio, Herbert Nicholson, was a part-time brickie and his methods of treatment were hardly cutting edge. Today, the injury would be repaired. Instead, Herbert encased the leg in plaster, immobilising it.

I didn't give in. I completed six laps of the training pitch each morning with my full-length cast on in a desperate bid to stay fit and keep my weight down.

I returned to the team too early and aggravated the problem. In truth, my leg was knackered. I never recovered full mobility but I battled to compensate and regained my place in the team.

Crucially, we did the double over Leyton Orient, the team locked with us in a struggle to fill the newly-created third promotion spot behind Luton and Middlesbrough.

We beat Aston Villa 2–0 in our final game but then had to wait six days to learn our fate. The following Friday night, Villa were to play at Leyton Orient who would overtake us if they won.

Some of the lads travelled to London to watch the game. The rest of Cumbria held its breath and switched on their radios.

It was 0–0 when the referee somehow contrived to add seven minutes of injury time. Eventually it was over. Orient couldn't find a winner.

Penniless, humble, unfashionable Carlisle had completed a remarkable rise from the Fourth Division basement to the First Division penthouse. Ashman was a modest hero, but another great manager, Bill Shankly, put his performance into perspective. 'What Carlisle have done,' said the Liverpool legend, 'is the greatest achievement in the history of football.'

I had a beer. Then they sold me.

After 200 league games for Carlisle, I was denied a chance to run out with the lads at Stamford Bridge for their first match in the big league. But I didn't care. I'd been poached by my favourite boss, Bob Stokoe, who was now managing Sunderland, the team I supported as a kid.

My dad didn't live to see it. He died months before the deal, so I never got the chance to make him the proudest Mackem alive.

Before I joined Sunderland, I decided to spend the summer playing for Denver in the USA, but on the plane from Heathrow I changed my mind. The minute I landed at New York's JFK Airport, I turned round and flew back home.

I went out there because my knee was knackered and fear for my future forced me to cast around for a role. But running off to

America was not the answer. Instead, I began to consider a career in management.

Stokoe knew I was crocked when he signed me. I lived three doors away from him and he kept a check on my health. Occasionally, he jumped on to his dustbin to peep over the fence to try to catch me having a crafty fag on the back doorstep.

He persuaded my lad Chris to act as his spy. If he caught me smoking, he'd run down the road shouting, 'I'm going to tell Uncle Bob.'

The fags did my playing career no harm. There was not much of it left. I played two pre-season Texaco Cup matches in the famous red-and-white shirt against Newcastle and Middlesbrough but my leg was still a wreck. I was hospitalised and wept with frustration.

A Sunderland fan in the bed opposite came and sat with me, producing a couple of bottles of beer. We drowned my sorrows and he hopped back into his bed the moment a ward sister marched through the doors.

'Have you been out of bed?' she asked as she pointed at me. 'Someone's broken into our fridge and stolen our Guinness.'

Club officials made sporadic visits. To liven things up, I used to persuade Kath to drape me in a white sheet so I could feign death.

I was finally released sporting another full-length plaster cast. Our striker Billy Hughes told me, 'Come on, we're going to see Rod Stewart tonight.'

Rod had a gig at Newcastle Odeon and had spent the previous week training with the lads. He was a decent player. His mate from The Faces, Ronnie Wood, tried to keep up but he was knackered and in the bath drawing on a fag after two minutes.

Rod became mates with Billy and sent a limo to take us to the theatre. We met the band in their dressing room before Stewart's people parked me in the wings in my wheelchair to watch the concert. Then we were chauffeured to the swanky Gosforth Park Hotel for the after-show party.

'What do you want to drink, Stan?' asked Rod.

'Dunno, Rod, mate. What have you got?'

'Whisky or beer,' he said.

'I'm not sure,' I said.

He walked to a cupboard and came back with a crate of each. 'Take your pick.'

Weeks later, the cast eventually came off ... but I was goosed.

Typically, on the very day I announced my official retirement from playing, the club announced the team's most ambitious tour ever, a glittering trip to Tahiti, New Zealand, Australia, Singapore and Los Angeles.

I was forced to stay at home. As compensation, Stokoe appointed me youth coach. The job gave me a start in management but my wage was more than halved to £60 a week after tax.

I was forced to ferry all 15 youth team players around the North-East in a leaky VW camper van while Kath cooked bacon butties for their lunch at our place after Saturday morning matches.

I had some good kids. Nick Pickering and Barry Venison went on to play for England.

When the youth team had no fixture, Stokoe lent me his silver Ford Granada so I could disappear on scouting missions for the first team. I tipped him off about a promising young lad called Paul Mariner at Plymouth but he chose not to buy him.

I also brought Graeme Souness over to Roker Park. He was fed up at Middlesbrough and ready to sign for £30,000, but Stokoe didn't make it happen. Souey went to Liverpool instead.

Bob's Second Division side had already famously won the FA Cup in 1973 beating Leeds United, and in 1976 they won the league and were promoted to the First Division. Amazingly, he then quit to rejoin Second Division Blackpool.

Don Revie was later to walk out on England for a job in the desert but nothing could match the shock felt in the North-East when Sunderland's saviour shot off to the seaside.

His replacement was Jimmy Adamson, who had been Burnley's skipper as I'd fought and failed to become a Turf Moor first team regular a decade earlier. He had recently taken Burnley into the First Division and promised to do the same for Sunderland. He appointed me to be his first team coach but by Christmas we had just nine points.

I rowed constantly with Jimmy, urging him to push some kids into the side. When he finally responded, we finished the season with a better points ratio than Liverpool, who won the title. But it wasn't enough. We were back in the Second Division.

A mediocre season followed in which we finished sixth. We were then due to fly to Kenya on an end-of-season tour. As we prepared to leave, I told Jimmy, 'I need a new contract.' I was still on only £100 a week.

He said, 'I'll sort it out.'

Nothing happened. I was impetuous and got the hump. I felt that he had let me down.

I was off. All he had had to do was make me feel wanted.

When he finally bothered to make me an offer, I was in no mood to consider it. He looked dumbfounded when he heard my response to his deal. 'Shove it up your arse, Jimmy.'

I left to rejoin Stokoe and become his assistant at Blackpool. They had been relegated to the Third Division in Bob's first disastrous season and I walked into a hellhole. There seemed to be 20 butchers, bakers and candlestickmakers on the Board jockeying for power and sticking their noses in.

When Bill Cartmell was Chairman, sessions began at 1.00pm each Monday. At 5.00pm he would place his pork pie hat on his head, leave and then return an hour later. 'I've just been home for my tea, lads.'

Gallons of PG Tips would be consumed as the room echoed to rows. They didn't just have general meetings. They held extra-extra-extra-extra-ordinary general meetings.

The club was in trauma and the Chairman appeared to change

every time we got a throw-in. At one point, warring factions behind the scenes unconnected with the Board threatened the local *Blackpool Gazette* sports reporter with being kneecapped. Crowds slumped to around 4,000 and Bloomfield Road was falling down around us. The fans who bothered to turn up at all proved judgemental and Stokoe was well aware of their moods.

During a fierce home match when we were being beaten 3–1 by Swansea, I was hit by a brick thrown from the crowd. Blood poured from a cut on my head. 'I'm going to the police,' I told Stokoe, as I slumped into the dugout. 'We need to find out who threw that.'

'Don't be stupid,' he said. 'It's probably one of ours.'

I'd earned this chance after years of hard work at Sunderland, yet I found myself embroiled in an anarchic power struggle at a madhouse.

When Peter Lawson was Chairman, he invited us to his huge house overlooking Stanley Park for nights of terrapin racing when we would make bets on the winner.

In our first season as a management duo, we finished mid-table but all the off-pitch chaos was too much for Stokoe, one of the most experienced managers in the Football League. He quit.

Before our first game of the 1979–80 season, he came to see me one Friday afternoon and said, 'I just can't handle all this any more, Stan. I'm off.'

Players wrote to the Board asking for me to get the job, but I didn't relish the prospect. Stokoe, who recommended me before he walked out, was Blackpool's third manager in 18 months. When I was appointed caretaker manager in his absence, it was forced medicine.

After nine games, I got the job full-time to become, at the age of 32, one of the youngest managers in the Football League. Quality players such as Bob Hatton and Mickey Walsh had cleared out soon after Stokoe arrived, so I turned to ex-Burnley stars Peter Noble and Paul Fletcher to help us avoid relegation.

Despite my best endeavours, supporters became as fickle as the

Board. I returned home one night, freezing and miserable after a 2–1 home defeat to Oxford, when a neighbour shouted, 'That's another nail in your coffin, Ternent.' I tried to grab him but he ran away into his house.

The Board began to lose faith, too. Almost immediately, whispers began to spread that ex-Blackpool player Alan Ball was being touted as the club's next Manager. I confronted the directors, who made reassuring noises, denied Ball had been approached and gave me a vote of confidence.

'Something needs to be sorted out long term,' I told them.

It was. I was sacked ... and replaced by Alan Ball.

The club even allowed him to begin work from his current home, 5,000 miles away at the Vancouver Whitecaps. It provoked John Sadler to launch a tirade against the club in his column in *The Sun* newspaper. 'The Blackpool Board have betrayed Stan Ternent by bringing in Ball behind his back,' he wrote. 'At one point, Ternent had to remind the players he was still their manager and his contract was valid until July 1980.'

It counted for nothing. I had been manager for six months, the longest six months of my life. The experience was invaluable. I learned exactly how not to run a football club. The whole set-up was a joke. It knocked my career back a mile.

To cap it all, when Ball finally arrived, his daughter was placed in the same class as my son Chris at school. It was cruel on the kid.

At a golf club function at Blackpool's Imperial Hotel soon after my sacking, Kath won a nest of tables in the raffle. I couldn't carry them so I was tempted to drive home.

Dressed in my second-hand dinner suit with Kath beside me in her fur coat, we set off along the seafront in our Austin 1300 at 1.30am. The police pulled us up after 500 yards. We looked like Bonnie and Clyde after a raid on MFI.

I was charged with drink-driving and speeding. In court, I was defended by lawyer Peter Lawson, the Chairman of Blackpool who had sacked me three weeks earlier.

I was eventually cleared of the alcohol charge, and when I got home, Kath tied a yellow ribbon around a tree in the garden.

Lawson soon followed me out of the door at Bloomfield Road.

When I was sacked, he sent a bouquet to my house with a note for Kath which said, 'Just to make sure you'll still let him out to play golf.'

We left the flowers to die. Six months later when Lawson was ousted, we sent him a wreath.

Within weeks of leaving Blackpool, I'd swapped one living nightmare for another. I accepted an offer from Jimmy Adamson, who was now at Leeds United, to become his reserve team coach, but the job was doomed. The side was mediocre. We finished mid-table in 1980 and were faring no better as we approached the start of 1981, losing 5–0 at home to Arsenal and 3–0 to Southampton. My kids Chris and Dan even stuck the knife in.

One night, they were watching the TV news about the hunt for the Yorkshire Ripper. Police announced he was a Geordie who regularly crossed the Pennines, was physically fit and drove a big car. The lads ticked off my credentials. I was a Geordie; I travelled from Lytham to Leeds every day; I was fit and I had been issued with a club car, a suitably big Granada. Only Kath's intervention stopped them ringing the police.

They realised their fears were groundless soon enough when my Pennine commuting days ended unexpectedly. Adamson was sacked by Leeds less than a year after I arrived. New manager Allan Clarke soon cleared his backroom staff out.

I thought, Bollocks to it. My pride was hurt. I was so sick of football I quit the game. I was offered jobs in Zambia and Bermuda but it was time to consider my family. The lads had constantly changed schools for years. They needed some stability.

To make ends meet I sold cars and frozen food. We helped out at the Queensway pub in Lytham. Kath learned how to do the paperwork. I learned how to hump crates of ale.

I pumped thousands of pounds into a fledgling frozen food

business but it folded and I lost a bundle. I was forced to do building work, a job I hadn't done since my days at Carlisle.

Our flat in Fairhaven Road became depressingly claustrophobic. We had a concertina door on the bog. You were forced to sit and whistle every time you took a crap. The TV ran on a meter. If we wanted an evening's entertainment, we had to build a mound of ten pences on top of the telly. The fabric on the settee was so cheap and nasty it could take the skin off your elbows.

One night, as all four of us lay in bed in the same room and I listened to Kath cry, I made a promise to her – 'This will never happen again.'

We tired of scraping a living at the coast and, four years after Leeds kicked me out, we moved back to Kath's home town of Burnley. I became licensee of the Thornton Arms, a newly-built pub just half-a-mile from our home on the outskirts of town.

I hated it. The police continually tried to catch me serving late drinks. No chance. I couldn't wait to shut. I'd barred half of the scrotes off the nearby council estate because they couldn't drink up quick enough.

A glue-sniffer nicked my golf clubs out of the van I parked behind the pub. They were found by amateur divers at the bottom of a local lake. Police told me their chief suspect had a crucifix tattoo. Weeks later, a bloke answering his description turned up at my bar.

'Pint of lager, please.'

I asked him, 'Did you break into my van?'

'Look,' said the lad, 'can I just have my pint?'

I hurdled the bar and chased him out. Minutes after I returned, the phone rang.

'Look,' said the same bloke, 'if I come back, can I have a pint?'

I looked out of the window and saw him in the phone box across the road. I passed the phone to Kath. 'Keep him talking.'

As she pressed the receiver to her ear, she heard every punch land after I'd cornered him. I made an intolerant landlord. Frankly, I didn't like customers.

One night, I embarked on a massive, costly promotional exercise to make peace with the locals. I announced a Burns Night party and spent £200 to provide free haggis for everyone.

I woke at 6am to begin preparations and by opening time we were still racing around knee deep in sheeps' bladders.

In the middle of the mayhem, an old bloke approached me at the bar. 'Excuse me, are you the landlord?' he asked.

'Why?'

'Well,' he explained, 'it's just that the wife doesn't like haggis. I was wondering if we could have a couple of free portions of scampi and chips.'

After telling the haggis-hater where to go, I wrote to the brewery and handed in my notice.

I was working out my last month behind the bar when Brian Flynn popped in for a pint. Flynny was at Leeds with me as a player and still lived in Burnley after playing for them in the Seventies. The Thornton Arms was his local. 'I hear there's a job going at Bradford,' he told me.

Apparently, manager Trevor Cherry, another player who had been at Elland Road with me five years earlier, was looking for a youth team coach. Flynn offered to have a word and, soon after, Trevor called me. We met with our wives at a pub in Huddersfield, where he offered me the job.

Only weeks into the position, Cherry's assistant manager, Terry Yorath, left to take charge at Swansea. Reserve coach Terry Dolan was promoted to work with the first team in his place while I got his job.

I had a glamorous life. The club couldn't afford to give me a car, so, for a scouting trip to Bournemouth, they booked me on to the Bolton Wanderers Supporters' Club bus.

When they eventually scraped some cash together, I was presented with a Fiat Panda that wouldn't go up hills.

One winter night after a reserve match, I was racing the Panda back over to Burnley, desperate to reach The Kettledrum for last orders. At 20mph, I could have pedalled faster.

As I reached a Yorkshire town called Mytholmroyd, I stopped for an emergency slash. I made my way precariously down a frosty pavement and positioned myself behind a derelict mill. In mid-flow, my loafers suddenly gave way on the ice and I fell to the ground with my hand trapped under my arse and my tackle flapping around in the freezing air. When I lifted my arm, I almost passed out. I'd broken my finger and it was already deformed.

In panic, I tried to re-set it myself but I was almost physically sick with pain. I couldn't even tuck myself back into my trousers and arrived home to a horrified welcome from Kath. My finger is still crooked today.

Those early months at Bradford were difficult. I was relieved to be back in football after an absence of five years, but the effects of that terrible fire still pervaded the club and the mood was grim.

After spells at Elland Road and Huddersfield's Leeds Road, our temporary home, the speedway and rugby stadium at Odsall, was a vast shit-tip. We could have attracted 60,000 fans and it would still have seemed empty.

At first, it was a novelty to watch the faces of visiting players as they registered their awful surroundings. But our fans hated it and our players hated it. The grass was so long that if little Flynny had joined us for training we would have lost him.

To survivors of Bradford's terrible tragedy, it never seemed like home and it was a major relief when the new, refurbished Valley Parade was officially reopened in front of 15,000 supporters who saw us win a friendly match 2–1 against an England XI starring Kevin Keegan and managed by Bobby Robson. Demand for tickets was so high that flat-roofed houses around the ground were lined with deckchairs.

As usual, I swapped two tickets for a free tandoori from my

mate Bashir, who lived opposite Valley Parade and would feed us when we had an afternoon to kill before a night match.

Even Maggie Thatcher toured our new ground, accompanied by the club's bowing and scraping hierarchy. My main concern was that the players might fart as she walked past.

After the redevelopment of sections of the ground, one of the old stands stood out like a spare prick at a wedding. It was only 10ft high with a capacity of 855. On match days, I trained the team to launch the ball over the roof where I knew a bunch of lads waited to nick it. With three minutes to go, defending a one-goal lead, an accurate clearance was a masterstroke.

The club paid a bloke to stand on the roof to try and direct the official ball boys but my team of urchins on the main road was quicker.

One day in training, our reserve keeper Rob Mauvely booted the ball over by mistake. 'Go and get it,' I told him.

Twenty minutes later, he staggered back into the ground pale and shaken. 'I fell over,' he said.

We ran to have a look at the spot where he'd tried to climb over and there was a 20ft drop on the other side. He'd broken his arm and was out for weeks.

Our first team performances could be just as stupid. A 5–0 home defeat to Nottingham Forest in the Milk Cup was followed by a 4–1 defeat by Stoke. When local rivals Huddersfield beat us 5–2 just after Christmas, it was curtains for Cherry, who got the boot. We had lost four games on the trot and were bottom of Division Two.

Some players had not worked too hard to help him out. A young apprentice from the reserve team claimed he had suffered a bad back injury and was sent to see a specialist. He was put in traction, and out of sympathy we gave him an extra year on his contract to give him time to recover.

One night, as I sipped my fourth Bacardi and Coke, watching ITV in my pyjamas at 1.00am, I almost choked. I shouted for my lad, who found me on all fours peering directly into the screen from two inches away. 'Chris, Chris! Look who that is!'

It was the crippled apprentice, in the audience on Pete Waterman's hit music show *The Hit Man and Her*, breakdancing on his head in some sort of jitterbugging contest.

After Cherry left, Terry Dolan put himself forward for the job and I gave him my backing. He had four different interviews with the Board until they narrowed it down to two candidates –Terry and Martin O'Neill, who was manager at non-league Grantham. The two of them were embarrassed to bump into each other during the final round of interviews, but it was Terry who got the nod to take up his first job in management. Chairman Stafford Hegginbotham backed my man. His Vice-Chairman Jack Tordoff wanted O'Neill.

Hegginbotham was a genial old buffer who owned a collection of three wigs. One short. One medium. One long. He would rotate them to imitate hair growth and remained convinced that none of us knew his secret. Stafford's victory over the selection of the new manager was never forgotten by Tordoff.

Even as Terry and Stafford sat around the Boardroom table on the night of the appointment quaffing champagne, dour Tordoff walked over to deliver his own damning verdict. He said to Terry and me, 'I'll tell you both now to your face before somebody else tells you behind my back. I didn't want you to have the job.'

We finished the season in tenth. With that sort of moral support, it was a miracle we stayed up at all.

Terry and I worked hard to stage a push for promotion in 1988 and strengthened the team big style. We switched John Hendrie from playing out wide to a more central role and his career took off.

We powered our way up the table scrapping with Middlesbrough, Aston Villa, Blackburn Rovers and Leeds United for one last promotion place.

Terry spent most matches in the stands and would dial me on an internal phone in the dugout to issue instructions. After two games, I left it off the hook.

During a 10-game unbeaten run in March, we lined up Andy Townsend and Keith Curle to join us for our final surge towards the top three, but the Board refused to fund the deals.

I told them, 'Speculate to accumulate. You can always get your money back if necessary by selling McCall and Hendrie.'

By now, Hegginbotham had been forced to retire. He had a dicky heart and could no longer dress in his knee-length shorts to take me and Terry golfing. He died on an operating table during a transplant.

In contrast to his predecessor's fun-filled attitude, Tordoff's ears were closed to our pleas for money. We were two matches away from the First Division. But instead of investing in the team, after a crucial 1–0 defeat at Aston Villa in our penultimate game we were left to our own devices. We needed to win our final match at home to Ipswich Town to stand any chance of going up automatically.

We lost 3–2.

As the other results came in, we realised that even a draw would have been enough.

Pitched into the play-offs against Middlesbrough, we were leading 2–0 in the first leg at Valley Parade when Trevor Senior scored a crucial goal for them in the last minute.

It was a disaster.

In the dressing room afterwards, even though we had won, the players were inconsolable. Hendrie said, 'We should have won by more. We pissed on them.'

The damage was done. After 90 minutes of the second leg, they were winning 1–0, but they scored another in extra time to knock us out.

The coach trip home was miserable. I sat with Terry and we faced the inevitable. McCall had a clause in his contract to allow him to leave if we failed to be promoted and Hendrie's contract had run out. Predictably, the pair of them wanted out.

Newcastle enquired about Hendrie and he told me, 'If I don't go now, I might never get a better chance. I've got to go, Stan.' He was sold for £500,000 while our other asset, home-grown McCall, joined Everton for £850,000.

Their team-mates deserved promotion after a strenuous season but their only reward was to see the side ripped apart. The club had rebuilt itself from a disaster of titanic proportions, only to begin to disintegrate immediately.

Stafford once told me that, as he toured local hospital wards 24 hours after the fire, one badly burned patient's only concern was for his favourite team. 'You won't sell McCall will you, Stafford?' he asked.

Now Stafford and McCall were both gone. Tordoff was in full control.

Terry was upbeat on that journey home, planning for the following season. I was more experienced. I knew we were doomed.

* * *

Tordoff waited five months. But his strike, when it came, was inevitable.

Our makeshift team was making a decent fist of clinging to a mid-table spot. We had knocked Spurs out of the FA Cup but then lost at home in the next round to Hull City. That night, Terry and I took our wives for a drink at the Coach and Horses in the nearby village of Luddendenfoot. We tried to forget the day's events, but Terry rose to leave too early.

> Terry: **I'll get off now. There's a Board meeting first thing in the morning and they want me there.'**
> Me: **A what?**
> Terry: **A Board meeting.**
> Me: **What time?**
> Terry: **First thing, why?**
> Me: **We're going to get sacked.**

The following morning, I was woken by a phone call from Tordoff. 'I've sacked Terry Dolan and I'm sacking you as well,' he said. 'I want your car back within a week.'

Terry was unprepared but I had rehearsed a thousand times all the shit I wanted to hurl at Tordoff. His lack of investment. His lack of encouragement.

In the end, his lack of bollocks kyboshed our row. He didn't even fire me to my face. I had turned down the job of Huddersfield manager three times while I was at Valley Parade. This was my reward.

Bradford refused to pay what was owing on my £25,000-a-year contract in one lump sum. Instead, they continued to pay me monthly in the hope I would soon get another job, and allow them to stop my wages entirely.

I grew to hate Tordoff but I had to wait eight years for revenge. During my final season at Bury, I went to watch a match at Valley Parade and sat next to a Bradford director during the first half. The conversation turned to Tordoff and I made my views clear. Sure enough, during the half-time break, when I refused to join everyone else in hospitality, Tordoff emerged and tried to shake hands with me. I told him straight: 'Fuck off.'

'Listen, Stan,' he said, 'it doesn't have to be like this.'

I raged, 'You didn't have the bollocks to tell me to my face I was sacked. You still owe me money. You tried to throw me on the scrapheap ...' By now my shouts had attracted the attention of hundreds of supporters. It didn't stop me. 'I'll never shake hands with you.'

Tordoff slunk away and I sat down, breathing heavily but relieved to have finally had my say.

Dave Bassett was sitting next to me and his face was drained. 'Jesus Christ, Stan,' he whispered, 'I only came here to watch a fucking game!'

6

'Bollocks to Pavarotti ...'

CRYSTAL PALACE, 1989;
HULL CITY, 1989–91

I held Steve Coppell's hand as we sat in the dugout and squeezed it. 'If he scores this penalty, we're running on,' I said.

Coppell deliberated for a second and then stared back at me. 'Load of bollocks that is, Stan. No chance.'

'I'm serious,' I shouted to him over the roar of the Anfield crowd.

It was only our fifth game together after we had won promotion to the First Division with Crystal Palace and we were already 6–0 down. But now, as our midfielder Geoff Thomas placed the ball on the spot, I tried to persuade our manager to make the most of the moment. My grip on Coppell's hand tightened.

Thomas stepped back and prepared to strike.

'I'm serious,' I said. I pointed towards the Kop. 'Look around you, Steve. We might never get a chance to be here again. I know we're 6–0 down but I'm telling you, if he scores this penalty we are both running on that pitch and dancing.'

Coppell nodded. He had decided to come with me.

In the dressing room afterwards, Coppell told me I had planted in his mind a vision of Butch Cassidy and the Sundance Kid at the top of a river gorge as we perched, hand in hand, at the edge of the dugout.

We moved closer to each other and, as Thomas attacked the ball, I readied myself to spring.

He struck his shot hard. I followed the flight path, involuntarily lifting Coppell's hand in readiness for our hornpipe on the touchline.

Oops. Thomas missed. Not only did he miss, he almost smashed a floodlight. The ball blazed so far over the bar that every Chinese acrobat on earth could have balanced on each other's shoulders and still not have headed it back.

I sagged. Coppell carefully freed his hand from mine and settled back into his seat. Liverpool scored three more to make it 9–0.

Their final goal was a penalty and manager Kenny Dalglish sent on substitute John Aldridge to take it.

'I'm not taking the piss, Stan,' he shouted. 'It's for a new record for Aldo.'

Our dressing room afterwards was a pitiful sight. A team of cocky youngsters who had stormed their way into the big league through the play-offs had just been taught a lesson by the masters. Our players had arrived with a laugh and a joke on their way into Anfield. Now they were embarrassed. The arrogance of youth coupled with the invincibility they felt after success last season intimidated plenty of other sides. But Liverpool had won the league title five times out of the previous seven.

Mark Bright, our scoring sensation who formed a deadly partnership with his best pal Ian Wright, hung his head and admitted, 'This is the worst moment of my career, Stan.'

'Take it from me,' I said. 'It can get worse. Lots worse. This sort of thing happens once in everyone's career, when everything goes right for them and not for you. Work at it. You've got to stick together.'

I left the lads to comfort each other and popped outside for a fag. Coppell had been speaking to the press and walked back towards me.

'Stan? About the holding hands and dancing thing ...' he said.

'What about it?'

He grimaced. 'Thank fuck we didn't score.'

* * *

Palace manager Coppell had made his rescue call as I sat at home after the Bradford débâcle and brooded over Tordoff sacking me. Due to the satisfyingly bizarre and incestuous circle of football life, he needed my help. His assistant Ian Evans had left suddenly to join Swansea after Terry Yorath had left Swansea to join Bradford after Terry and I were sacked. You see?

There was an unexpected vacancy for a first team coach at Selhurst Park and it had my name on it. Coppell told me over the phone, 'Whenever we played Bradford you were well organised and I know it was you who did the coaching. Now I want you to do a job for me. Bring some experience and northern grit to the place.'

He invited me for talks at a hotel in Oxford before a match, and allowed me to sit on the bench. They lost 1–0 but I met the squad over their pre-match meal and I knew we could do business.

I was reluctant to leave home. I missed Kath. I missed my lads and I missed my garden. But the deprivations we suffered when I was out of football were still fresh in my memory.

I had promised we would never sink so low again. There was no alternative.

I got on the train to Euston and arrived at the training ground in Mitcham to take my first session. And after just 20 minutes I walked away.

Coppell let me get on with things because he trusted me as a coach but, typically, the players had tried it on.

Born-again Christian John Salako said to me, 'Coach, can you not swear as much when you train us.'

'Fuck off,' I replied.

They took the mickey out of my northern accent, but I expected that. Ian Wright admitted afterwards that he had never even heard of me but I forced myself to be so brash and confident he thought, Who the bloody hell is this geezer? But his mate, Brighty, went a step too far and verbally abused me. I halted the session, walked up to the kid and looked him in the eye. I said, 'I'm not taking this from anyone,' and walked away to get showered.

I could tell some other lads in the squad, Eddie McGoldrick, Andy Gray, Thomas and Wrighty, were shocked and the next day they showed more respect. From that moment, so did Brighty.

He and Wrighty had enough raw talent and energy to storm the First Division and it was thrilling for me to work with them. They were never more than 10ft away from each other on the pitch and great friends off it.

After normal training was over, I stayed late, organising scoring contests and honing their competitiveness.

Their desire was frightening. At one stage, my teenage son Dan came to watch us practise and offered to knock over some crosses so Brighty could practise headers. After three out of the first four went astray, Bright stormed over to Dan and yelled, 'If you can't fucking do it right, fuck off!'

Dan was shocked, but Brighty had a point. He and Wright knew they had enough ability to become leading Premiership players and took their frustrations out on anyone who let them down. I deliberately used to light their fuse.

During training, I barked at them, 'You two just stay in the box. You'll score a million goals.' Then I'd shout to the wingers, 'You get the ball into box for them. I don't care how many we concede, we'll score more.'

Wright and Bright were on their way to scoring 50 goals that season and eagerly adopted this as their mantra. If crosses came in late or inaccurately, they used to try to kick the shit out of their team-mates. Brawls and screaming matches erupted regularly in the dressing room.

McGoldrick and Phil Barber were their usual victims. John Salako got it, too. Wright and Bright had enormous self-belief and I physically had to restrain them from tearing lumps out of people who they felt had let them down during a game. If it kicked off, I'd barge into the middle and shout, 'I've knocked bigger people out than you to get *into* a fight!' I regularly told the team, 'We've got to stick together and all piss in the same pot.'

It was the most competitive squad I ever worked with and those two were the brilliant powerhouses at the heart of a line-up of hard-working pros like Dave Madden, John Pemberton and Alan Pardew.

If we scored four and Wright had not hit the net, he acted as though we had lost 10–0. The team would give each other high fives and say, 'Well done', but Wrighty would be distraught. 'Bollocks,' he'd shout. 'That's not well done.'

The place buzzed when they were around. Wright would use his mountain bike to get to training and regularly scuffed along the freshly polished wooden floors of the clubhouse squirting a trail of shite behind him. He would dismount and swan into the dressing room wearing tailored short trousers and £600 crocodile shoes. Wrighty thought he was a fashion icon but, where I came from, I only saw that sort of gear in panto.

> **Wrighty:** Look at these shoes, Stan.
> **Me:** How much did you pay for them?
> **Wrighty:** Eighty quid.
> **Me:** *Eighty quid*? You're wasting your money. Give it to me and I can get three pairs for that from Tommy Ball's on Accrington Market.

Soon after I arrived, we played Brighton at home. Wright headed the ball down in our half, crossed into theirs and hit a screamer from 20 yards. I said to Coppell, 'I don't believe it.'

Steve laughed and replied, 'He does that every week.'

Palace were in the thick of a fight for automatic promotion but to do it we had to win our last game of the season at home to Birmingham by five or six goals and hope Manchester City would not win at Bradford.

After 25 minutes, we were 4–0 up. Birmingham had already been relegated and their fans were resigned to wearing fancy dress to brighten up their day. At one point, they invaded the pitch and the match was delayed by 20 minutes. When it restarted, the mood of anti-climax was suffocating.

City's game was already over and Trevor Morley had hit their late winner.

They were up. We weren't. We could have won by ten that afternoon and it would not have mattered, so we took a couple of players off to rest before the play-offs.

We lost the semi-final first leg at Swindon 1–0, but it was no great concern. We had the fire-power to brush them aside and won 2–0 at Palace to reach the first ever final, against Blackburn Rovers.

A promotion was at stake, and I'd been hired to win it. What a pity we were crap.

After 20 minutes of the first leg at Ewood Park, Coppell turned to me and shouted, 'Blimey, we're being overrun!'

Blackburn battered us and went 2–0 up. McGoldrick pulled one back but then, stupidly, we allowed Howard Gayle to get their third. They even missed a penalty. We were gutted.

Wrighty stormed into the dressing room and booted a hole in the door. The whole team went potty. I nipped out for a fag and bumped into Rovers' assistant manager, Tony Parkes, who invited me for a quick beer.

He slurped on a bottle of lager and said, 'Well, I think we've done enough, Stan. It's a good lead.'

I said, 'It'll be a different story at Selhurst, pal.'

But he looked content. Smug. His team were automatically made red-hot favourites.

The mood on our coach travelling back to London was flat. But as the miles ticked away, the players began to react positively. They said, 'No one beats us at our place ...' and 'We can beat these.'

Over the next few days in training, the players were desperate to work hard and show determination. 'Stick to your tasks,' I warned them constantly. 'This lot are there for the taking.' I was positive we would win the second leg, but could we score enough goals?

On the eve of the match, we had a quiet Greek meal at the Mythos restaurant in Thornton Heath, owned by my old pal Jack. I had no doubts we would do it. Wright and Bright were even more adamant. Their destiny was to play in the First Division.

Only 16,000 fans watched the first leg at Ewood. Selhurst Park was packed with twice as many for our big day.

The players arrived at 10.30am that morning and were hyperactive. We got changed into training gear and loosened up on the pitch under a boiling sun. We put on our club tracksuits, had a light pre-match meal and waited.

The noise from the terraces began to filter through. As part of our psychological warfare against Blackburn, the tannoy system had been doctored to play our club song 'Glad All Over' at twice its normal volume. The effect shook my bones.

Thousands of balloons were dished out to home fans. A neutral observer would have thought that *we* were winning 3–1 instead of them. The roar as we walked out was so loud the hairs stood up on my tracksuit.

It was 2–0 to us at full time. We needed to play an extra 30 minutes to settle the tie and the tension was unbearable. Fans spilled out from the terraces and crowded around the touchlines. Rovers manager Don Mackay had his leg in plaster and found it hard to raise himself off the bench to see.

Every so often, I heard his Scottish accent above the roar of the crowd as he shouted at the ref. 'Courtney! Courtney! They're on the fucking pitch again!'

It was a madhouse. I dragged my lad Dan into the dugout with me for protection.

When we hit the winner, my view was immediately obliterated by a sea of tight jeans and floppy haircuts as Palace supporters exploded with happiness.

Seconds from the end, Rovers' dangerman Simon Garner struck a sweet volley and my heart stopped ... before I saw Perry Suckling tip it over the bar for a corner.

When the whistle went, I hardly had the energy to draw on my fag. I gave Coppell a hug and I shook the hand of Chairman Ron Noades. I'd bet him £5,000 we would go up and he still owes me! Both of them spent the first half in the stands but stood by the dugout after the interval.

As I disappeared up the tunnel to smoke in peace, I saw both sets of players swallowed by a full-scale pitch invasion. Wrighty's minder, 25st Big Charlie, waded out towards the centre circle to wrestle his pal away from supporters who were stripping him of his kit. I was sprayed with champagne as the lads bundled themselves back into the dressing room.

Then I walked away. I had fulfilled my contract with Coppell and got his lads up. They were back in the First Division after a gap of eight years. Now it was their party.

In the car park as I prepared to set off up the M1, I saw Rovers Chairman Bill Fox. He looked as though he had been in tears. In contrast, the Palace boys celebrated with a booze bender in London's West End.

I can't stand discotheques. I went to one in Burnley once and couldn't see 3ft in front of me. By 10.30pm that night I was back in my favourite seat in The Kettledrum. When the landlord caught sight of me, he shouted to his barmaid, 'Oi! Don't serve him!'

I thought I'd been barred. Instead, a bottle of chilled

champagne was brought to my table. I realised why. I had helped to defeat Burnley's biggest enemy, Blackburn Rovers. The misery I'd heaped on Ewood Park that afternoon meant I wouldn't have to buy another drink all year.

Instead of a long, hot summer of job-hunting, Coppell soon telephoned to ask me back. We worked on the list of players he ought to retain and I recommended that a youngster who was a candidate for the sack should be given another chance. It was Gareth Southgate.

I also went on the pre-season trip to Sweden but the players could focus on nothing else other than their first game in the First Division against QPR.

Unlike them, I was distracted. I hated being number two. The thrill of pitting my wits against other top coaches in the big league was constantly eroded by frustration I felt at taking orders every day.

I was also unhappy living in Croydon. The club paid for a poxy one-room studio flat with a pull-down bed. I had to wrestle with the mattress to strap it down every night before I could go to sleep. If I had guests, they went to bed when I did whether they wanted to or not.

To the players' annoyance, Monday morning training could not begin until well after lunch because I had to make my way back from Burnley.

I missed my garden. I missed my wife. I missed my lads. I ached with loneliness. Each night I would pester the staff after training and say, 'Who's coming for a schooner down the pub with me?'

But they all had family lives. They joined me at first but eventually I noticed that they had begun to avoid me. Instead of enjoying life in the First Division, I was miserable.

It is no surprise that, in this disastrous frame of mind, I made the biggest mistake of my career.

'Hull City?' Coppell couldn't believe his ears. We had just lost three consecutive games to Aston Villa, Nottingham Forest and

Manchester City. We had conceded ten goals and scored only one. Now, after two months of the new season, I hit him with a low blow. I told him I wanted to quit.

Coppell warned me, 'There are 70 clubs in the Football League that you do not want to manage. Looking at Hull, they are one of them.'

His arguments were pointless. I had been offered the manager's job at the Second Division club and I was going. It was closer to home and I would, at last, be in a position to make my own decisions.

Coppell asked me to work out a two-week notice period but in training the very next Friday I said to him, 'Why is the manager of Hull on the bench at Palace?'

I wanted out. He was angry and he was right to be. I had snatched at the first job I had been offered instead of developing my reputation in the First Division.

Coppell said, 'You've been my mate, my mucker. I wouldn't have expected you to do it this way, Stan. I gave you the job in the first place. It's been cloak and dagger. Not even slow cloak and dagger.'

I was adamant. 'I've been offered a job and I'm going.'

I didn't even say goodbye to the players and sloped off to the railway station to get out of their way. I pretended to myself that I didn't want to disrupt their concentration before a crucial relegation clash against Luton, but it was bollocks. I was actually worried they would talk me out of the move.

'Why are you going to Hull, Stan?' ... 'Where is it?' I could imagine Wrighty and Brighty wearing me down with questions.

That night, as I sat at home with Kath, I became convinced I had made the decision in haste and for all the wrong reasons. She wrote a telegram to send to the Palace players before their game the next afternoon. It said: ALL THE BEST. WIN FOR ME. STAN.

I was going to miss those lads. When Kath read the message to me, I was overcome by a sense of overwhelming regret and I cried.

Palace survived. Just. They avoided relegation by five points. I was not blackballed either.

They reached the semi-finals of the FA Cup against Liverpool five months after I left, and Coppell got in touch. 'I want you to do me a favour.'

It was wonderful to hear that he didn't hold a grudge. I said, 'If I can, I will.'

Coppell asked, 'Come down and see the boys before the game. It'll give them a massive boost. Bring Kath.'

The tie was to be played at noon on an April Sunday at Villa Park and Kath and I arrived at the impressive eighteenth-century New Hall Hotel in Sutton Coldfield in time for breakfast.

The receptionist directed me towards the restaurant and I saw the lads tucking in at the same time as they saw me. I was worried I would be an imposition but Kath said she heard their cheers from out in the car park.

Coppell explained how he thought Liverpool were vulnerable at set pieces, and after the fuss died down I spoke to his players. 'Hey, I haven't come down here for nothing. I haven't come down here to see you lose.'

We wandered out into the reception area where I lit a Silk Cut. As the players watched, an officious short-arsed bloke in a tight-fitting suit approached and tapped me on the shoulder.

> **Short Arse:** Excuse me, sir.
> **Me:** What?
> **Short Arse:** Excuse me, you'll have to put that cigarette out.
> **Me:** Why?
> **Short Arse:** Because Mr Pavarotti is performing in Birmingham this evening and he is about to walk through this area. We simply cannot risk his lungs.
> **Me:** Well, tell him to go out the back way.

> **Assorted Players:** Who does he think he's talking to, Stan?
> ... You're Stan Ternent!
> **Short Arse:** I must insist ...
> **Me:** He's not in Italy now, you know.
> Bollocks to Pavarotti.

The players collapsed into fits of laughter. They were suitably relaxed.

Incredibly, Palace won the memorable semi-final 4–3. Brighty got one. Wrighty was injured.

When it was over, before I made my way into the dressing room, I sat in the stand and continued to regret my decision to leave. I was part of their success. The lads invited me to their party, but I could have been leading their charge instead of following it.

Since my time at Palace, Mark Bright has said, 'You don't come across many people like Stan in football. You are lucky to touch on one in your career.'

Wrighty has said, 'Stan was a real pivotal force in my career. He has always been honest. He's been like a dad to me. I feel like one of his lads.'

As Coppell said farewell, shook my hand and gave Kath a peck on the cheek, I smiled ruefully. I'd cocked it up. He and the boys were off to Wembley. I had to return to the living hell of Hull.

* * *

Coppell was right to warn me about going to Humberside. The best thing ever to come out of that place is the M62.

I took the damn job in the knowledge that they had not won a game all season and were bottom of the league. I soon realised far more than surgery was needed. Hull City required a cull.

I became the club's third manager in 19 months after Eddie Gray and Colin Appleton. If I was to survive, they needed to start winning. That's why I ran away from Palace. I couldn't bear to think of my new team kicking off one more match without my input.

The day after I left Coppell in the lurch, I arrived unannounced for our next game. It was at Bradford City. I had a priceless chance for revenge against Tordoff and the club that had shafted me less than a year earlier. I couldn't resist it.

The Hull staff had expected me to arrive on the following Monday but I'd thought, Bollocks to that. I sat on the bench and took over that afternoon.

I thought I ought to make my presence felt. After only three minutes I signalled for striker Peter Swan to come off.

He couldn't believe it and did a double-take. He even checked the number on the back of his shirt to see if it matched the one I held up.

I've since re-signed him twice at other clubs but that day, after 180 seconds, he had moved so little he was paying ground rent.

Swan was fuming as he walked past me towards the showers. I later sent Andy Payton and Ian McParland on from the bench who both scored. We won 3–2 with a last-minute winner.

There was better to come. As we made our way off the pitch, the Bradford fans began a huge protest and held a 15-minute sit-in as they sang 'Sack the Board!' until the police took them away.

The next morning, I divided my time between reading our match report in the Sunday papers and laughing at accounts of Tordoff's desperate defence against his own supporters. He said, 'We are all bitterly disappointed but it is towards the team where we should direct our attention – not the Board!'

Hull's revival continued. We were 14 points adrift at the bottom before that game at Valley Parade. I brought in eight new players for just over £500,000 and, by the end of the first season, we were mid-table, ten points clear of the relegation zone.

Amidst all the euphoria, I was promised everything from the keys to the city to a budget that would satisfy Manchester United.

In reality, I got bugger all.

When the next season began, I felt like a virgin who had just given her all for a can of pop and a free ticket to the cinema. I was offered the job as manager of Sunderland during the summer but, like a prat, I told them, 'Nope, I'll stay at Hull. I've been promised a few quid.'

Everything quickly began to fall apart. I set a 50-point survival target but it took us nine games to win our first match. A week after that first narrow 3–2 victory, over Port Vale, we were stuffed 7–1 by West Ham United.

I had been forced to sell Richard Jobson to Oldham to raise £450,000, so my defensive plans were ruined. Sheffield Wednesday put five past us, too, and chaos ensued.

During training in the gym, I gave a decision against Billy Whitehurst. He's a big man, well over 6ft tall and 15st. His forearms were the size of Tyson's neck. I gave him a forfeit of ten press-ups.

'I'm not doing them,' he said.

'You fucking are.'

'I'm fucking not,' he said.

Twenty minutes later ... 'You fucking are.'

'I'm fucking NOT!'

'Listen,' I said. 'I'll do them with you.'

'Fuck off. You can do them.'

It was a matter of principle for us both and when Whitehurst stepped up to within an inch of my face, for the first time in my football career I thought I was going to get battered. I delivered my nuclear option. 'Look, I'll do them with you ... or I'll phone your wife.'

He thought for a moment. 'OK.'

Billy's wife was the only person in the world who he was scared of.

Other players had similar problems. We came back from one away trip only for one player to find his car had been nicked by his missus who telephoned later that night to say she wanted a divorce.

I had my own personal problems. The stress of successive defeats and the fear of failure had eaten away at my nerves. I was ready to erupt. One afternoon, two scumbags knocked on the door of our house in Burnley and asked Kath for directions. As she talked, they snatched her handbag and ran off.

A few months later, they tried again. This time I was in. Kath shouted and I charged through the back door and into the yard. I locked the gate and booted them around until the police arrived.

A week later, I was at home again doing the washing up one night, when I heard a commotion outside on the road. I looked through the window to see Kath clutching six shopping bags from the local Spar, arguing heatedly with a bloke from nearby.

I walked outside to the doorstep. Kath was trying to park and this prick was refusing to budge his car.

He had plenty of space outside his house yet he had left his motor on our land.

I yelled, 'My wife is trying to park.'

The bloke shouted to me, 'You think you own the place. I'll move in a minute.'

'You wait,' I said and marched up to him, the tea towel from the kitchen still draped over my arm. He prodded me in the chest.

'Don't prod me,' I said. Then I launched myself at him and we kicked up a cloud of dust as we rolled in the road. His glasses flew off and Kath fled inside. We fought for a few minutes and then I made my way back into the house.

'Kath, er, the police are going to come.'

She went pale. 'If this gets out you're really going to be in it.'

A constable arrived. 'Mr Ternent? We're going to have to take you to the station.'

I turned to Kath. 'I'll sort it. Just ring my solicitor.'

The neighbour had officially complained and I was escorted to the nick in the back of a squad car.

'You're going in the cells, Mr Ternent,' said the desk sergeant. 'I want your shoes in case you use the laces to hang yourself.'

'But they're slip-ons,' I protested.

The next morning, I emerged to find my solicitor waiting outside.

'Good news,' he said. 'The charges have been dropped.'

The press in Hull never found out, but they didn't have to wait long for their next headline. We crashed to the bottom of the league with a 2–1 defeat at home to Barnsley. The next game was a vital away trip to Portsmouth, who were second-to-bottom and hadn't won for 13 games. We were stuffed 5–1.

After the game, I had a row in the dressing room with Steve Doyle, one of my players. I bawled him out. He hurled himself at me. Cups, boots and players went flying. We had to be separated.

I yelled at him, 'You'll never kick another ball for me ... ever!'

I was right. The next day I was sacked.

The Board met in emergency session at Boothferry Park two days into 1991. We were bottom of the league and £300,000 in debt. I was out. Happy New Year.

Chairman Richard Chetham, who resembled a tousled, bouffanted relic from *Brideshead Revisited*, at least had the guts to meet me at the ground to deliver his verdict.

He told the press, 'I have not interfered, and allowed the manager to do what he wanted.'

Bollocks. I had rescued a crap team from certain relegation and then been tossed aside after only 13 months with nothing but unfulfilled promises over money. None of the cash from Jobson's sale was made available to me. I was just another statistic.

I walked away from a football disaster with my sanity in question. I was exhausted, disillusioned and depressed. The confusion was so great that within five months I would be even worse off at Chelsea.

Back at Hull, Chetham turned to my old Bradford boss Terry Dolan after I left. They went straight down to Division Three.

7

'I Want to See It on Grandstand ...'

BURY, 1993–96

I clambered into the cramped hatchback car and drew on a fag, wedged myself into the passenger seat and struggled to house my outstretched leg which was encased in a plaster cast. 'Is there a chance we might get there today?' Dan, my lad, got behind the wheel and set off.

My foot was temporarily knackered, so I had to rely on family chauffeurs to get around and my frustrations were showing. Too fast. Too slow. Too fast again. For 20 miles.

As we careered down the M66 towards Manchester, an idiot overtook us and swerved in front, causing Dan to brake violently. My leg bashed against the dashboard and spasms of pain erupted from my ankle.

'Keep driving,' I urged. 'After him.'

'Leave it, Dad,' said Dan.

'Never mind leave it. Catch him up!'

We chased the roadhog's car for another six miles, on to the M62 heading towards Leeds. Gradually, Dan caught up with the moron.

'Pull alongside,' I shouted.

At speeds of up to 90mph, we dodged and weaved from the middle to the fast lanes as we fought to overtake. After minutes of manoeuvring, he became stuck behind a lorry and we pulled abreast in the outside lane. I mouthed an obscenity to the driver from my passenger seat. He flashed a V-sign and triggered an explosion of rage inside me which I had been expecting ever since Ian Porterfield's time at Chelsea and I had walked away without revenge.

As Dan clung desperately to the steering wheel with whitening knuckles, I wound down the window and reached for my NHS crutch. The pillock in the other car got the fright of his life as I thrust it outside and began bashing it against his window in a high-speed joust.

Dan flushed with embarrassment as I shouted to the maniac across the carriageway, 'Get ... the ... fuck ... out ... of ... our ... way ... in ... future.'

Satisfied by the look of terror on his face, I withdrew my weapon, signalled Dan to slow down and ordered him to find a junction where we could turn round. In all the excitement, we had driven at least 15 miles past Gigg Lane, which was a pity. This was my first day in a new job as assistant manager of Bury and it would be a shame to be late.

I had been out of full-time football work since the nightmare at Chelsea with Porterfield. Now, after two years in exile, I knew it was time to return. I was adamant that he was not going to write the epitaph to my career.

Bury's ground was within easy commuting range of my Burnley home and I was a good friend of their manager, Mike Walsh. For months I had been helping him out with training, free of charge. That's why my leg was in plaster.

We always ended our morning sessions in the gym with a game

of football tennis. My partner, as usual, was Walshy.

We played against Bury's chief scout, Cliff Roberts, and our mutual pal Peter Reid, who was also out of work after being sacked by Manchester City. The game was a regular feature of our day. It had become ritualistic. It was serious. It was competitive. There was pride at stake. More importantly, a lot of money rode on the outcome.

Reidy lobbed the ball high and, as I ran back to take a shot at it, I tripped and fell over a low bench. It was match point but I was writhing in agony. Walshy saw the wretched look on my face and begged for the game to be abandoned. Reidy had other ideas. 'Fuck him,' he said and took the points.

He took great pleasure in playing out the final rally over my prone body and then voted to fine me for interfering with play. The Bury physio examined me and said, 'You've just bruised your ankle.'

I hobbled home with Reidy's voice echoing, 'Old woman!' and 'Poof!'

My foot went bluer by the day until it was eventually diagnosed as a ruptured achilles. My services as a free coach to Bury were over, so I was surprised a week later when Walshy, a rugged Mancunian with a shock of blond hair, knocked on my kitchen door. 'Have you got an hour?' he said.

Walshy's assistant, John King, had announced he was leaving to manage non-league Altrincham and Mike wanted me as his replacement. I resisted the urge to say 'Yes' immediately and pondered what I knew about Bury.

They were near the bottom of the Third Division. They employed nine professionals and nine amateur players. Overshadowed by nearby Manchester, which is only 12 miles away, Bury is an unfashionable club with a ground capacity of 11,000. It was only ever going to be filled at gunpoint.

Most people who live in Bury moved there from the Manchester suburbs 40 years earlier and still passionately support

City or United. Never mind all that. When I join clubs, I don't consider the size of the dog. I consider the fight that is in it. And I had a good feeling about little Bury's tenacity.

Hopping across my living room, I shook Walshy by the hand and accepted his job offer. I would have accepted anything to avoid the daily humiliation I suffered when I was out of work.

After the Chelsea disaster, I found myself on the dole at the same time as my son Chris. He signed on at 9.45am every Wednesday. I signed on at 10.15am.

I was placed on a Jobcentre 'Back to Work' initiative. One morning, I arrived for my weekly interview dressed in a full-length soccer manager's coat.

'What is it you do?' asked the girl behind the bullet-proof window.

'Football coach.'

'What does that entail?'

'Coaching footballers.'

'What is the region of salary you are looking for?'

'Fifty thousand pounds.'

'Sorry?'

'Well, of course it depends on what division, but I think a grand a week is reasonable.'

'My husband's a fireman. He works 50 hours a week for £12,000 a year.

'Well, I'm not your husband.'

Chris disappeared. Rapid.

I was informed that I was not actively seeking work and told to go on a basket-weaving course. It was full of dead legs who couldn't even afford fags for me to cadge.

At that time, I bumped into Howard Wilkinson who said, 'What happened to you, Stan? You passed out at Lilleshall with the highest results we've ever had.'

Thank Christ for Bury.

After day one on the M66, Dan refused to give me any more

lifts so I spent my initial two months plotting their revival at the end of the '93–'94 season commuting to the ground in the disabled seat of the single-decker X43 Timesaver from Burnley bus station. My wait for a company car would be a little longer.

We ended without a win in ten matches, finishing in the bottom half of the division. Most Chairmen would have fretted, but ex-wrestler Terry Robinson is a breed apart. He is a huge bloke in every sense. His blind devotion to Bury was only matched by his appetite.

Once, at a party at my house, Terry sat at the table, tucked a napkin under his chin and began ripping the legs off a turkey like Henry VIII until I reminded him it was supposed to feed everyone.

His secretary, Jill Neville, mother of the Manchester United stars Phil and Gary, was well used to his ways. Occasionally, we'd be talking in her office close to Terry's, when a cry would erupt in his gruff northern accent. 'Jiiiilllll?!'

She would be required to tie the big man's shoelaces because his belly was too large to allow him to bend down easily.

It wasn't just Terry's trousers that were tight. Bury's budget more suited players sleeping on park benches than hotel beds. Horrified by the size of his family's grocery bills, he once informed his wife that he would be taking over shopping duties and bragged to us all how he had bought a bag of beef ribs for £3 that would last him all week. Two days later, he broke a tooth on them which cost him £60 to repair.

Bury's misfortunes reflected Terry's. After a pre-season during which I worked the players hard, we were motoring, heading for the play-offs. We had to play a rearranged night match at Scarborough and heard that Bury's VIP director, Hugh Eaves, was due to attend.

London-based Eaves was a genuine Bury fan and our most generous benefactor. He ploughed millions into the club to keep it afloat. He was no Jack Walker; Bury always seemed permanently skint. But the club would have been bankrupt without the scholarly, bespectacled Eaves's regular donations.

As we struggled on the rock-hard and rutted pitch at the McCain Stadium that night, I suddenly heard a commotion from the stands. Eaves had arrived late. He'd had a nap on the train and had woken up in Darlington, forcing him to take a taxi back to Scarborough. He seemed pissed off. Even the players heard his performance.

'Come along, Bury,' he shouted in his posh accent, 'they are a fucking pub team.'

He tripped up and his wig slipped.

Luckily we won 2–1, but he warned us afterwards, 'The P45s would have been flying if we'd lost.'

After a superhuman effort on our unrealistic budget, we reached the play-offs. We faced Preston in the semi-final, the team that had stuffed us 5–0 earlier in the season. Mind you, the driving force behind that performance was a confident if slightly skinny kid on loan from Manchester United ... David Beckham! Thankfully, he'd had his fill of trips to Walsall by May and had trotted back to Old Trafford before we played them again.

1–0 wins in each leg saw us overcome North End to reach the final at Wembley but, despite being the form team, we lost catastrophically 2–0 to Chesterfield, a side who had failed to beat us in their last six attempts.

The hangover into the following season was severe. It turned out to be terminal for Walshy. I saw warning signs with just four games gone of the 1995–96 season.

Playing away at Hereford, we were 3–0 down by half-time. Walshy despaired but I felt real anger. I refused to let the team in the dressing room at the interval. 'Get back on to the pitch, the lot of you.' I didn't even give them a cup of tea. It was purely a gut reaction.

We won 4–3. But the revival was short-lived. Two games later we were thumped 5–0 at home to Plymouth, who hadn't scored an away goal in five matches and were managed by my nemesis, Neil bloody Warnock.

The following Monday, I arrived at Gigg Lane to be told Walshy was upstairs in Terry's office. He eventually came back down to see me. 'I'm going.'

He was quite matter-of-fact for a man who had just been sacked.

My first thought was, Right. I'll be going as well.

Out of respect for a mate, I was prepared to walk away with him, even if I wasn't pushed. But Walshy said, 'You should stay.'

I wasn't sure if I had the option. Walshy was a good manager. He had been working with a paltry budget and, like most bosses at Bury, had had to fight against a home crowd who were hyper-critical at best and downright disloyal at worst.

Moments after Walshy left the building, Terry summoned me to his office and asked me to be caretaker manager. I didn't kid myself. It was an easy option, a fact which was hardly likely to stop the vultures circling. Sammy McIlroy and Frank Stapleton were both touted for the job but I was better qualified than any of them.

My stint as caretaker lasted for two games. We drew 2–2 at Lincoln and lost 2–1 at home to Cambridge, a game which certainly made an impact on our supporters, who had allowed their frustrations to ferment since Wembley. They rioted.

After the match, Terry was sharing a tin of lager in our Boardroom with visiting directors. A Bury fan found his way past the pensioner on the door, walked up to the Chairman and spat in his wife's face. Terry, already suffering with his leg in plaster after an accident, took it upon himself to escort the moron outside. As they walked across the car park directly behind the main stand, the thug struggled out of Terry's grip and kicked his good leg.

As usual, I was having a drink with the players in the supporters' bar overlooking the car park and we saw everything. It was a race between the whole squad to see who could reach the hooligan first. We all waded in, some trying to restrain him, most of us trying to knock him out.

Terry was shaken but he witnessed a spirit of togetherness

amongst his players which he had thought was lacking, and which he perhaps imagined might help us progress.

The following Monday, I was appointed full-time manager. The players wanted me. Terry wanted me.

As the Chairman tucked into a lunchtime chip barm cake, he spat, 'There's no doubt in my mind. You're the only man for the job.' It was a pity that many of the fans didn't agree.

A local DJ applied for the post and, when he didn't get it, he popped a note through one of the director's letterboxes listing '20 reasons why Ternent is crap'.

Other supporters believed that they had sussed Terry. They certainly knew him better than I did. In the pages of the *Bury Times*, they argued he had gone for the cheapest deal, employing a man who may have been known within the game but not on the terraces. That's me.

I preferred Terry's privately-held view. 'Stan,' he said. 'I have a strong philosophy about football. There are special people to do a specific job at a particular moment in time. This time, it's you.'

* * *

Thank God for Ian Porterfield. In one excruciating season at Chelsea, he had taught me something about how not to run a football team. After I had witnessed first-hand how things operated at a Premiership club, I knew that it was a waste of my time and a waste of my life to ever be an assistant again.

Obeying orders from some people left me stymied. Terry's offer gave me what could be my last chance to reach the Premiership as a manager. Not a realistic chance, I admit. It was a huge great, undercooked, heavy-on-the-pastry, pie-in-the-sky chance. But I was taking it.

I was determined not to leave anything to chance and began by tightening my grip on all aspects of life at Bury, on and off the pitch. I'm not a diplomat and the staff soon realised it. Question and answer sessions are for an episode of *Trisha*, not a football club. I resolved to be a dictator.

Huge swathes of my professional life had been dominated by clueless individuals who, either by sheer luck or the size of their wallets, had held sway over me.

I'd seen players steamroller managers and I had seen chinless wonders from the Boardroom ignore specialists they employed to run the team in the first place and impose ridiculous schemes on stressed professionals. That wasn't for me and I left Terry in no doubt.

Bury chose to place their trust in Stan Ternent. I had to be single-minded enough to ignite a radical relaunch of the Football League's most unglamorous club or I would regret it for ever.

I started in the laundry. Each morning, I marched down to the washroom to butter up kit lady Pat Holt. Nothing moved at Gigg Lane without Pat's knowledge. I soon found out who was doing what behind my back, and who was having it off with who. Gradually, I tightened my grip by being first with the gossip.

To thank Pat, I forced the players to wash their own training kits. Call it Stan's National Service. I embraced the role of sergeant major.

My first game in charge was a 2–1 away defeat at First Division Sheffield United in the Coca Cola Cup. To my disgust, fans patted me on the back afterwards saying I had at least given the club their pride back.

Pride in defeat? Bollocks. What about my personal pride?

My volatile temper is easily ignited and, before the second leg two weeks later, I tore into the players in the dressing room.

'What are we doing here, eh? We are twenty-first in the bottom division and about to go out of the Cup. What's the point? Do you want to piss off home now and I'll go and forfeit the game?'

They were silent. But were they thinking? 'I wouldn't have come here if I thought you lot were happy to piss around pretending to be professional footballers when you're only one step up from a pub team.

'Look at Sheffield United tonight. Big boys, eh? They think we don't belong on the same pitch. No one thinks you're any good. They think we are the poor relations. They'll probably wipe their feet when they walk out of here. I'll tell you something. We might be poor relations, but we are not poorer players.'

It also helped that I raved like a madman at half-time. I gauged the real men amongst my players by counting those who could look me straight in the eye as I picked apart their miserable performances.

To get the attention of the other more bashful players, I slapped so hard on the treatment table that I had to bite my tongue to cope with the pain ... and the players could see my hand swelling by the second.

We won 4–2. David Johnson, a lightning-quick black kid we'd brought in from Manchester United, scored his first ever goal. Johnno was a typical Bury purchase. Bought for peanuts, he had to adjust quickly to life at the arse-end of football, streets away from his pampered existence amongst the youngsters at Old Trafford. His signing-on fee was a whopping £500 before tax. And he even had to wait for that. Our club couldn't afford so much at such short notice. After a week without pay, Johnno bravely marched into Terry's office to complain and said he caught the Chairman eating a potato pie in a butty with a side order of chips. Johnson thought, If you cut out one course a day I might get paid a bit quicker.

Eventually, like many deals at our cash-strapped club, he accepted payment in instalments using contributions from petty-cash, topped up by money funnelled directly from fans as they came through the turnstiles on match day. It took weeks for culture-shocked Johnson to get his old club out of his system.

We were making a training trip to a spartan military camp at RAF Valley on Anglesey and I told him to meet the rest of the squad at the club at noon.

Johnno: What time's the bus arriving?
   Me: There is no bus.
Johnno: Are we going in our own cars?
   Me: Look, it's Bury, not Barcelona.

The journey to Wales took five hours along tortuous B-roads and Johnson spilled out of the passenger door at the other end, horrified that each player was only due a fiver for expenses and that settlement would take one calendar month.

'It's a shambles,' he said.

He was lucky actually. Five quid was double the normal rate because we had travelled abroad.

The fact we were skint played into my hands. I used Blitz mentality to bond the lads together, relying on camaraderie in adversity. If we travelled to Torquay, we would make the 500-mile round trip on the same day we played, eating soup and sandwiches on the coach rather than tucking into a £30-a-head pre-match plate of pasta en-route.

We were forced to train on Goshen, desolate public playing fields half-a-mile from the ground overlooked on one side by a *Brookside* housing estate and bordered by a rusting metal fence held up by huge concrete posts. Our match preparations were frequently hampered by dog shit, kites and kids playing cricket.

Training never went too smoothly. In warmer months, I'd patrol Goshen dressed in shorts and socks, clutching my whistle. I never wore a shirt if I could help it. I knew the players sometimes took the piss and called me 'Arnold Schwarzenegger', so I gave them extra work whether I heard them or not. Best to be safe.

Physio Alan Raw was their more frequent target. He was late one day and burst into the dressing room, eager to apologise. Too eager. His false teeth spilled out on to the floor and the players formed a rugby scrum and nicked them.

As Goshen became packed with punters, a bloke with a bad swing constantly sliced golf balls in our direction. I strode over to give him a free lesson with his two iron.

To cries of 'Fuck me, it's Gary Player' from the lads, I showed him the ropes. Every time he saw me afterwards, he ran off.

When we weren't ducking golf balls, I forced the players to count the balls we used in training every morning. At £30 each, we couldn't afford to lose them.

Peter Thompson, a 6ft 3in-tall lad, let rip during shooting practice and constantly skied his efforts. Our keeper needed stilts.

I shouted, 'Just sidefoot it!'

Inevitably, one of his ballooned volleys cleared the fence and plopped into the River Roch, which flowed behind one of our goals.

'Go and get it.'

He stripped off and waded in. At one point, only his head was visible. He looked like a luggage bearer in an old *Tarzan* film. He clambered out exhausted and frozen stiff, but he'd saved the club £30. We'd probably saved the life of a spectator who would have been decapitated if Thompson's shooting had been allowed to continue unchecked.

The lads took the piss about our cost-cutting but they knew the drill and agreed with me that if we were ever to spend any money on better players we had to forego the luxuries that most teams take for granted.

It's not easy trying to be a major force on a limited budget and, because any potential new recruits were likely to be rare, I was prepared to investigate thoroughly the calibre of any man I was about to bring in to my new set-up.

I made the final decision to sign Chris Lucketti because he had built his own house from scratch, brick by brick. That told me far more about his strength of character than 1,000 words of bullshit on a poxy agent's CV.

Using similar intuition, I began to rebuild Bury in my own

tenacious image. Showboaters were no good to me. I was already having to stomach one of the lowest salaries in the Football League, so there was no way I was going to line the pockets of unreliable players who could be brilliant for 20 seconds and then spend the rest of the game refusing to track back across the halfway line. My team would not be pretty, but it would become hard to beat.

My first deal brought in Dean West, a sinewy, determined full-back from Lincoln City whom I swapped for Kevin Hulme. Thanks to a handout from Hugh Eaves, we broke the Bank of Bury to buy Rob Matthews for £100,000 from York City. He repaid us immediately by scoring on his début against Chester to earn us a point, and then by hitting the winner two games later at Doncaster.

I spent weeks searching for others to match our budget. Inevitably, they were either rejects from higher divisions or amateurs trawled by Scouser Cliff Roberts, the silver-haired chief scout I had inherited. Vitally, Cliff knew the non-league scene intimately and I was indebted to Eaves once again when he funded a £120,000 deal to buy uncompromising Gary Brabin from Runcorn, a player I eventually sold to Blackpool in a deal which recouped every penny.

Brabin's début appearances for Bury matched Matthews's for drama, if not success. He was stretchered off in his first match and sent off in his second.

These new boys linked up with some of the characters already in our ranks, fighters like former squaddie Phil Stant who scored a hat-trick in my eighth game in charge when we stuffed Mansfield 5–1 at their place.

I was convinced Stanty used to be linked to the SAS and I spent hours on away trips sitting next to him on the team bus to pick his brain about strategies – how organised groups can outmanoeuvre opposition forces when outnumbered; how to maintain morale in difficult circumstances; and how to hold on to a hard-won objective – all of which I intended to adapt to the way we played football. If they failed, we always had our fists.

A third round Coca-Cola Cup tie at Reading soon tested our resilience. We were winning 2–0 when torrential rain started to pour and the ref, John Kirkby, took the players off. I sensed what was coming, so I raced to his room to persuade him not to call it off.

'We've travelled a long way,' I pleaded with him. 'Don't abandon it. Let's give it ten minutes and then we can fork the pitch.'

To his credit, the ref agreed to try and salvage the game. There were 10,000 supporters inside the ground that he had to consider, after all.

Luckily, the storm began to die down and the heavy rain faded into fine drizzle, so I marched on to the pitch to inspect the groundsman's efforts and to estimate how long it would take to achieve a restart.

I realised within seconds that it was over for good. There were just two groundsmen wandering aimlessly around one of the penalty boxes with one fork between them. Their limp-wristed efforts wouldn't have been enough to remove the surface water from a window box.

Reading had obviously made a decision. They were losing so they were prepared to have the match written off.

Predictably, after 20 more minutes of gardening from Tommy Titchmarch and his pal, word emerged from the referee's room. Replay.

I ran to find Kirkby. 'You can't call it off!'

He read me the rule book but I was convinced we'd been stitched up by Reading's inactivity.

The decision sparked chaos. Players from both sides were soon fighting with each other. I had to be held back from physically attacking the ref and the groundsman. In the end, policemen were posted on doors to both dressing rooms as the Reading players laughed into their hot tea while we sat and brooded.

I was still bitter when we had to yomp back down for the replay, and persuaded a couple of the lads to help me achieve a moral victory. When the teams ran out on to the pitch, Stanty and Gary Kelly were waving a couple of pitchforks I had nicked from the groundsman's cupboard.

That was the pinnacle of our night's work. We lost 2–1.

Three days later, we were beaten 2–0 at home in the FA Cup by Blyth Spartans from the Unibond League and the sections of the crowd who disagreed with my appointment grew more vociferous. There were always ferocious critics at Bury, blinkered prats whose aspirations would test even that lot in red further down the road. I resented them. I despised their attitude and their sneering air of superiority.

Even so, it came as something of a shock when me and my backroom staff ended up brawling with them.

* * *

Terry blanched. He grimaced and clenched his fists before placing his head in his hands. We had been having a convivial discussion about recruiting a number two for me and all was going swimmingly until I mentioned my favourite's name. It was as devastating for the Chairman as if he'd been served a hot dog without a sausage.

> Terry: **Have you found a number two yet?**
> Me: **I've got one in mind.**
> Terry: **Who is it?**
> Me: **Big Sam.**
> Terry: **Oh good. Allardyce?**
> Me: **No. Ellis.**
> Terry: **Fucking hell, I wish I'd never asked.**

I had just presented Terry with a nightmare scenario. Tough. Sam Ellis knew Bury intimately. And that was the problem for some. He managed the team himself during the late '80s and took them to the top of the league. Abruptly, much to the anger and disbelief of the fans, he upped and left to become Peter Reid's assistant at Maine Road.

To some people in the Gigg Lane crowd, he transformed from saviour to sod overnight. They demonised him. Terry knew these donkeys with long memories would not welcome Sam back easily ... if at all.

'Listen, Stan,' he said, 'the fans aren't too keen on *you* yet. Bring Sam back and it could go seriously pear-shaped. I don't doubt his ability but it's going to be hair-raising.'

I was adamant about my choice and every time I refused to budge, another worry wrinkle creased Terry's forehead. I understood his reservations but, honestly, did the fans care about the good of the team or some petty grudge that could ultimately wreck any hopes we had of promotion?

The petty grudge, obviously.

Our own supporters booed Sam on to the pitch as he made his way to sit beside me on the bench for our first game.

Once that particular murmur of disapproval faded, individuals hurled dog's abuse at him throughout the match.

Sam's a strong man with broad shoulders. Whenever we play Sheffield United, their fans call him a 'pig' to his face because he used to play for Sheffield Wednesday, but he always nods, smiles and brushes away their frothing hatred with grace.

Yet at Bury, he quickly began to wilt under a ferocious barrage of 'traitor' and 'bastard'.

Sam had two major grievances: (1) he felt it was overly harsh for our own fans to encourage their kids to wave at him on his way to the ground using just two fingers; (2) his enemies at Bury were basing their campaign on lies.

The general consensus among his tormentors was that he had walked out on Bury. The truth was, he had been pushed.

Just as his team began to achieve in the league, Terry called Sam into his office and told him, 'We're going to have to sell some of our players.'

Sam replied diplomatically: 'Fuck off!'

'I'm serious,' said Terry.

Hugh Eaves was experiencing an unexpected financial blip and had slowed down Bury's money tap, temporarily causing financial problems for the club. Players would have to be flogged to pay the wage bill for those who were left.

Sam's disbelief was compounded by the fact that, in order to remain loyal, he had just turned down a lucrative offer from Reidy to be number two at City. 'I'm selling nobody,' he promised.

Terry knew the situation was impossible. Sam's team would have to be dismantled, with or without his co-operation. The Chairman bowed to the inevitable. 'Ring Reidy and ask him if the job is still available.'

It was, and Sam left to work for the club he had supported as a boy. Bury's fortunes went on a downward spiral. More players than ever were forced to become part-time, training after work on Tuesday and Thursday nights.

Disillusioned supporters released their venom on Sam, vilifying him for tripling his salary while they refused to accept the obvious – their club was poverty stricken.

Following his return at my side, the bile heaped on Sam worsened each week. At one point, he grabbed a Bury supporter by the throat for hurling personal insults from a spot on the terraces just a few feet from where his dad watched every game. After that incident, I accepted an invite to visit his house.

'I'm not staying, Stan,' were his first words.

His dad, sat by his side, chipped in. 'No one deserves that sort of abuse.'

The constant tirade from the terraces had obviously forced both Ellises to reconsider their position. I didn't blame them. Sam continued, 'The whole situation is putting too much pressure on the players. Their job is hard enough already without the dickheads in the crowd. They only have you for 90 minutes. I'm not letting them ruin my life.'

I replied, 'One thing's for sure. If you walk, so do I.'

At a Board meeting called to discuss the problem, club director Neville Neville refused to accept his resignation. Neville was devoted to Bury. Terry's secretary, Jill, was his wife and his lads Gary and Phil were huge fans who watched Bury whenever they were off duty from Manchester United. Sam had become a family friend. Gary and Phil even caddied for him on the golf course. Accordingly, Neville's support was total. He understood Sam's suffering well enough. Brain-dead fans gave *him* stick because his lads played for United and they couldn't understand why they wouldn't sacrifice their careers and personal riches to leave Old Trafford and come and play for us for ten bob a match.

Neville told the directors, 'If we let Sam go, we let the animals win. We might as well all pack it in.'

I had my own methods for persuading Sam to change his mind. After I left his house that night, I telephoned some of our mutual friends in football – Reidy, Ian Greaves, Sam Allardyce and Paul Bracewell – and told them to give him some stick.

One by one over the next few hours, they telephoned to slaughter him – 'You big daft bastard,' ... 'Mummy's boy,' ... They really got into his ribs.

Sam returned to work and we were ruthless with anybody who challenged our authority. A South African forward called John Paskin refused to take part in a training session in which each player donated a quid and the winner took the pot. Sam told him, 'Go and see the gaffer.'

This was our Dennis Wise moment. At Chelsea, Porterfield failed to support me against the players and they crucified me. As a result, from the moment Paskin set foot in my office, his fate was sealed. He had challenged Sam. Whatever the circumstances, I had to display unwavering faith in my assistant.

Paskin got both barrels. I heard his version of events and then explained to him, 'You won't play for me again, son.'

One more battle was needed before we could truly say we had overcome all our enemies at Bury. Sections of the supporters were still revolting. Quietly, at half-time during the next home match, we arranged for the violent ringleaders of the anti-Sam faction to meet with some of our own, more violent acquaintances.

They got the message.

I have never fought so hard to be accepted by my own team's supporters, and their bitterness soured our relationship. Every success Sam and I had subsequently at Bury was motivated partly by the fact I wanted to ram their treatment of us right back down their throats.

The team started to click. Over the Christmas period, we were beaten once in eight games and went seven matches without conceding a goal, cruising to sixth in the league. Our begrudging fans even got off my back for once, but I couldn't please everybody.

We were winning 1–0 at Doncaster and I'd been getting some stick from their supporters behind my dugout. With ten minutes to go, the loudest mouth offered me a fag and I decided to accept it. An Embassy Number Six would serve as our peace pipe.

As I reached for the tab, he yanked it away and flicked a V-sign at me. His mates started to laugh but he didn't have a chance to enjoy his own joke before I jumped over the advertising hoarding and set on him.

Sam eventually hauled me back on to the pitch side. I never got my fag but at least I crushed his while it was still between his lips.

I had to accept that my stress levels were not likely to improve as the season progressed as a promotion place became less of a dream and more of a possibility.

We put seven past Lincoln, four past Cambridge and three past Scunthorpe. I was Manager of the Month in March, gratefully wolfing down a free meal provided for me and my staff by the Football League which was way beyond the normal reaches of my scabby Bury FC expense account.

We became embroiled in a bitter dogfight for the final promotion spot with Darlington and, with three games to go, we were scheduled to travel to their place for a decider.

I invited my mate Peter Reid, who had just won promotion to the Premiership with Sunderland, to come to the game with his assistant Bob Saxton.

Hopefully, anything he could do, I could do, too.

We were tubbed 4–0. As the game churned on, the pair of them showed no mercy. Their seats were close to the Bury dugout and I heard every word Reidy uttered, as I was supposed to. 'Promotion? No fucking chance, mate,' ... 'In your fucking dreams,' ... 'You fucking blew it.'

The final whistle shut them up and I buggered off to the dressing room without a backward glance. I couldn't believe my team had allowed themselves to be bent over and rogered when we were so close to success.

I was in mid-bollocking when there was a knock at the door and the ref Gurnam Singh popped his head in to see one of our players whom he knew. 'Is Stanty in?'

I told him to fuck off, and he did. He even had the good grace to seem surprised.

I was supposed to be staying the weekend at Reidy's house but I couldn't face any more piss-taking. I sneaked away from the ground and smuggled myself aboard the team bus. I wanted to brood. I was convinced we had thrown away our best chance of a miracle promotion in my first season.

As punishment, the players were all dragged, kicking and screaming, into training the next day. We had two games left, starting with a trip to Exeter, and I wasn't going to let them lose concentration.

The journey down to the south coast was tiring and tense. We tried to loosen up and relax on arrival by warming up in a local park. Terry and his directors joined in, toe-poking crosses to the far post in their brogues while Sam ripped their efforts to pieces.

Our unusual pre-match kickabout seemed to have worked. We took the lead with a Mark Carter penalty after half-an-hour and we heard Darlington were losing in their match. At one point, we were just 23 minutes from automatic promotion.

At that moment, crucially, Lee Bracey lost his head. That was a major problem ... because Bracey was my goalkeeper.

Exeter's Mark Chamberlain had looped a soft cross into our box. I watched it approach the peak of its arc and begin to drop. I saw Bracey follow its path intently. It floated closer. Ever so close. Go on, catch it, I thought. He didn't. Go on, jump, I thought. He didn't. At least punch it, I thought. He didn't.

Their centre-half Noel Blake strolled over, waved to the crowd, smiled at the photographers, signed a couple of autographs, adjusted his shorts, thought about combing his hair and still had time to head it into our net.

1–1.

A point was not enough. Not by a mile.

It secured us a play-off spot but Darlington had beaten Chester 3–1 and were now a point ahead of us in the last promotion spot that we had occupied for almost a month. If they won their last game at Scunthorpe we would miss out.

The coach on the trip home had all the atmosphere of a 50ft-long hearse. I reflected on the cruelty of our game. Months of effort, the ruination of players' lives when they are sold against their will, the abuse I'd endured, the sacrifices I'd made to adhere to our absurd budget. All of it. Everything and anything that could meaningfully affect our status rested on a poofy cross that I could have cleared with my knob end.

We approached our last match of the season knowing our fate rested over the Yorkshire border at Scunthorpe. That lot owed us nothing. We had put five past Mick Buxton's team during the season; they were mid-table and dreaming about summer holidays. Darlington, with players such as Sean Gregan, Phil Bennett and Robbie Blake, were expected to knock them over.

We had to beat Phil Neal's Cardiff at Gigg Lane to stand any chance of snatching promotion but our impotence bred an air of nervous anti-climax before kick-off.

Just over 5,000 fans out of a total population of 170,000 turned up to bite their nails with us, an indication of our constant struggle to generate enthusiasm in the town. Floating supporters could not even be persuaded to turn up for a promotion showdown on the final day of the season.

Some of those who did attend were the same gloating bastards who had hounded me from the moment I was made manager and who had almost forced Sam to quit.

As I walked to my dugout, I stared squarely into the faces of the crowd, hoping at that moment that some of them had the decency to be ashamed. I was relieved to get out of the dressing room. The whole club had been going stir-crazy for a week. We had held so many 'what-if' discussions, we covered every option from going up to staying down to being struck by a meteor in the last minute.

Hugh Eaves went to extraordinary lengths to please the gods of good luck. Earlier in the season, he had been in Brussels for a business meeting on the day we beat Lincoln City 7–1. So, hours before kick-off against Cardiff, he sacrificed his seat in the stand for our biggest match in years and flew out to Belgium again, desperate to see if his superstition would work.

The players were over-anxious, too. We worked on our game plan in the frantic minutes leading up to kick-off, but my most difficult task was to keep them calm. There was an extra-long queue for the khazi.

The only player immune to all the fuss was Mark Carter, the coolest striker on the planet. As everyone else jigged, jogged, paced and prowled around the dressing room, Carter sat calmly in his dress shirt and socks doing a crossword. With just minutes to go, he threw on his kit, one sock up, one sock down, and strolled out on to the pitch.

Not everyone could be so relaxed. Watching from the stands

were the Neville brothers, Gary and Phil, both big Bury supporters. Both of them joined in with the celebrations when we heard unbelievable news from Scunthorpe ... Darlington had gone behind to two early goals.

Our fans reacted immediately. Local radio was broadcasting bulletins from the game and there were so many transistors on the terraces they would have generated enough battery power to run the floodlights.

As news of the goals spread, a general hubbub developed into a swell of backslapping, hugging and cheering which swept around the ground. Minutes later, David Pugh put us 1–0 up and the place erupted.

After the interval, David Johnson scored our second and Tony Rigby got the third. We'd done our bit.

Our game petered out. Instead, everyone focused on events at Scunthorpe. The Neville brothers had been forced to leave the ground after our first goal to catch the Manchester United team bus for a trip to Middlesbrough. They were due to collect their hard-won Premiership trophy there the next day.

As they walked down the aisle to take their seats, the other United players, who were listening to full-match commentary on local BBC radio and already knew we were winning, began to cheer. The only dissenting voice belonged to Gary Pallister who had once been on loan at Darlington. Suddenly, he brightened up.

Simultaneously, a sick silence descended on Gigg Lane. Darlington had scored. Even more hands clasped even more radios to even more ears. Their faces fell further. Darlington had equalised.

By now, our game was a distraction. We had it won. The players were playing keep-ball, more interested in shouting to the bench to ask for the Scunthorpe score.

I told them to concentrate and get on with it, but as I sent the subs out to warm up, I noticed that one of them was wearing radio earphones under his bobble hat. He was determined to keep his mates informed.

Cheers? Was it? Yes! Suddenly, huge cheers broke out. Another Mexican wave of grins and applause washed over our heads and around three sides of the stadium. Andy McFarlane had put Scunthorpe ahead again. Those boys must have been fighting men.

Moments later, we were crushed, emotionally mangled, as Darlo managed to equalise. The torture increased as visiting Cardiff fans cried out that Darlo had scored a winner, triggering panic. They were taking the piss but Darlington had definitely hit the bar.

Our referee, Alan Butler, had had enough and blew his final whistle. None of the players were the slightest bit interested in our game and it showed.

Half of the Bury supporters invaded the pitch, desperate to celebrate. But we knew the Scunthorpe match still had at least five minutes to run.

On the Manchester United coach, they had travelled out of local radio reception range at a crucial stage in both games so Alex Ferguson telephoned Scunthorpe Clubcall and relayed the commentary to his frantic full-backs.

As the seconds ticked away, I sat in the dugout for a couple of minutes watching various bouts of madness break out in the centre circle. Legions of kids were careering around, yelling their heads off and prematurely kissing the turf.

Behind me, still in their seats, many of Bury's more seasoned supporters, well used to being hoofed in the goolies at moments like these, sat and prayed silently that finally, on just this one precious occasion, we might actually enjoy some good fortune.

I said to Sam, 'I'm going to my office.' I couldn't bear to watch if they bagged one.

As I was halfway up the tunnel, all hell broke loose.

Word emerged that the final whistle had been blown at Scunthorpe. The game was drawn. We were promoted!

I refused to acknowledge the file of friends and strangers who queued to shake my hand. Instead, I barged into my office dragging my son Chris inside, too, before locking the door.

I told him, 'I won't believe it until I see it on *Grandstand*.'

Almost immediately, I had my wish. The caption did not, could not, lie. Division Three. Champions: Preston North End. Promoted: Gillingham and Bury.

If lovely, lovely, lovely Steve Ryder said it, it must be true. We were twenty-first in October. Now we were up.

I was chuffed for Terry, Neville and Hugh Eaves. I was pleased, too, for the minority of supporters who'd refused to condemn me and allowed me time to exert my influence instead of incessantly begging the Board to appoint McIlroy like many of their mates. More than any other single emotion, I felt vindicated. Rather like that famous Norwegian commentator, I had my own list: Harry Potts ... Jack Tordoff ... Richard Chetham ... Ian Porterfield ... were you watching?

My own personal scores aside, it is never my style to bathe in glory. We achieved a small measure of success but I was determined not to allow the players to wallow in the crazy adulation of the crowd and become distracted. Typically, the fickle folk of Bury beat me to it and refused point-blank to offer any form of crazy adulation whatsoever.

* * *

'Where is everybody?'

Not exactly the phrase you want to hear on an open-top bus during a celebratory cavalcade. I stood with the players as our promotion parade began its triumphant tour of Bury and we crawled along empty roads searching desperately for supporters to wave at.

Indeed. Where was everybody?

In a masterstroke of organisation, our parade had been arranged for the same Sunday afternoon that Manchester United had chosen to hold their party.

It was a fiasco.

As we urged our underwhelmed driver to trawl deserted streets in search of supporters, people washing their cars in the bright sunshine looked up to see a squad of 18 men frantically giving them the thumbs-up, desperate to be acknowledged by anyone.

Old ladies stuck their arms out as we approached, assuming we were the town centre service. There was no indication to tell them otherwise. No crowds six-deep at the roadside. No young children being handed up by their fathers for me to kiss. I'd seen more people in The Kettledrum on a Saturday night. What did me and Sam have to do to be accepted?

The bus driver became so confused by the lack of crowds he turned in the wrong direction down a one-way street. As a result, our central defender, Michael Jackson, was almost decapitated by a tree branch as it whiplashed across us outside Bury College.

We eventually arrived at the town hall for our civic reception to be met by just over 1,000 fans who had gathered to wish us well. One out of every 170 people in Bury felt motivated enough to come along and congratulate us.

As we paraded out on to the stone balcony overhanging the entrance behind a 'Well Done Shakers' banner, Hugh Eaves and I were given a standing ovation. The crowd spotted Terry and shouted, 'Sumo!'

After the dramatic events at Scunthorpe, I sent their manager a crate of champagne. Now, despite the reluctance of the people of Bury to party, I realised it was time for my lot to celebrate.

As we made our way to the Player of the Season awards at the Gigg Lane Social Club, I pulled the lads to one side.

Hugh Eaves had generously donated a wad of cash to pay for an end-of-season trip and I decided to allow the players to enjoy the responsibility of choosing our destination.

'We've got just two words to say to you, gaffer.'

What? Monte Carlo? The Algarve? Black Forest? They looked at me as though I was barking mad.

8

'F*** me, another Wig ...'

BURY, 1996–98

'Get out of here, you slappers!'

The two startled women stared at me blankly. Obviously foreign. Obviously about to shag two of my best players and fleece them, too. I wasn't having it. More to the point, they weren't having it either.

My lads looked on in shock as I tore into the birds. 'Get out of this hotel! Go on, piss off. Leave my players alone.'

'But, gaffer ...' stammered one of the lads.

'But, gaffer, nothing! Get to bed. I'll sort you two in the morning.'

I'd warned the squad on arrival. If there was to be any sex on this trip, it needed to be well away from our hotel. We were representing Bury Football Club and while I was manager, that meant obeying my rules and upholding my standards.

I'd enjoyed a brandy or two myself that night and had been in bed for barely an hour when this foursome tumbled giggling out of the lift. They woke me up with their squealing and the click-clack of the girls' high-heeled shoes on tiled corridor floors.

The club's directors were in rooms on the same floor and, promotion winners or not, I didn't want them swanning around in Don Estelle shorts on the way to breakfast and bumping into a couple of Spanish tarts performing nude flamenco dancing with two of our best players.

Dressed in my pyjamas and wrapped in a duvet, I bawled the two women out and dragged them into the lift. Despite their drunken protests, I pressed the button marked ground floor before I stepped out. The doors closed and hid their astonished faces. I was taking no chances. I wanted them out of the hotel.

When I got back to my room, I was seething. I grabbed the phone and dialled reception.

'Get me the manager,' I shouted. 'I want him to know that there are women of the night operating in his hotel and trying to interfere with employees of Bury Football Club.' Satisfied, I stomped off back to bed, the dignity of the squad intact.

The next morning, I dragged the whole squad from their beds for a round-up at 6.30am and gave them a monstering. Later, I was enjoying a coffee in the early morning sunshine by the swimming pool, still fuming. I bent down to put out a fag under my flip-flop and spotted the two players in their trunks, mingling with the rest of the lads close to the deep end.

Every so often, they glanced nervously in my direction. They understood punishment was on its way. They just didn't know what form it would take. Neither did I.

I was tempted to send them home for being stupid enough to get caught. If they wanted sex, there were hundreds of better dives in Magaluf rather than traipsing back to the club's official hotel with a couple of two-bob tarts in tow. The whole town is an accident waiting to happen.

I believed the players had earned the right to choose their destination and bravely agreed to abide by their decision. I even clung to a forlorn hope they would pick somewhere cultural. Not likely.

Magaluf is a string of bars held together by strips of neon lighting and blobs of hardened vomit. I'd been there before with other clubs and the pattern is always the same. Players go mad for 36 hours, fall over each other to find drink and then women or even straw donkeys to fornicate with. Whatever takes their fancy is available.

In the late 1990s, league clubs from all over England turned up to sample the delights of Magaluf at the same time every season. A diligent slapper with an autograph book could make a fortune.

I knew what went on but I preferred for it not to happen under my nose. Perhaps I would banish the two lads to their rooms for a day. Ground them.

As I contemplated their fate, I saw our skipper David Pugh make his way towards my sun-lounger. As captain, he had come to argue the guilty players' case.

'Forget it, Pughy lad. I'm not interested. I caught 'em. They've had it.'

'But, gaffer ...'

'I said forget it, lad.'

'But, gaffer ...'

I sat up and gave him my look. Shoulders square. It usually worked.

'But, gaffer ...' He was insistent.

'What?'

'There are two women here who want an apology off you.'

'Who?'

He pointed towards the revolving door that led to the hotel reception area. It was them! The hookers! Dressed in skimpy skirts and spilling out of bikini tops. I rose to my feet. If the manager wouldn't throw them out, I would.

'Gaffer! Gaffer!' Pugh pulled on my arm. 'They're staying here,' he explained.

'They're residents, not hookers! They had the room next to the lads and they shared a lift after separate nights out. They're from Liverpool. They were only going back to their own room when they said a madman wearing a duvet threw them out. They said it was you and they're going to complain.'

I sat down again quickly. I didn't dare look towards the team. If I had, and they were laughing, I would have front-crawled across the pool and knocked the lot of them clean out. I knew I was in for plenty of stick off the lads. They were loving it.

Two bottles of champagne and an extremely red face later, I managed to calm the women down. In my haste in the early hours of the morning, I mistakenly called them slappers. To be fair to the lasses, they were anxious to point out that there was 'little chance of them ever preying on my players anyway' because they were all such 'ugly bastards'.

Various other misdemeanours as the holiday progressed – including coming in late, coming in on all fours and coming in naked – meant I was still able to levy record fines against all the players. Naturally, they didn't pay up.

Once we were back in Bury, I asked Jill Neville to type official letters addressed to their wives explaining why fine money was being docked from their husbands' wages. I told her to leave them in clear view, face up on the corner of the desk in my office.

Two days later, in a state of total panic, every single one of them settled in full.

I eventually made them pay in triplicate for my embarrassment in Magaluf. Oh yes!

As we moved into the 1996–97 pre-season period, I ran the squad hard over the forbidding slopes of Tandle Hill and then enjoyed a cappuccino at my favourite Roma coffee house watching their tans pale as they heaved and strained through dozens of push-ups.

To recover completely from my Spanish trauma, I squeezed in a quick break to Portugal with Kath and a group of family friends.

We drank wine, talked nonsense and I slept well. At the same time, I underwent a transformation.

I resolved to change things.

Too many people at Bury were approaching our new season in Division Two discussing aspects of consolidation. As far as I was concerned, people who settle for second best usually end up with nothing. There was too much fear and trepidation at the club. Too many timid people. The prospect of playing Watford, Preston and Burnley didn't frighten me.

If my ambition outstretched Bury's imagination, so be it. I was one step nearer to my goal of managing a club in the Premiership. With a few adjustments, this team could take me even closer.

The Board had plenty of opportunities to see the results of positive thinking first hand. To boost our finances, we rented our ground to Manchester United who paid handsomely for the privilege of using Gigg Lane for their reserve matches.

I used to go along and watch. Brian Kidd was in charge and occasionally recruited me as a motivator.

'Give Andy Cole a bit of stick, will you, Stan?'

'Coley!' I shouted. 'Get yourself moving, you lazy, flat-footed bastard.'

Kidd laughed and Cole took it in the spirit it was meant.

'Fuck off,' he told me.

What I would give for a few lazy, flat-footed bastards like him in my team. Whatever meagre resources Hugh Eaves did make available, I spent wisely. Formidable centre-half Paul Butler joined from Rochdale for £130,000. I bought Ronnie Jepson, a huge, impressive, influential, ginger-haired, tattooed powerhouse of a human being from Huddersfield at a snip for £40,000. Gordon Armstrong, a utility player who was slightly mad and totally dedicated came on a free transfer from Sunderland.

All my new recruits were capable individuals who would strengthen the spirit of the team, though I had a problem with Jeppo ... keeping him off fags.

The dressing room doors at Bury have portholes in them and I used to lie in wait, peeping through to catch him sneaking down to the laundry with Stanty for a crafty drag.

I'd follow them on tiptoe down the corridor and cough loudly outside the washroom door, listening as Jeppo fought to squeeze his bulky frame into the 6in gap behind the industrial-size tumble dryers. It became a routine. If I was feeling particularly kind, I'd stay for half-an-hour and catch up with the gossip from kit woman Pat. Jeppo could lose up to a stone sweating in his alcove with jets of steam squirting up his arse.

It was during a Jeppo-hunt that I decided I needed a team-bonding session. I've met plenty of deluded managers who experience small amounts of success and are tempted to organise pre-season tours of Scandinavian outposts, harbouring stupid illusions about their team's new-found prestige. We didn't need fancy plans.

My physio Matt Radcliffe had contacts in the South-West of England through his dad and, as a result, we received an invite to visit Exeter. I felt a shiver of pleasure as I informed the players of our destination. The further their faces fell, the bigger the thrill I got from outlining the spartan details of our grand tour.

Most professional footballers are pampered from the moment they enter the game. Arse-wiping would be a cottage industry if they had their way.

Not at Bury. We based ourselves at Exeter University for a week and played a series of tough matches against competent local teams. It was unglamorous. It was gruelling. Just the way I like it.

The only distraction I allowed the players was a sightseeing trip to Dartmoor Prison and the odd round of golf. Even that was not without trauma.

As we hacked our way around a links course at Bridgeport, a golfer putting for his par on the ninth hole collapsed with a heart-attack.

We rushed over to give him the kiss of life, but when I turned to ask Sam for advice, he was running off up the fairway faster than Benny Hill. One of the toughest men in football was as squeamish as a schoolgirl with spiders in her pants. If he'd been one of my players, I'd have fined him.

That night, as we left for home, I sensed the players and staff were very knackered and slightly depressed.

To give them a lift, I made a surprise announcement. We would, after all, be spending a week abroad playing in a prestigious European tournament. They gave a spirited cheer. It wasn't until we pulled up at the Gigg Lane car park that I revealed we were actually off to the Isle of Man.

One week and two games later, I sensed we were on the verge of one of Bury's biggest seasons ever.

I changed my formation during the tournament to play three at the back, and we satisfyingly thumped the Isle of Man 8–0. We lost 1–0 to First Division West Bromwich Albion but, by then, I was satisfied I had a good team. We were mobile, we were aggressive, we were strong in the air. Just as importantly, all the players had a desire to play in a higher league. At last, I had recruited 11 men whose ambitions matched my own.

It was just a shame their off-field behaviour didn't. A condition of entry for the competition was that we had to attend several official functions on the island, meeting with fans and dignitaries over glasses of warm beer. Like most football bashes, half of the guests are perfectly normal, the other 50 per cent consist of know-alls, piss-heads, crashing bores or prats who imagine they could manage England if only they had the chance.

Neville Neville, who had brought his lad Phil on the trip, had a decent approach to coping with these functions that he had developed over the years along with Terry. The pair of them, both big lads, would use the events as excuses to gorge themselves. They once drew an appreciative crowd to their table when they each ordered 32oz steaks and ate the lot without fainting.

I drew an even bigger crowd when I started a ruck. I was

already fed up of fixing my smile and listening to inane chat when I turned from Terry and Neville's feast and spotted a Bury supporter who wrote one of the club's fanzines. In his last issue, he had slaughtered one of my players, Kevin Hulme.

I made my way towards him. He actually thought I wanted to be his pal and was preening himself as I approached. His self-important smile crumpled when I told him, 'You owe the player and his family an apology. You've printed a disgraceful character assassination.'

The fella, who had a club foot, shifted uncomfortably. 'I'm sorry,' he mumbled.

'Sorry?' I said. 'You'll have two fucking club feet if you do it again.'

Terry overheard our row and picked an argument with me. I didn't hang around to listen to his reasons. I knew them well. The attendances at Bury were so pitiful he was afraid to alienate any supporters whatsoever.

Bollocks to that! I'd rather have ten genuine fans watch a team of mine than have a full house of sniping, booing, miserable hypocrites.

Back at the hotel, I was not good company. Gradually, the directors and coaching staff returned, we said our desultory good nights and they left me in the bar area nursing a coffee and a brandy. I watched the clock.

The deadline for players to return passed, yet I'd only seen one or two of the lads wander through reception. It was Magaluf all over again.

This time I was ready. I searched out the night porter and persuaded him, with the help of a few fivers, to bolt the front door.

They could sleep out on the streets.

As I made my way to bed, I heard scuffling noises through the outside wall in the corridor close to my room. The strange scraping noises moved gradually along. Too noisy for mice. Then a window popped up, prised open from the outside. Seconds later, one of my midfielders poked his head through.

He looked left ... the coast was clear. He looked right ... and saw me. 'Gaffer!'

'That's right. See me in the morning.'

After hauling him through the window and packing him off to his room, I locked it and took the lift back down to reception.

I complained to the caretaker that the building was not watertight and warned him that there could be quite a few other 'break-ins' over the next few hours.

'Do you want to watch them trying on telly?' he asked.

The chap led me to a back office and switched on a small portable black-and-white television. The picture changed constantly, each frame an exterior view of the hotel from a different angle. Smile, lads, you're on CCTV.

Slowly, they came. One or two up the fire escape, others trying windows, a couple even clumsily helping each other up a drainpipe. I noted their names.

The next morning at breakfast, I shopped them all and handed out whopping fines. None of them knew how I'd found out.

I had another shock for them back in Bury. Just 24 hours before our first game, a trip to Brentford, I completed a £125,000 deal to sign a sensational goalkeeper I'd spotted playing for York City, Dean Keily, currently in the Premiership with Charlton.

He was tremendous but his only drawback was sulking. If someone scored past him in training, he dwelled on it for too long, but I tolerated it. Conceding goals mattered to him and, with his contribution, we were soon up and running.

We earned a 1–1 draw at Brentford thanks to a goal from Jeppo, followed by wins at Chesterfield and Wycombe and home wins against Bristol City, Notts County and Rotherham. Before a ball had been kicked, my team were favourites to be relegated. Pundits had queued up to slag us off.

I've no time for commentators and critics. David Pleat can talk under water. What did they know? Game seven and we were already in the top three.

We beat our big neighbours from Burnley. Jeppo did the business again but, frustratingly, the Bury public still refused to show. That night, we opened a flash new stand and it was full, top to bottom ... with Burnley fans.

Despite being outnumbered at most matches, we continued to pick up points and some of our rivals found our hard-fought, no-frills success hard to stomach.

We hit second place in October with a 2–1 win at Peterborough, but David Johnson, who was racially abused for most of the match, became the first player *ever* to be sent off for over-celebrating a goal when he hit the winner with seven minutes left and took the mick out of their supporters.

It started going pear-shaped. Dean Keily was arrested two weeks later after we beat Bristol Rovers 2–1 at Gigg Lane. A group of their fans claimed he had made gestures at them. The police released him without charge.

I wasn't upset. I actively encouraged occasional displays of defiance. It embodied the essence of our half-arsed outfit to turn up at bigger, better supported, better funded clubs and beat them. We got in their faces.

The Board announced record losses of £820,264 in December but I barely noticed. As far as I was concerned, I was delivering an adventure and the price had to be paid. Hugh Eaves was worth millions. He could afford it.

I spent another £140,000 on midfielder Adrian Randall, a tricky player who scored on his début at Gillingham with his first touch.

I began to believe nothing would stop us, and I relished a trip to Burnley, the club that had rejected me as a player and refused to consider me as a manager, even though I lived within spitting distance of their ground.

The match was on Sky TV and, I hate to admit, I was unusually tense. During a live interview in the tunnel before kick-off I was asked, 'Stan, you've come back to Burnley as a manager for the first time in 29 years. You started here as a player, but now you find yourself as manager of Bury. You have dropped leading goalscorer Mark Carter and you are missing your captain David Pugh with injury, yet your goalkeeper Dean Keily is in a rich vein of form. You are sitting pretty in the Second Division challenging your local rivals Stockport County, and now you face the team where you have strong and binding emotional ties. Is this a huge game for Stan Ternent and Bury Football Club?'

What did he expect me to say to that? I barked, 'No,' and stomped off on to the pitch.

Stupidly, I changed our system from a pattern of three centre-halves, which had served us well, to a flat back four. I had some notion of Rob Matthews breaking wide down their right but it didn't come off and we were 3–1 down at half-time. Burnley fans yelled, 'Ternent, Ternent, what's the score?' Taunted in my own backyard!

I switched tactics back for the second half and there were no more goals, but I was inconsolable at the end. I was furious with myself. For months afterwards I tried to convince myself that I'd played the game normally, but it was a lie. I despised myself for trying too hard to impress the people at Burnley. I had nothing whatsoever to prove to them but, in my haste to show my home club what they had missed, I sacrificed a winning formula.

That game haunted me for weeks, more so because the TV people hadn't given a toss about us throughout our run from Division Three, yet the first time we had ever appeared live on the box I mucked it up.

Even worse, Burnley leapfrogged over us in the table.

I gave the usual bullshit to the press afterwards. 'You learn something from every match,' ... 'I thought we showed resilience,' ... 'We've no complaints.' The truth was, I made myself a solemn promise that if we didn't finish above Burnley that season, I would quit football for ever.

I needn't have worried. Burnley faded away and *we* challenged for the leadership, climaxing in an Easter showdown at Brentford.

We were second. They were top. We battered them, won 2–0 and earned the highest praise any team of mine could ever aspire to. The *Daily Telegraph* reported, 'Bury played with a frightening determination and a desire to win.'

It was an intensive, attritional performance. Chris Luketti played on with ten stitches in a severe wound. Tellingly, their fans applauded us off.

Now we were top, and we would protect that spot as if our lives depended on it. Even the enforced sale of one of our best players, defender Michael Jackson, to Preston North End couldn't deflect us.

But we suffered minor setbacks. After a 2–1 defeat at Stockport, I lost patience with the players and warned them, 'Get back on the bus by 5.30pm or it will leave you behind.'

I left the ground after a chat with County manager Dave Jones and the coach had gone! The car park was empty. At first, I thought the players had hidden it round the corner but they had pissed off back to Bury without me. I scuttled back inside Edgeley Park and had to accept a lift home off Jonesy.

A month later we were losing 2–0 at Blackpool, when there was a commotion in the directors' box. Our officials were packed in tightly, doing their best to become anonymous as we faced defeat against delighted local rivals.

The directors slid further and further down in their seats, desperately trying to hide behind a low wooden partition separating them from the paying public.

However, idiots in the crowd turned to give our lot some abuse and soon spotted one of our directors. He wore a wig.

'Fuck me, a wig!' they shouted.

Then they spotted Hugh Eaves. He wore a wig.

'Fuck me, another wig!' they shouted.

Then they spotted another one of our directors. He wore a wig.

'Fuck me, three wigs!'

Our lot didn't know where to look. Sadly, the rest of the crowd did. From the front, it was like staring at a family of hamsters on a pet shop shelf. Hugh's wig was so dodgy that if you ran your finger down the parting you'd need stitches. At least it diverted attention from our performance. We'd now lost two away matches in succession, but I refused to acknowledge we were letting things slip.

We managed to scrape a point at promotion rivals Luton and then travelled to Watford for the penultimate game of the season knowing we needed just a point to go up. It was unprecedented.

We were one single point away from the club's first double promotion in its 112-year history. The side had developed a momentum which I felt was destined to carry us to Division One and maybe beyond.

No one fancied us. No one wanted us in the higher division. Our average attendance of 4,502 was pathetic. But being nonconformists had become our trademark. No luxury training ground, no five-star hotels, no Porsches in the car park, no big-name superstars, no compromises. And no prisoners.

It was ironic that, as we ran on to the pitch at Watford, the PA announcer was informing their fans that Elton John had retaken control of the club. It was the complete antithesis of everything Bury stood for. 'Candle in the Wind'? He could have been singing about our knackered Gigg Lane floodlights.

A huge roar greeted the teams as we emerged from the tunnel and I was pleasantly surprised to see at least 1,500 fans had travelled down from Bury. That meant one-third of our normal home crowd had made the trip. Glory-grabbers? I preferred to regard it as a new dawn.

The match was goalless and uneventful until the 88th minute. The precious point we needed was barely two minutes away. We had battled hard for the first 70 minutes and been subjected to a barrage of attacks towards the end. Now, we were 120 seconds away from glory.

Graham Taylor's team swarmed forward. They still had a chance to reach the play-offs. Their defender Richard Johnson found himself in our penalty area and lifted his leg to shoot ... He missed.

But the reason he missed was because Gordon Armstrong had clattered into him. Good tackle, surely?

The ref seemed unmoved. I glanced along the touchline to the linesman. Except it was a lines*woman*. Wendy Tomms. Keep your flag down, love, keep your flag down. I was beyond prayer. My eyes widened like a pair of Elton's specs as I focused on the woman who stood between me and the First Division. She flagged. Backwards and forwards, up and down, went that flag.

The ref blew and gave the penalty. We scampered down the touchline.

'Never a penner, that!'

She said nothing.

'You've cost us promotion, love!'

Still nothing.

'Oi! Can I ask you a question? While you're here knackering our chances, who's making your husband's tea?'

It was pointless abuse, but I'd be lying if I said it didn't make us feel better.

On the pitch, Watford's lethal goalscoring machine Tommy Mooney placed the ball on the spot. I began to plan for next Saturday's game against Millwall. It would now be a must-win match.

Mooney hit it to our keeper's left. Our players were too disheartened to even follow it up. Two Bury midfielders were stood on the edge of the box with their arms around each other like schoolboys summoning the courage to buy their first Durex.

Then, Keily saved it! Bloody hell, he saved it!

He's lost it! Bloody hell, he's lost it!

He's caught it again!

I was ecstatic. Dean Keily had blocked the first shot, fumbled the ball and then smothered it with his body.

Our fans went potty. Our players went potty. I stared towards the directors' box expecting to see wigs being tossed into the air like straw boaters. Instead, I met Terry's gaze and gave him a wink.

When the final whistle sounded 90 seconds later, it felt as though we had played an hour of injury time. My players hugged each other and fell to the ground in exhaustion.

I shook hands with my coaching staff and succumbed to a sense of tremendous relief. More ghosts from my past had been exorcised. Enough of those who had cursed the name of Ternent in the past would now envy it.

The bus trip home summed up our season. We stopped at the first chip shop we could find and ordered 25 fish suppers. If the champagne was on ice, it was because it was still in the fridges at Asda. There was no extra money for bubbly.

Instead, we had a quick whip round and bought as many bottles of cheap wine as we could muster. Quantity not quality was the order and by the time we reached the outskirts of Bury that night everyone was rat-arsed on Watford's finest Concord.

I didn't touch a drop. I sat throughout the journey in my usual seat behind the driver, happy to savour the moment. Neville Neville plonked himself beside me for a while and had to shout to be heard above the players' singing.

'I'll tell you what, Stan,' he said. 'Both of my lads have played for England but today has been one of the most amazing moments of my life.'

The coach arrived at The Windmill pub, one of our normal pre-arranged dropping-off points, where some of the players had left their cars.

Waiting for us was Michael Jackson. I'd sold him to Preston weeks earlier but he desperately wanted to be part of our big day and drove along specially. He had done more than enough to earn his share of the praise and I was glad to see him.

As soon as he clambered up the steps, he came straight over and gave me a big hug. I only let the soppy sod get away with it because, technically, I was no longer his gaffer. He had been waiting two hours. Everything I ever told my players about forging team spirit was embodied in that gesture from Jackson. I was delighted for him and the rest of the lads but my bones were weary.

During my chats with Stanty about life with the SAS, I discussed aspects of their approach to combat and concluded that I operated similarly. Our long battle for promotion was over; I was proud of our achievements but had no desire whatsoever to revel in the glory.

As we finally arrived at the Gigg Lane Social Club to be welcomed by hundreds of deliriously drunken fans, I felt a little uncomfortable.

Out of duty, I gave a small speech. 'Thanks for coming. See you next season.'

Then I scrounged a fag off Jeppo and legged it home to bed.

* * *

I couldn't see anything through my car windscreen except for a wall of flabby arses in baggy jeans and the faces of snot-nosed kids. Dads, lads, mums, too. Everyone draped in blue-and-white.

Normally on match days, you could swing a giraffe around by the neck in the car park at Gigg Lane and you'd only hit the fella with the flat cap who sold programmes. Today was the last day of the season, our chance to clinch the Second Division title, and they were queuing around the block.

Was this more evidence of Ternent's new dawn, when huge swathes of the population finally had the scales removed from their eyes and realised their lives were not complete without a visit every fortnight to Gigg Lane? Or was the bingo shut? It was debatable.

Terry wasn't fussy. The turnstiles became slot machines and bulged with coins and notes as supporters tussled to get inside. After a desperate struggle to attract crowds all season, stewards

Top: My second consecutive promotion with Bury. I was soaked in water, not champagne! Jeppo (*third left, back row*), Gordon Armstrong (*sixth left, back row*) Sam Ellis (*extreme right, back row*) Dean West (*third left front row*), David Johnson (*fourth left, front row*) and Lennie Johnrose (*extreme right, front row*) share our one can of lager.

Bottom: F*** me, another wig! A hair-raising day for Hugh Eaves.

Top left: Terry Robinson with his latest free drink.

Top right: Promotion silverware.

Bottom: Day one at Burnley as Frank Teasdale's chosen one.

BFC saviour Barry Kilby welcomes new signing Ian Wright.

Top: Wrighty almost broke my back after breaking his duck at Gillingham.

Bottom: Promotion for Burnley and I almost plunge to my death at Scunthorpe.

Top: Wrighty's farewell photo. One for his private collection.

Bottom: A hard day in a hard life, at Stockport. (*left to right*) Sam Ellis, me, Mick Docherty and Cliff Roberts.

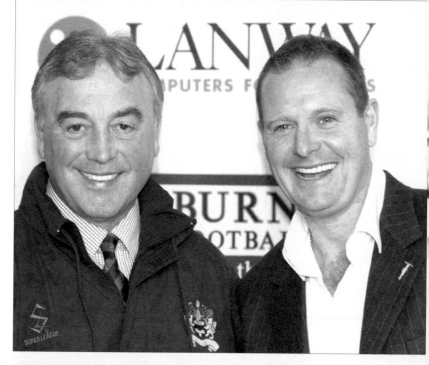

Top: Gazza signs and another legend prepares to wear the claret and blue of Burnley FC.

Bottom: The usual suspects at a manager's dinner. (*left to right*) Danny Wilson, Dario Gradi, Colin Todd, me, John Duncan, Dave Jones, John Deehan and the seated Brian Kidd.

Kath flies the colours.

My favourite supporters ... Chris, Kath, me and seated, Yogi, Olivia and Dan.

Inset: What a beauty ... Olivia on a trip to Turf Moor.

now had to lock out 2,000 fans as the capacity of 10,000 was reached well before kick-off.

In 20 months I had taken attendances from around 3,000 and more than tripled them. Cynics said that filling Gigg Lane was an achievement on a par with back-to-back promotions.

The newcomers all went home happy, too. We won 2–0, clinching the title to snatch it from Stockport. All sorts of records were smashed in the process. We hadn't conceded a goal in seven games; the last time Bury did that was in 1923. We had been unbeaten at home all season, a record not equalled since 1895 when players had very long shorts. We also achieved the unthinkable with a set of players other managers thought were unusable.

The lads paraded the trophy around the ground, alternately shouting, 'We've done it!' and 'Fucking Magaluf!' I accepted my medal, grabbed the cup and clambered on to the roof of my dugout. In front of the cheering crowd, many of whom had never been to our ground before, I wanted them to see who was responsible for Bury's continued existence and handed it over to Terry and Hugh Eaves.

Those two men had bravely persevered with an unfashionable club when the rest of the town had turned its back. Eaves refused to listen to doom-mongers who had predicted we would fail and collected £25,000 from the bookies who had offered odds of 25–1 against us winning the title. He and Terry deserved this day more than any of us and for once even *I* must have looked cheerful.

Jeppo announced to the press, 'Stan isn't really smiling. It's wind.'

Despite the uproar, or possibly because of it, I began to settle scores with relish. In the programme that day, I'd announced, 'I would like to thank Sky Sports for not showing any live games from Gigg Lane this season. I would like to thank Elton Welsby for only mentioning us once on his TV show. And I would like to thank the PFA for not putting any of our players in their end-of-season league team.'

As the party on the pitch continued, I made my way to the Boardroom for a quiet pint with Terry, only to be confronted by a huge crowd of men in suits with strange faces, all clamouring to touch Terry or the trophy, slap each other's backs and hijack our big day. I wasn't standing for it.

I enjoyed scrapping as the underdog. All I wanted to do was to celebrate with the loyal staff who had devoted their lives to the club. I found all this mock Bury-worship from virgin outsiders sickening. Terry felt the full force of my anger as I rounded on them all at the top of my voice. 'Where were all you lot when we were struggling, eh? Where were you when we were in the Third Division? Fucking hangers-on!'

I shattered the silence that followed by slamming the Boardroom door as I stomped off, out of the stand and across the car park.

I was nudging towards the exit in my Merc when Terry, huffing and puffing, caught up and signalled me to wind down the window by tapping on the roof.

'Don't bother, Terry,' I said. 'I know you feel you've got to suck up to these scumbags but I wish you wouldn't. They're only here for the big game. They won't be back.'

'I know,' he admitted. 'They are the officials from the Football League who have come to present the fucking trophy.'

* * *

As we scrabbled for seats on the team bus at Manchester Airport for the short trip back to Bury, I totted it up. Not a bad body count for Magaluf – one player missing, one wounded, one warned for trying to explode an aeroplane.

Soon after winning the title, I had booked our traditional week in the sun without even bothering to ask the players for their preferred destination. They'd made it clear in which hellhole they wanted to party.

Most of them arrived in Spain wearing baggy Bermuda shorts and sandals and were all over the first bar they saw like safari park monkeys on a Ford Sierra.

I gave my usual lecture. 'Keep your wits about you. Don't embarrass the club. Don't get too drunk in public.'

I popped out for a walk and returned to find Gordon Armstrong and my son Dan holding lager races across the pool, upending kids in rubber rings in their wake. Last one to finish had to down a pint and, in the mêlée, Dan gashed his face and was bleeding heavily as they both emerged from the shallow end. Everyone started talking at once.

'Pipe down the lot of you,' I told them. 'First warning.'

We'd been in the resort for exactly two hours and ten minutes.

That afternoon, desperate to avoid any more scenes, I 'advised' the squad to relax by the pool. The hotel entertainment manager was holding bingo sessions for the other guests but we bowed out. Or so I thought.

There was a sudden commotion when an argument developed a few tables away from us. I was too chilled out to remove my sunglasses but I could hear volleys in an agitated Spanish accent compete with expletives barked by a bloke from Stoke.

I was out of my seat instantly. I found Ronnie Jepson, luxuriating full-length on a sun-lounger with 23 bingo cards arranged over his sunburn-pink chest and stomach. Next to him on a small side-table was a half-empty packet of Silk Cut and a pint of beer.

He was in heaven. Jeppo is an ex-miner, built like a brick shithouse, who just happens to love bingo. He's as big as two fat ladies.

'All right, gaffer!'

'What's going on, Jeppo?'

'I'll tell you what is going on, sir ...' A dapper midget appeared alongside me with an immaculately trimmed moustache and hair that looked like shoe polish. He was wearing a white suit with epaulettes. 'He has been cheating.'

Not surprisingly, Jeppo bristled. I knew he was a man of honour. If he farted in a lift, instead of acting innocent he was more than likely to try and light it.

As soon as the bingo session had been announced, Jeppo tried to interest his team-mates, but they wanted none of it. So he collected their cards together and, using skills honed in all sorts of colliery clubs in the 1970s, played 23 games at once. He wasn't cheating. I made my views clear and left.

The argument continued as I headed to the bar. 'You cheated.'

'I didn't.'

'You cheated.'

'I didn't.'

'You cheated.'

The last words I made out as the door to the pool closed gently behind me were uttered by Jeppo. 'Look. Fuck off, pal, or I'll lob you in the pool.'

The next morning, my midfielder Adrian Randall had disappeared.

'Where is he?' I asked David Pugh.

'Dunno. No one has seen him for two days. He was last spotted coming out of Bananas Disco and heading for Palma Airport.'

Randall had only been with us for five months but I was certain he knew the rules. No one is allowed on an early flight home without my express permission. That's if he had actually left on a plane. He could have been lost or locked up.

Like others in my team, Randall was hardly the sharpest tool in the box. Earlier that day, one of my players was about to try his hand at go-karting when the rest of the lads convinced him he needed a driving licence. He had borrowed mine and had spent 24 hours practising how to forge my signature. Then, just as he was about to get in a kart, the same players convinced him not to bother because the licence he was using had points for speeding.

Based on that sort of stupidity, Randall could have been

anywhere. During our bar-to-bar search, I bumped into players from Tranmere, Wrexham, Wigan and York.

I saw a useful lad called Mark Patterson. He let slip he was available on a free transfer from Sheffield United, who were managed by Howard Kendall.

'Where's your gaffer?' I asked him.

Patterson pointed further along the strip. 'Third pub on the left.'

As I wandered towards the bar, I heard a shout. 'Stan! Over here, mate!'

Howard had spotted me first and was already hitting the hard stuff. 'Brandy?'

I was only in there for an hour but, by the time I emerged with a promise over the Patterson deal, I was walking sideways. I also agreed to sign Andy Gray from Falkirk in Mano's Bar.

As a result of all these 'negotiations', the search for Randall was quickly abandoned. Two days later, when we reached the airport to catch our flight home, I was forced to wait for an hour on the tarmac in case the pillock showed up at the last minute. There was no sign.

There was also almost no plane left for him to catch, in any case. As I squinted into the afternoon sun, looking for my AWOL midfielder, I caught sight of the squad making their way off the shuttle bus towards the aeroplane steps. Jeppo turned for a last look towards the terminal and I almost fainted.

He was little more than 6ft from a wing laden with tons of highly flammable aviation fuel ... and was furiously dragging on a Benson and Hedges. King size.

'Jeppo, for fuck's sake!'

Holidaymakers stared at me in shock.

'Jeppo!'

The big lump saw me and waved, the short sleeves of his Hawaiian shirt flapping in the slight breeze. He was about to flick the fag away on to the ground. The whole place could have gone up.

'Jeppo, man! What're you doing? There's aviation fuel everywhere!'

The message, relayed via other players, finally got through. Jeppo pinched the fag out with his fingers and laughed as he entered the plane. The cabin crew were about to hammer him to death with their inflatable jackets.

Safely back in Bury, I found Randall. 'Why did you leave Spain? You should have told me.'

The jug-eared midfielder looked at me as though I was stupid. 'I had to get back, gaffer. The wife booked us a big holiday and would never have forgiven me if we'd missed it.'

'I'm fining you,' I told him automatically. 'Anyway, where did you go that was so important?'

'Blackpool, boss,' Randall explained gravely.

The jaunt over without too many disasters, I was fresh, tanned, relaxed and looking forward to mixing it with the big boys.

Lining up against Bury in Division One for the '97–'98 season were Sunderland, Manchester City, Wolves and Nottingham Forest.

It was my crack at reaching the Premiership, my biggest test as a manager and it was vital we began positively.

Officials at the club were beside themselves with the news that we had sold 2,500 advance season tickets, the highest figure since World War II.

Director John Smith officially announced that Sam and I were 'miracle workers'. And ... that's as good as it got.

Days before our first game, I was summoned to Terry's office and I found him in deep discussion with Neville Neville. Both of them looked devastated. I hoped to God it wasn't the RSPCA again.

We used to have an adopted team cat that was supposed to be lucky. Fans and staff got to know it and would stroke it as it perched in the stand. In reality, the moth-eaten creature spent most of its time shitting on everything we owned and ripping up the kit.

One day it disappeared. The RSPCA heard that someone at the club had put it in a sack, lobbed it into the boot of their car and hurled it over a fence into nearby Heaton Park in Manchester. They threatened to hold an inquiry but the allegations were never proved. Had they found some evidence?

'We've had some bad news, Stan,' said Terry.

'I had nothing to do with that cat.'

They both looked at me. 'It's Hugh Eaves,' said Neville. 'He's pulled out. We've no money left and our assets have been frozen.'

Wow! Apart from hearing that my back three had been eaten by tigers, this was the most shocking news I could have imagined.

I had already been devastated once that morning, long before I'd reached Terry's office. The muppets at the Football League had broken with a decade of tradition and refused to award me the Manager of the Year trophy for winning the Second Division.

Despite being champs, 12 months after winning promotion from the Third Division, they claimed Dave Jones at runners-up Stockport County deserved it more.

I felt betrayed, the victim of a carve-up which was a slur on myself and Bury. It reinforced my opinion of the prejudice I felt they held towards our unfashionable club. If they could hear the news I was receiving about Eaves, Christ, they'd probably piss themselves.

'What happened?'

It transpired that Hugh had made some poor financial investments. He had subsequently withdrawn from the club and gone to Hong Kong for a short while. What this meant for us was that the money he was investing in the club was gone, leaving us in an awkward financial situation.

Eaves had placed the club up for sale at £6m at one stage. If it had been sold, it would have made £2m profit.

No one bought it. No one even bothered to ask for a guided tour.

Eaves's departure laid bare the delusions we all harboured about Bury. As soon as we'd achieved promotion to the First

Division, players' contracts expanded and expenditure went haywire. We were up shit creek without a paddle. Or a boat.

Everyone at the club regarded Eaves as a kindly benefactor who had arrived as a supporter in 1985 and became a saviour. Now that he had been exposed, I got the distinct feeling that the Board mourned their own misfortune far more than the fate of the people he had let down.

'We had no idea what he was doing, but he has given us ten wonderful years,' said Neville. 'We would never have reached the First Division without him.'

There was little option but to allow the systematic rape of the club's minimal assets. We beat eventual champions Nottingham Forest 2–0 at Gigg Lane and then, depressingly, had to sell one of our scorers, David Johnson – the brilliant forward we had pinched from Manchester United reserves – for £1 million.

Johnno was a huge talent. As soon as I was forced to sell him to Ipswich, terminal decline set in. He epitomised Bury's battling spirit. He is 3ft-nothing, yet ran defences ragged and stood his corner.

We once returned from an away match and I let the lads have a drink to relax, as usual. Halfway home, I slaughtered Johnno about an aspect of his game and he decided to defend himself. We travelled between Junctions 8 and 9 on the M1 standing toe to toe in the centre aisle of the bus taking it in turns to shout 'Fuck off!' into each other's face.

Johnno went home that night feeling guilty and, after a heart-to-heart with his missus, turned up at training the following Monday to say sorry.

I was a realist. I could hardly ask the little fella to play with balls if I didn't expect him to show them to me occasionally. He imagined he was going to be sacked. I told him, 'It was the wine talking. But you were out of order.'

Johnno cringed as he awaited my verdict.

'Now, about Saturday, can you play against Birmingham?'

He wasn't the only enforced sale. I had to flog Ian Hughes to Blackpool for £200,000.

If our double promotion had been a miracle, staying up was now impossible. The door to the Premiership had not only been slammed in my face, it was wedged shut by Billy Bunter's bigger brother.

The fans were the first to give up. Despite the record season-ticket sale, only 5,000 could be bothered to show up for our first game against Reading. The full-house for our championship-winning match just weeks earlier was a tease, a stroke, a one-off mirage, a bloody day-out for glory-hunters with their picnic baskets who had no intention of backing their home-town team.

As the season progressed, we only filled the ground once, against Manchester City. Out of the 11,000 fans packing into Gigg Lane, 6,000 were from Maine Road. When Sunderland brought 8,000 supporters, we couldn't even fill our own end.

The club tried everything. Over 15 per cent of the population around Gigg Lane are from ethnic minorities, so an Indian lad was signed and we took an English Asian on loan from Leeds. The crowd soared by four – their parents.

Frustrations increased. A bonus I was promised for winning the title took two years to materialise. The players felt betrayed, too. They objected to their bonus structure which paid £75 for each point achieved.

In the First Division, playing against millionaires and multi-million-pound clubs, such a figure was insulting. Crap. We knew Bury couldn't afford much more but the air of poverty began to pollute every aspect of life at the club.

Facilities had always been poor. Johnson's wife brought their new-born baby to the first game, but any spare rooms had been hired to corporate guests in a desperate bid to raise money. There were no nappy-changing facilities in the ladies' bogs so she started to look after the kid in one of the lounges, but was ordered to leave by a flunky. In protest, she and Johnno walked out and changed the kid's dirty nappy in the car park. The press got involved and they ended up on *GMTV*.

Things began to fall apart. The fixture list decreed that we had to travel backwards and forwards to Ipswich *and* Norwich in the space of six days. It was laughable.

The club had a rush of blood and bought the squad new blazers which were hardly Savile Row quality. On the way down, we stopped at a motorway service station and I was tucking into my pasta when a bloke tapped me on the shoulder. 'Where do we park, mate?'

He thought we were bus drivers.

Despite the swanky outfits, there was zero chance of an overnight stay. We would have to pay for our own hotel rooms. I paid the first set of bills from the Ipswich trip out of the players' kitty, collected from fines levied during the season.

After the match, which we lost 2–0 and during which Andy Gray and Ian Hughes were sent off, I told them, 'You've done me proud. We've come to a big club, the conditions were crap, you've paid for your own travel.' I looked in my pocket. 'We've got £24 left in the kitty. Let's have some beers.'

The following week, for the long haul to Norwich, where we drew 2–2, I paid for everything out of my own pocket.

In September, we beat Tranmere 1–0 to reach seventh in the table. That's as high as we got. We beat Birmingham 3–1 to cling on in mid-table as we reached October, but after the Forest win at the start of November, we went 14 games without a victory, hitting bottom spot on Boxing Day.

The press became negative and upped the ante in our battle for survival. As a diversion, I played games with reporters. Normally, my mantra has all the allure of a stuck record: 'Well, 50 points to safety, lads,' ... 'Well, 47 points to safety, lads,' ...'Well ...'

'We know, Stan,' they'd say.

Suddenly, I began quoting ridiculous psycho-babble to see if they'd print it. I preferred to talk about the clematis in my garden rather than my centre-half. 'Well, I thought we were one tomato short of a salad today, boys.'

I treat most sport reporters with barely-concealed contempt. Too many kids these days know nothing about football. Even worse, most of them know nothing about real life. Their trade requires negativity above all else, always looking to destroy, always looking for cock-ups.

There's an old saying: 'There are two men in prison, looking through bars. One sees mud, the other sees stars.' Most football hacks choose to see mud. They only consider themselves to be in heaven when they're knee-deep in shite.

Tensions rose inside the privacy of our dressing room, too. Inevitably, the players searched for a release. I took Kenny Dalglish's lad on loan but he had his nose broken and his cheek smashed during a nasty challenge against Sheffield United. The lads were incensed and brawls erupted all over the pitch. I could do nothing to stop it. I didn't want to.

Things got worse. We were losing 1–0 at Bradford when Peter Swan tangled with one of their forwards. Swan claimed he'd been headbutted but their guy came off worse and collapsed on to the deck. Swanny stood in the centre circle, unhurt and laughing, imagining the incident had escaped the ref's attention.

It had, briefly, due to the fact that a 20-man riot had broken out. Everyone was at it. Only the goalkeepers weren't swinging punches. My centre-half Paul Butler waded in, along with others. Months of frustration were being exorcised by a good old scrap. From nowhere, Paul Jewell, who was assistant manager to Chris Kamara at Bradford, appeared and got stuck in.

No one touches my players. I wasn't having it. I always fight for my corner and my players. I dragged him into the dugout, dug him in the ribs and bashed his head against the roof. Suddenly he didn't want to get stuck in any more.

On the short journey home, a vague notion that I had outgrown Bury, which had begun to dawn after the Eaves débâcle and the first few matches of the season, developed into a certainty. I accepted that, without a superhuman effort, relegation was guaranteed. Worse, there was no telling where the fall would eventually halt once Bury began to slide down the league.

I wasn't packing it in. My years of hardship, sacrifice and ideological battles against the countless divs I've come across in football saw to that. My spirit is stronger than most managers I have ever met. But I decided that my self-preservation and Bury's survival were entwined. If I wanted to resurrect my chances of mounting a realistic challenge for the Premiership with any club, Bury had to stay up. It would be a bigger achievement than the back-to-back promotions. It would also send out a message to other clubs. It would be the greatest last stand since Custer's.

The fightback began with a 1–0 win at Manchester City and we lost only once in the next nine games. The lads made the mind-boggling return trip to Portsmouth for a night match without any overnight stays and still came away with a point.

Despite these sacrifices and my achievements since joining Bury, I found it harder to win over the supporters. Our relationship was uneasy. From day one they waited for success before offering any signs of acceptance. Their football education was not extensive enough for them to understand the limitations within which we were operating. During a home game against Oxford, they loudly booed when I substituted Rob Matthews for Tony Rigby. Abuse poured down from the stands.

With his first kick, Matthews laid on our winning goal. I stomped off up the tunnel, refusing to acknowledge their hypocritical applause.

They printed a public apology in the match programme two weeks later. It read:

> *We humble supporters of Bury FC wish to express our deep regret in daring to question your superior judgement and*

*knowledge of the game of football and we should be grateful
if you would kindly accept our most sincere apologies.
Please rest assured that this kind of outburst shall never
occur again.*

Your loyal servants, Bury FC supporters.

It was far too little, far too late. With three games to go, we were
desperately trying to claw our way out of trouble. What was the
point of their stupid, self-defeating protests? Did they imagine
booing players was the motivation we needed?

We lost 3–0 at Sheffield United and then, disastrously, 1–0 at
home to Ipswich Town. Everything, all our hard work over the
past four years, rested on the final game, a trip to Queen's Park
Rangers who were level on points with us and in real danger of
relegation themselves.

Defeat would send us down, rendering our last promotion
worthless and hurtling the club towards bankruptcy.

Gordon Armstrong scored after 24 minutes and we clung on for
three points. The 1,000 fans who had followed us down partied
harder than when we had won the title.

I sat in the dressing room and reflected on a campaign which
had drained me. I stared at the lads, a motley collection of
experienced pros, kids unhindered by the scepticism of years
journeying around the lower divisions and coaching staff who had
almost sacrificed their sanity to help me achieve the impossible.

We had survived while giants Manchester City and Stoke City
had been relegated. If that was in any script, it must have been a
Carry On film.

I was elated. I was the most successful manager in Bury's
history. I was also concerned. With no money available, next
season would be a write-off. As it transpired, it didn't matter a jot.
I'd managed my last game at Bury.

As I recovered from our fight for survival, Chris Waddle had lost his at Turf Moor. The Burnley Board finally removed their blinkers and waited for me to rescue their club.

Before they formally pounced, I disappeared from Bury for a week or two to collect my thoughts. There was no point wasting valuable time wondering where to head for. The shouts I could hear from the players in the showers after our last match win at QPR told me all I needed to know.

'Fucking Magaluf!'

Where else?

9

'Keep Going, Son, You'll Get It Right Eventually ...'

BURNLEY, 1999–2000

My new Burnley players had to pinch themselves to believe it. We had barely survived in Division Two during our first traumatic season together after I quit Bury. I was forced to sack more players than I signed.

With a motley crew of ageing pros, stage-struck kids and inadequates who would struggle to get a game for Holby City, we limped over the finishing line to avoid relegation only after their complete ineptitude forced me to fight for my job when we were drubbed by Manchester City and Gillingham.

Bookies queued up to write us off for the following 1999–2000 season. You could get odds of 2–1 on the cones beating us in training. What did they know?

With 17 games to go, our resurgence was in full flow. We were fourth and pushing hard for the play-offs. No wonder the players found it hard to accept.

Most difficult of all to grasp was that across from them in the dressing room, wearing the same claret-and-blue colours that had been disgraced too often over the previous decade, was Ian Wright. *The* Ian Wright. Or, to give him his full title, Ian Wright-Wright-Wright Esquire, MBE. A fully minted football legend.

I'd spent weeks persuading him to sign for Burnley. It had started as a joke. After the work I'd done with him at Crystal Palace, he publicly acknowledged that I played a major role in furthering his career, and the man I knew as Satchmo had stayed in touch.

During an emotional phone call at a stage when he was getting abuse from Neanderthals in the crowd after his move to Celtic, I offered him an opportunity to play for us merely to divert the conversation and cheer him up. Except he didn't laugh. He actually signed.

The town went potty. In the days surrounding his Turf Moor début against Wigan, we easily sold every ticket and earned thousands of pounds pushing out genuine Wrighty merchandise.

Apart from his Ferrari, Wrighty willingly checked in most of the trappings from his superstar lifestyle at the border with Accrington and pledged himself to fight to help my club win promotion. 'I'll do it for you, Stan,' was the promise of a man who I knew always kept his word.

I beamed as I watched him banter with the rest of the team during the warm-up for his second game. We had arrived for a match in Colchester at the arse-end of a knackering 300-mile bus trip but Wrighty was fresh after driving himself over from his house in London.

Typically, he was buzzing. Whether running out for Arsenal at Wembley or for us in an Essex fleapit, with his jokes and his gold-tooth smile, he gave everyone the impression it didn't matter a damn.

We won 2–1. The play-offs were still on. Even automatic promotion couldn't be ruled out. But as we returned to the dressing room after the final whistle, I no longer gave a monkey's toss. The game was a complete disaster.

Throughout each of the previous 90 minutes, the Colchester crowd hurled at Wrighty the foulest racist abuse I'd ever heard at a football match. My face was red with shame as I stood on the touchline, powerless to stop the narrow-minded scum chanting sick songs at one of England's greatest players.

The pride I'd felt for Ian as he'd run out on to the pitch in Burnley colours rapidly became embarrassment. I'd persuaded him to play in a league where I believed he would be afforded dignity and respect. Yet all those dickheads at Colchester had to offer was jealousy, bile and bitter insults based on his skin colour. It was bollocks.

The ignorant bastards had had the chance to watch one of the most talented players our country has ever produced, yet they chose to barrack him instead. No home fan at Layer Road that day was innocent. Everyone could clearly hear the filth but not one of them tried to stop it.

Wrighty was uncharacteristically silent and withdrawn as he showered. Outside the ground, a group of ignorant Colchester fans tried to ask for his autograph and jostled him as he struggled to get through the car park to his waiting Audi for the lonely drive back to his home in Croydon. They abused him further when he treated them with contempt.

The party on the coach among the rest of our players to celebrate winning three vital points was muted and eventually subsided into silence, each of them lost in their own thoughts as we clocked up more motorway miles. I was devastated.

The conversation I'd had with Wrighty as he'd barged out of the dressing room door constantly replayed in my mind. 'Listen, Satch,' I told him, 'that was crap today. They are ignorant morons. It's scandalous. I'll complain officially to the club. Just try and calm down, have a good night's kip and push them out of your mind.'

Wrighty stared at me. 'I can't, Stan ... I've had enough.' It was only his second game for us. He added, 'I'm quitting.'

How had it come to this? It had all begun so well. Following the abortion of my first season, I'd cleared out 12 dumbfounded players in a ruthless cull that was bloody and necessary. Players cried. Players begged me to change my mind. Not too many other managers would have been brave enough to eviscerate the dressing room as I had. But I knew Burnley had floundered for years due to half-hearted approaches.

Terry's last words to me at Bury were, 'We are better run than Burnley, you'll find out.' He was right. But in new Chairman Barry Kilby, I had an ally at Turf Moor who at least had the balls to back my revolution.

I secured the full-time services of lippy Scouser and part-time bookie Paul Cook who had played on loan for us and had done so well at the end of the previous season.

Ex-Burnley midfielder John Mullin rejoined us on another free transfer after my mate Reidy let him go from Sunderland, and I also nicked Dean West from Bury under the Bosman ruling. Served Terry right.

Most of the time I managed to avoid agents. I tried to sign a defender from Wimbledon and he brought his money man along, a young kid in a baseball cap clutching a computer, poncing into Turf Moor in his open-top car.

'That's the deal,' I said as I slapped a contract on the table.

The agent said, 'But according to this ...'.

'What's that?' I asked.

'It's my laptop,' said the agent.

I closed negotiations rapidly. 'Well take your laptop and fuck off. I've been stuck in here for half-an-hour with you and we haven't discussed football once.'

Thankfully, former England defender Mitchell Thomas, who arrived on a free transfer, was much easier to deal with. He was getting on a bit at 34 but brought with him vast experience from his days in the Premiership with Spurs and West Ham. Mitch had played for years under Terry Venables, David Pleat, Billy Bonds and Bobby Robson. He had also heard everything about me from my days at Palace with his best pal Wrighty. Or so he thought.

He arrived at our Gawthorpe training ground for his first day's work as eager as a teenage apprentice, but the session was only 45 seconds old when it all kicked off. I'd gathered the squad together to issue them with instructions but, instead of listening attentively, they carried on gibbering to each other about Playstations, horse-racing and last night's totty.

Sod the lot of them. I wasn't in the best of moods. I'd just had an operation on varicose veins on my shin. The doctor had promised me a minor op but I hadn't been able to move for a fortnight thanks to 100 stitches and a surgical stocking. I was going to sue the specialist but he had died leaving my leg looking worse than Deirdre Barlow's neck.

It was not a good day for the players to wind me up by chattering. We were trying to win promotion, not recreate an episode of *Parkinson*. Their socks weren't even sweaty when I told them, 'Go home. Fuck off, the lot of you.'

I could tell from Mitchell's reaction that he couldn't believe what he was hearing. Like a true pro, he worked out on his own for half-an-hour on the treadmill before he showered, changed and drove away but, like the others, he learned his lessons quickly and the next day's training was an improvement.

There were no hefty transfer fees involved for any of my new recruits because we are always skint. I'd signed big ginger Jeppo from Bury the previous season and he was forced to double as our reserve keeper on match days because I couldn't afford to buy one.

Even the directors became experts at penny-pinching. We were training on the Turf Moor pitch one morning when Clive Holt gave me a shout. 'Have you got a minute, Stan?'

He stood in front of the giant Cricket Field stand and pointed up towards some advertising hoardings bolted to the front edge of the roof, 80ft high.

> Clive: Who's the best shot you've got?
> Me: Why?
> Clive: See that advertising board there, for Hansen Offset?
> Me: Yes.
> Clive: It's hanging off. If your best shot could just kick the ball up there and knock it off, it would save me the cost of a crane.
> Me: What do you want him to hit, the 'O' or the 'T'? Pay up. Andy McNab couldn't hit that with a fucking rifle.

Despite our lack of resources, we won five out of our first eight games and, confounding everybody, were top of Division Two by late September.

Naturally, we conceded our customary hatful of goals to Manchester City along the way. Life just wouldn't have been the same without that. In only our second game, we travelled to Maine Road for a Worthington Cup tie. Not for the first time, we surrendered pathetically and were stuffed 5–0.

However, unlike the 6–0 drubbing at Turf Moor five months earlier when I offered to resign, I refused to let this latest scalping affect us critically, even though it emerged that whenever City beat anyone heavily, their fans now always sang, 'Are you Burnley in disguise?' They were our bogey team.

In interviews, Shaun Goater even described Turf Moor as his favourite ground. City had top-quality players and had spent fortunes.

I told my low-cost players to forget it, and we fought on. Setbacks? We had a few. We dropped two points at home to Brentford when they equalised by lobbing our goalkeeper Paul Crichton from a million yards out. But we began to win more than we lost.

The players transformed themselves into a unit that expected success rather than a caning at some of the shocking stadiums we had to visit. On the journey to Cambridge, I illustrated to the squad how perfection had to be sought in all aspects of our lives if we were to succeed. I am obsessive about levels of service afforded to any team under my control.

We stopped at a four-star hotel in Peterborough for lunch. I refuse to accept trashy treatment and when they served up slop in the restaurant I lost control.

'We are a professional outfit. We're not paying for any of this. Get me the manager. The eggs have been runny, the beans are tepid ... We are Burnley FC and we are going to eat as much as we want for free.'

I could see players sniggering into their sandwiches but they had to develop self-respect, even if it meant learning from the master how to profit from public scenes. I am never shy to crucify those who let me down.

Food fights happen frequently. I've made Michelin chefs cook their whole menu again because pasta is underdone. These numbskulls aren't feeding an army when Burnley FC pop in for lunch. They are servicing finely-tuned athletes.

I'm just as strict with packed lunches. When we travel to distant away matches, chefs at Burnley are ordered to stock the bus with plates of butties. After picking up members of the squad at various points en route, I only give permission to eat when I know everyone is on board and entitled to a fair share of the grub.

On a trip to Bournemouth, as we approached Wigan I asked for a tuna sandwich and was told we had none left. None fucking left? The greedy gets had scoffed the lot before we were a mile from Turf Moor.

I stormed up the aisle and delivered a ten-minute rant at the team, spitting bits of crappy crisps in anger. I saw Clive Holt staring open-mouthed as I lost my rag over a sandwich filling, but the wider issue was one of discipline. Running a football team requires order, structure and rules. If players take the piss they will overrun you.

Returning from one defeat, Clive was too scared to wake me up to ask if we could stop for fish and chips.

I won't compromise if the good of the club is at stake. It seemed to work. We were beaten only once in the next nine matches, at Luton.

Before the game, Vinnie Jones telephoned me to say he would be popping along to check us out. I knew his style and warned him, 'Don't bring one of your fancy cars, my lads only drive Fiestas.'

It had no effect. He pulled up in front of the Luton Posthouse Hotel and swanked around in his Bentley Convertible. At least he had the decency to get the first round in for the lads to commiserate with them in defeat.

Another six-game unbeaten run followed but ended dismally, away on Boxing Day. Missing four crucial players through illness and injury, we were 4–0 down by half-time and skipper Steve Davis had been sent off for deliberate handball. Four thousand Burnley fans made the trip. Half of them left at the interval.

Of all the places in all the world to get stuffed. Bury. They were mediocre and in mid-table at the time but, of course, they played like Real Madrid against me. I was cursed. I expected it. Whenever life chooses to be cruel, I generally get double helpings.

A Burnley fan who'd died left me a legacy which I was instructed to collect from his lawyer. When I arrived, I was informed my inheritance consisted of two goldfish.

I suppose the Bury mauling could have been worse. Until days before the game, Neil Warnock, had been in charge of them.

Warnock had inherited my team after I'd left Bury. His achievement in his first season was for them to be relegated. He then left Gigg Lane to join Sheffield United, claiming some Bury fans had threatened to set his wife on fire in an account remarkably similar to the attack by Burnley supporters on Jimmy Mullen years earlier.

We bounced back from the Bury defeat with a home win against Oxford but then lost heavily at Notts County and Coventry.

Once again we revived, winning three and drawing two out of the next five games. We clung to fourth spot but were still eight points away from the leaders. I ached to succeed.

I had issues with Terry. I had issues with Warnock. I had issues with Barry, whom I was desperate to impress. Most of all, I had issues with myself. I was desperate to work in the Premiership in my own right.

I felt uneasy at the prospect of a bunfight in the play-offs. ITV Digital were offering fortunes to any club that reached the promised land of the First Division within two years. Three million pounds in hard cash was the reward. It had to be an automatic spot or nothing. I needed to give Turf Moor an adrenalin injection to force us over the finishing line ahead of the pack.

One afternoon, as I listened to my car radio, I knew I had succeeded. Howard Booth, a sports presenter on Radio Lancashire, announced tantalisingly, 'We're just about to go to a travel bulletin but, if you're a Burnley fan, stay around because we've got news that will blow your mind.'

The news of Ian Wright's signing wasn't universally celebrated. There is always one merchant of doom. This one had a very big nose. I was watching Granada TV's Sunday afternoon football highlights show when Liverpool's Phil Thompson popped up in the interviewee's seat. He was asked about Wrighty's arrival and said, 'I just hope Stan knows what he is doing.'

What I was doing was building my own team to succeed on my own terms. And Wrighty was the icing on the cake.

Three weeks earlier, I began to hear mutterings from his best mate Mitchell Thomas in training that Wrighty wasn't happy at Celtic. He had only played eight games and was getting stick from some of the home crowd, an experience he never underwent in his time at Arsenal.

I rang him a few times to cheer him up. I also put a call in to his agent, Jerome Anderson, and suggested that a trip to Burnley might enliven the end of his season. I knew Mitchell had already told Wrighty, 'You'll love it at Burnley. The fans and the people are great. We're in a promotion campaign. Come on, mate, they'll love you.'

I took advantage and worked at it, too, until finally, at the end of a ten-minute chat with Wrighty one night, I came straight out with it. 'Come and play for me. Come and give the lads a lift. We need promotion.'

There was silence before Wrighty answered, 'All right, Stan.'

The decision had to remain confidential. That night, I spoke to the only person I could trust. 'How do you think Ian Wright would go down at Burnley?' I asked Kath as she cooked us some supper in the kitchen.

Her eyes widened. Kath has experienced first-hand everything that I have undertaken in football and was immune to surprises. Like the time we had a dog and it had taken a dump in our kitchen. Years of playing football had hardened the skin on my feet and when I stood in the stuff late one night, I couldn't feel it. Next morning, we awoke with the bed looking like a cell wall after a dirty protest. Yet I could tell the thought of bringing Wrighty to town impressed her.

She laughed, looked me straight in the eyes and said, 'Stan, love, the whole place will lift off.'

My gut feeling was, she's right. I convinced Barry and his deputy, Ray Ingleby, that funding Ian's wages was not a problem. Higher crowds as fans fought to see him play meant he would pay for himself. They agreed.

I also knew what *they* didn't. Wrighty has an infectious personality that was bound to inspire his new team-mates.

News of his move leaked on Valentine's Day. I had taken Kath to the Toby restaurant in Edgeworth for a bottle of Chablis and a prawn cocktail when we found our loving meal interrupted by the arrival of Sky TV cameras.

Most of the country thought the whole deal was an early April Fool's gag. Cockney Wrighty, three buttons short of being a Pearly King, style guru, TV presenter, fashion icon, pin-up, London boy and Premiership hero, was off to *Coronation Street* to play in the Second Division. Four days later, it was no joke.

Ian travelled up from Euston Station on the train with Ray. I met them at the Tickled Trout Hotel near Preston to sign the deal. I always finalise contracts at my house or local hotels; the punters around Turf Moor are better at spreading news than CNN.

After shaking hands over the deal, our cub secretary, Cathy Pickup, drove me and Wrighty to Burnley for a press conference. His reaction as we travelled through Whalley, Accrington and Burnley was a joy.

'You know, with everything I've done in football, I've never been in the north like this. I've only seen it on the telly. It's weird. Like going back in time.'

As the country's media lapped up Wrighty's arrival, and packs of over-excited Burnley fans had to be kept at a distance using crowd-control barriers, he set the tone as he impersonated my accent for the cameras. How long had I sounded like Compo from *Last of the Summer Wine*?

Wrighty moved in with Mitchell and they settled down to life as the Odd Couple in a sparsely furnished, modern semi-detached house on an estate in Harle Syke, a hillside suburb of Burnley. They called it 'The Den' and it became Ian's sanctuary.

After training, they headed back, drew the curtains and tried to cut themselves off from the outside world. Mitch would get into his robe and then kip on the settee while Wrighty cooked a meal and settled down to watch a movie or play computer games. That peaceful routine lasted for a day. Their address soon became public knowledge and they were besieged.

Autograph-hunters called constantly. Often, Mitch was too knackered to roll off his couch but Wrighty never turned one of them down. He signed books, programmes, posters and even babies.

As winter gave way to spring, they began to bicker like a married couple. Whatever the weather, Wrighty insisted on turning the gas fire on to full power and cranked the central heating up to its highest level. When he answered the door to local kids, they almost fainted with the heat.

He came over to my house every Sunday to hide from his adoring fans and scrounge breakfast. As Kath rustled up some grub, Wrighty hugged our fire as though we lived in the Arctic. He'd return to The Den for the afternoon and then come back for dinner.

He admitted, 'I've got culture shock, man. It's a nice shock. This place seems like those old mining towns I've seen on TV. Everybody seems to work in the same factory. That's the vibe I'm getting.'

The guys tried to settle down anonymously, with about as much success as Bill Clinton attempting to set up home in Emmerdale.

When Wrighty went to the small corner-shop grocers in Harle Syke, within minutes there would be more people cramming the aisles than could fit into Sainsbury's.

It was no better when he and Mitch sneaked into the town centre's Marks and Spencer store to stock up their trolley with Wrighty's favourite pasta, water biscuits and toiletries. Within seconds, there would be a trail of locals behind them. Training became his only escape.

On Wrighty's first day, our skipper Steve Davis took him into the dressing rooms at Gawthorpe. Behind their expectant smiles, I knew some of our players were nervous, worried that Wrighty's powerful personality would overpower them. Many of them were not used to the TV attention that accompanied him even if he only picked his nose.

Their nerves were calmed instantly. Wrighty wooed the lads and impressed them by demanding no special treatment. In fact, they began to take the piss out of him for being teacher's pet. He was one of the few players I allowed to call me Stan instead of Gaffer. I could see him laughing quietly to himself as I bollocked them. Despite the good-natured abuse, or probably because of it, he was accepted.

That Saturday, nudging against pie-sellers outside Turf Moor, was a new phenomenon at Burnley games – ticket touts. Our end-of-season run-in was suddenly the hottest event in the Nationwide League. Wrighty emerged from the tunnel, proudly wearing the number 33 shirt I gave him to mark his 33 England appearances.

The occasion deserved a better game and we drew 0–0. But Wright-Wright-Wright fans in Burnley were so obsessed that the result was academic to many of them.

The following Tuesday he tried to relax with a game of tennis in nearby Queen's Park. He arrived at the council-run courts in his £200 trainers and Wimbledon outfit, clutching a top dollar racket. It was 40-love in the first game when it was abandoned due to a court invasion by hundreds of kids.

It got to the stage where Wrighty could not move around Burnley in daylight without being mobbed. He was used to being idolised incessantly during his days at Arsenal, but in London there were enough safe havens to allow him to disappear. In Burnley, if he flushed his toilet after 10.00pm people took notes.

Wrighty lived for match day. His whole demeanour lightened as kick-off approached. And he expected great things for himself away from the intense Burnley spotlight as we headed to Colchester.

Part of our mutual pact when he signed for the club was flexibility over his schedule. His TV commitments included presenting the *Guinness World of Records* and *Friday Night's Alwright*. I knew it was important for Ian to be with his family as much as possible, so I allowed him to travel to the match from his home.

Disastrously, he left the loving bosom of his family to be confronted with those racist morons in Essex. As a result, 90 minutes later, my prized asset and Burnley's newly-adopted son turned his back on the town and decided to quit.

Do you know what? I couldn't blame him.

I spoke to Wrighty for hours over the next few days and urged him to reconsider. Phone calls from Mitch and some of the other lads helped persuade him to stay. The stubborn, driven and dedicated Ian Wright I knew so well had never run away from a fight. I would happily have fought alongside him against those Colchester bigots who abused a wonderful, genuine football legend by calling him a 'black bastard'.

But that was not the way. Ian's proud life is worth ten times more than any of those scum. They were not fit to see him play. So they were certainly not fit to force him out of the game. He returned to Burnley upset, but determined to persevere.

The events of the following week did nothing to help his confidence. Within three days, we lost two home games on the trot, 3–0 to bitter local rivals and runaway leaders Preston, and 2–0 to mid-table Luton.

We were four games into Wrighty's stint at Turf Moor and he still hadn't scored. Critics told him he was finished. Visiting fans hurled abuse. I could see bewilderment and hurt in his eyes. Wrighty was desperate to do well for himself. He exists to score goals. He knew I'd gambled on him and I could tell he was tearing himself apart with guilt because he felt he'd let me down. I forced myself to be cruel to be kind and dropped him from the team. He cut a forlorn figure among our substitutes, even though we won 1–0 at Wrexham with Andy Payton scoring the winner, his 200th career goal.

The headlines in the papers the next day predictably focused on the 'superstar who can't even get a game for Burnley'.

On the journey back from Wales, Wrighty sat beside me on the coach and urged, 'I really want to play in the games, Stan. I know it's not gone well for me, but I want to play through it.'

I told him, 'Take it easy. You have got nothing to prove to anybody, least of all me. I just want you to come on and do something for me every now and again. Now that you are here, a lot of people expect us to go up. They are all saying it, "We'll get promotion now Wrighty's here!" We've got to dampen their enthusiasm. It's unrealistic.' I tried to protect him.

Privately, he was very disappointed with me, angry even. I overheard even our most loyal fans begin to complain, 'Bloody hell, what's going on? Wrighty came here to help us go up and we're losing games.'

Lesser players of Premiership standard would have exited stage left. Rapid. Yet it had exactly the effect I was looking for.

Our next game was a showdown at promotion rivals Gillingham. Out of the six teams scrapping for the one remaining automatic spot, leaders Preston were already out of reach, the Gills were closest to us.

We were losing 2–1 on a bitterly cold Tuesday night in Kent with just four minutes left. I winked at Ian who shot up off the bench, threw his tracksuit top to the ground and sprang to the touchline. He yelled at the linesman that it was time for him to go to work.

As soon as he was waved on to the pitch by the referee, he tore forward ready to take ball, defenders and goalkeeper into the net if necessary. He was desperate. We were desperate. A defeat against the Gills would leave us floundering in the play-off zone, vulnerable to the rest of the chasing pack.

In panic, with barely seconds left to play, Mitchell Thomas lobbed the ball hopefully into their penalty area in the general direction of his best pal.

Wrighty watched it coming. He steadied himself. He balanced himself. He shrugged off a full-back, controlled the ball and battered it into the net in one fluid movement.

That's why I paid the money for his wages. That's why I was nursing him through his stay. That's why I gambled on one of the most natural goalscorers the game has ever seen.

The moment he scored, Wrighty loped along in front of disbelieving Burnley fans who were, by now, a seething, heaving mass of steaming bodies rolling around their enclosure with bunched fists thrust out in delight. It looked like a cartoon fight in the *Beano*.

He raced towards me and bounced into my arms. We jigged around like extras from a tracksuit version of the *Kama Sutra*.

His beaming smile exuded relief. 'I got it for you, Stan. I got the fucker!'

We had a valuable point. More importantly, Wrighty was off the mark. Thankfully, he began to relax. I couldn't.

The lads normally bugger off to Cheltenham races at this point during each season but, on instinct, I banned the trip. We couldn't risk losing our concentration.

That didn't stop Jeppo, Paul Cook and Gordon Armstrong. They took a risk and set off secretly for a day at the races. Following a comfy win on the third race, they barged into one of the bars for an afternoon session.

'Bollocks,' shouted Jeppo, 'it's the Chairman!'

'All right, lads?' said Barry. 'What brings you here?'

Not me, that was for sure. I fined the lot of them.

Thankfully, they didn't get their claws into Wrighty and he settled into a cosy domestic routine with Mitchell. Each Monday morning, he left home in Croydon at 6.00am, picked Mitchell up in Luton and arrived at Gawthorpe for training at 10.30am. After a workout, he headed to The Den for a kip, visited my house and chatted to my family or drove up to the North-East to see his mate Paul Ince.

The lads in the team encouraged him to join in their social lives. Occasionally, he clambered into a minibus for a drive over to Paul Cook's pub on Merseyside, The Fantail, where they had an off-duty blow-out away from prying eyes.

Ian helped me out in training, teaching young strikers like Andy Cooke the secrets of his success. His ability was awesome.

After a while, he began to take the piss out of the locals' northern accents. 'Tha fans have ony got two songs tha' knows,' he said, doing his Compo impersonation again. 'Andy, Andy Payton,' and 'Stevey, Stevey Davis.'

I educated him in the ways of small-town Lancashire. Wrighty was no big-time Charlie. He was a working-class lad who achieved success beyond his wildest dreams. He was in the FA Hall of Fame. His wallet was the size of a baby's head. Consequently, he had spare money by the fistful. He would arrive for training behind the Cricket Field stand in his big blue Bentley continental coupé worth over £200,000.

Once I'd made myself heard over his hi-fi, I explained, 'You can't come up in that. This is Burnley!'

A week later, he jetted to the ground in his silver Ferrari 360 Modena. What a waste of money.

'You can see the bloody engine,' I told him. 'Don't you get a bonnet included in the price? It stinks of petrol. If you drive it around some of the terraced streets near here it will be worth more than all the houses put together.'

He finally took the hint and swapped it for a black mini and a BMX bike.

Hills were a novelty to Ian. He was genuinely astounded to be living in an area that was lumpy, and he took advantage. He set off for training on his pushbike one hour earlier than Mitch, who eventually overtook him, pedalling furiously through a traffic jam outside a Happy Eater a mile from Gawthorpe.

Occasionally, the hills would tax even Wrighty's enormous energy reserves and he would flag Mitch's car down and persuade him to ride the bike home while Ian got behind the wheel and drove.

As he settled into life up north, life on the pitch continued to improve. He scored again in our next game after coming on as a substitute, heading our third against Reading in the last minute to complete an easy win.

But with eight games left, we were still only fifth, seven points away from a promotion place. The last news I needed came one afternoon as I prepared to leave my office and head for home.

A Scottish FA disciplinary panel, meeting in Glasgow, banned Wrighty for two matches for an incident when he pushed a match official while playing for Celtic. I couldn't believe it. Fine him. Put him in the stocks, by all means. But to ban him when he was now playing in England at a critical stage of the season was crazy.

We scraped a home draw against Bury and won at Cardiff while he was out. Our next game, against Notts County at Turf Moor, was crucial. They were challenging us to reach the play-offs.

I kept Wrighty on the bench and all seemed well when Payton put us into an early lead. We ran the game, we bossed every tackle, we dominated. Then they scrambled an equaliser with 60 seconds of the match left. I was frantic. Wrighty was already on the pitch; I had decided to give him the final ten minutes to help his match fitness. We were stunned. The players were rocked back on their heels by County's sucker punch.

Steve Davis punted the ball forward as the referee looked at his watch. Wrighty collected the pass, controlled the ball, skinned a defender and launched the ball into the top corner from 25 yards.

His smile eclipsed the floodlights. His yells drowned out the public address system. Hundreds of fans, who'd left when County equalised, missed the goal of the season from the signing of the decade.

Once again, he galloped to the dugout and we embraced. I think he kissed me but I've tried to block that from my mind.

The Wrighty phenomenon developed its own momentum, carrying us towards that elusive automatic promotion spot with the force of his personality and his hunger for victory at any level.

We were losing 1–0 at Oxford the following Saturday when we equalised in the last minute. Then, with only seconds to go, Wrighty chased a hopeless ball towards the corner flag, kept it in play, turned and crossed for Paul Weller to head the winner with the very last touch of the game.

Thousands of Burnley fans who remained faithful in an open terrace section throughout 90 minutes of rain, hail and shite saluted the team and acknowledged our new-found belief.

We went eight games unbeaten. We agreed we were unstoppable, until Gillingham turned up again three days later. Big crowd. Big atmosphere. Big let-down.

A defensive cock-up in the first few minutes cost us dearly and they swamped us 3–0. The Burnley crowd looked as though they had witnessed a road accident. Gillingham worked harder than us, looked more determined than us. Perhaps they sensed that my players believed we had done enough hard work for the season.

I was furious. Out of courtesy, I shook hands with their manager, Peter Taylor. What happened next almost caused me to knock him clean out. He put his arm around my shoulders as we walked off the pitch and squeezed me tight. 'Never mind, Stan,' he said in his cheery cockney twang. 'Keep going. You'll get it right eventually.'

Who did he think he was he talking to? Some retard from the Beazer Homes League? I'd performed two-footed tackles on Graeme Souness when he was still wetting the bed. I'd managed my first team at the age of 33. Did he mistake me for some journeyman, happy to settle for second best and the odd away win?

I was incredulous.

He wandered off up the tunnel and left me staring after him in disbelief. Allowed to ferment much longer, it would have reached the critical level required for nuclear fission. That clever sod would be hearing from me again. First, I had to get up that tunnel and take it out on the lads.

Due to Peter's infuriating attempt to comfort me that night, I threw everything into preparing for our last four games.

We won the first three but, agonisingly, it still only guaranteed us a play-off spot. We had to face our last match at Scunthorpe knowing even a win would not guarantee us automatic promotion. They were already relegated so the odds were surely in our favour.

But glorious success in my first real season at Burnley depended on another crucial factor. Because of their better goal difference, if Peter Taylor's precious Gillingham won at Wrexham, they would go up to the First Division instead of us.

I felt quite sure that would kill me.

I expected a sleepless night before the Scunthorpe match, but a trusty extra-strength Bacardi and Coke at bedtime put me out.

I woke early, wandered to the bathroom and stared hard at myself in the mirror. Here I was again, on the verge of the First Division, the penultimate rung on the ladder to the Premiership.

When I reached the First with Bury, it was a miracle. People in wheelchairs who couldn't afford the bus trip to Lourdes turned up at Gigg Lane for weeks. With Burnley, promotion was expected.

The pressure told. Already prematurely grey, I knew my health had suffered over the past two years at Turf Moor. I didn't want to worry Kath, but I had begun to feel weary. Some mornings, it was an effort to light my first fag. I left the bathroom and bumped into Kath on the stairs.

'How are you feeling?' she asked.

'It's funny, love,' I said, 'but I haven't got an ounce of nerves.'

Sam arrived and we drove down to our ground together. The players gathered in the laundry room, scrounged brews and bantered nervously.

'Come on,' I told them. 'We're a better side than them. We're going to be all right.'

The bus trip to Scunthorpe was a quiet affair. A small group of the players formed a card school, others dozed, others sat alone listening to their personal stereos. I parked myself behind the driver and discussed with Sam all the permutations for our formation that afternoon. He sketches different line-ups on sheets of A4 paper and we go through the pros and cons of each as he withdraws them from a brown envelope. The routine is always the same.

Final decision made, I sat back and watched a procession of cars carrying Burnley fans stream past us into Yorkshire, yet another reminder of the huge burden of expectation loaded upon our backs.

Ping! Was that another grey hair to add to the collection?

As we paced around the dressing room, I reminded the lads of their individual tactical instructions while Sam, as always, stuck a large sheet of paper to the wall with details to tell our lot who they were supposed to mark at corners and free kicks.

It was a low-key moment. I couldn't afford for the squad to lose their heads because it was anything but a low-key event.

Back at Turf Moor, a huge screen had been installed on the pitch and 7,000 fans had paid to watch the game beamed live by satellite from Scunthorpe. I just wanted to get on with it.

Our fans were packed into an L-shaped area behind one of the goals and they roared deafeningly as we ran on to the pitch.

Exactly like Bury, when we needed Darlington to lose at Scunthorpe on the last day of the season, there were more radios on show per square foot than at Dixons. This time, it was Burnley fans who were tuning into Radio Five, straining for any mention of events at Wrexham v Gillingham.

Our game was a frustrating stalemate but there was a disturbance among the Burnley supporters. I tried not to pay any attention but I couldn't resist a quick look. They were cheering as word spread. Unbelievably, Wrexham had scored.

The Welsh club was managed by ex-Burnley hero Brian Flynn. He is 4ft-nothing in his socks, and I resolved to drown him in champagne if they could hold on. At that stage, we were up.

Within minutes, the mood changed. Scunthorpe's Lee Hodge hit a belter which bounced in past Crichton off the underside of our bar. The Scunthorpe fans rejoiced. They wanted to see us suffer. At that stage, we were down.

Then, minutes before half-time, Mickey Mellon equalised for us with a volley from the edge of the box. At that stage we were up again.

Throughout the interval, I urged the lads to stay calm. We knew if Gillingham equalised at Wrexham we would need a winner, but we hadn't to rush things and concede a goal ourselves. It was tempting to rely on Flynny's lads to hold on in Wales but no one expected them to.

I spent the first 30 minutes of the second half waiting for groans of disappointment to emerge from the Burnley fans as they heard of an equaliser for Peter Taylor's team. It didn't come.

Instead, they forgot their radios as they celebrated our winner from Glen Little who found the top corner from 20 yards after I sent him on as a substitute to do precisely that. At that stage, we were still up.

The whistle went. The Burnley fans invaded the pitch. We'd won 2–1. Supporters stripped off my shirt and tracksuit bottoms. I reached the dressing room in my underpants and watched as Mitchell Thomas staggered in wearing just his jockstrap.

I could only imagine the scenes at Turf Moor. I was later told there was also a pitch invasion. Short of players to mob, fans began kissing the giant screen.

There was a problem. At this stage, the Wrexham game was still going on. Gillingham still had a chance.

I paced around outside the dressing room, patting each of my players on the back as they passed me. From inside, I heard them jump around, cheering. That Wrexham game still wasn't over ... didn't they realise?

I crashed through the door. 'Oi!'

Most of them looked up, some of them seemed not to hear and carried on partying, giggling at each other, searching for cans of lager.

'Sit down, lads, calm it down.' They began to get the message. 'Listen,' I told them, 'I've been here before. Let's get it official before we start celebrating, eh?'

Some of the younger lads couldn't give a toss and continued to go crazy. But seasoned professionals like Mitchell sat back and patiently waited for the news. He knew enough about football to appreciate that heart-ache can arrive at any point before the final whistle blows.

Hadn't they all watched Manchester United rip the European Cup from Bayern Munich with two goals in the last minute just 12 months earlier?

Various busybodies continued to appear and poke their heads around the door. 'Still no change.'

Then another announcement. 'Still no change.'

Jesus Christ! I jumped to my feet. I'd go and get the bloody result myself. As soon as the dressing room door closed behind me, Sam pulled me to one side in the corridor. The full-time whistle had sounded in Wrexham and he had the result.

I let a long, painful, 30 seconds elapse before I walked slowly back into our dressing room looking drawn, tired and thoroughly depressed. The players registered my expression and their eyes widened in shock. Surely not? Surely not, gaffer? They thought something had gone horribly wrong.

It had. But it was only my joke that had failed. I couldn't keep a straight face. Through muffled laughter, I announced, 'Well done, lads. You're up!'

Immediately, all hell broke loose. I was drenched in champagne which appeared by the crateful the moment we were confirmed as a promoted side.

Mitch shouted, 'It's like a rave!' as Wrighty took piggy-back rides around the treatment table. Everyone guzzled bubbly.

Normally, I don't allow directors within a mile of my dressing room, but John Turkington appeared at the door, desperate to join in. He was dressed in a white suit and all the players began shouting, 'Fucking hell, it's Schnorbitz!'

Bizarrely, that was the name of comedian Bernie Winters's dog, but by this time they'd lost the plot completely. John was so delighted he promised me a new Bentley car if I won promotion to the Premier League. I had it recorded in the minutes of the next Board meeting and he went white with fear.

As the Scunthorpe party went on, Chief Executive Andrew Watson almost fell into the dressing room, dragging my two lads Dan and Chris behind him. It was bedlam. We linked arms for a family hug in the centre of the room. The players bounced around us spraying champagne on to our backs and at that point I started to crack.

A manager can tear lumps out of his players, his directors, his supporters and even his Chairman but, ultimately, his family suffers most. Mood swings are part of our job description.

I missed seeing my great boys grow up. Years of irreplaceable memories sacrificed for football. Thank God we are now closer than ever. At that point, I was the proudest man alive.

We smiled at each other and the noise subsided as the players barged back out into the stands to greet the Burnley fans who beseeched them to reappear. Dan and Chris went, too.

It was a relief. I felt I was about to break down. Alone in the dressing room, I had a fag, sipped at a plastic cup full of bubbly and decided to call Kath. My mobile took a while to connect but she finally answered.

I said, 'Hello, love, it's me.'

Kath was excited and delighted. I could tell. 'I didn't expect to hear from you until later,' she said. 'I've been doing the ironing, listening to it on the radio. I'm so proud of you.'

At that point I cried. Kath heard my sobs. 'Don't worry, Stan, I understand. Give me a ring when you're on the coach. Go and enjoy it with your lads.'

That was the cue for more tears. I thanked God I was on my own. If any of the players returned and caught me blubbing, I'd have had to fine myself for being a poof. I scanned the room and listened to muffled cheers from our fans who were clattering around in the stand directly above my head.

The day belonged to the players. I was happy to leave them to it until a Scunthorpe steward walked in and said, 'The fans are shouting for you, Stan. They won't go home until you go out there.'

As I made my way on to a raised balcony above the tunnel where the Board waited. I was overcome with emotion.

I heard supporters sing, 'Stan Ternent's claret-and-blue army.' When I appeared in front of them as they massed on the pitch, their roar almost knocked me off my feet. In the past, I shied away from taking any personal acclaim at moments like this but here, in exotic Scunthorpe, at 5.15pm, I officially went loopy.

As the supporters shouted, 'We want Stan!' I inhaled deeply to try to contain any more tears and a thousand thoughts cascaded through my mind. I remembered the boos as I'd tried to rebuild Burnley. I remembered the jeers as I'd switched on the Christmas lights. I remembered the abuse as I'd sacked players. I remembered the insults when we shipped 11 goals in two home games.

But I understood it all. Man's inhumanity to man is a remarkably depressing phenomenon but the people of Burnley live for football or, more specifically, for their team. Their treatment of me in the early days was the only way they could express themselves.

Today, gloriously, I finally realised that I was one of them all along.

As they acclaimed me, I rose to greet them, the veins on my neck visible as I strained every muscle to give them a clenched fist salute. At that moment, as I stood before the Burnley public, I was Churchill, I was Lord Nelson, I was even Rocky Balboa. Parts I, II, III, IV and V.

Most of all, as they took my salute, they recognised me as Stan, a Burnley fan. Exactly like them.

As their cheers reverberated around the stadium, I became so carried away I almost fell to my death over the balcony. As I toppled forward, John Turkington and Ray Ingleby grabbed the back of my trousers to hold me up. My part in the public proceedings ended abruptly with two grown men grimacing as they grappled with my arse.

I made my way back to the dressing room where I was ambushed by radio and newspaper reporters desperate to hear my reaction. When they offered me their congratulations, I felt more tears begin to prick my eyes. 'Thanks, fellas,' I said. My voice cracked with emotion. 'I want to go and see my lads. You'll have to give me ten minutes.'

Coming so soon after speaking to Kath, I couldn't trust myself not to start blubbing live on Radio Lancashire. That would put the tin lid on it.

I went to find the Chairman. He was dazed. I saw him staring at events on the pitch as though he could not believe his eyes. We shook hands and hugged. Above all else, Barry Kilby is a massive Burnley supporter. He backed me when things were rough in my first season and refused to listen to the hundreds of people who lined up to tell him, 'Get rid of Ternent.' This promotion was my personal thank you to him.

The bus trip home was a wild blur of singing, dancing and drinking. I let the players get on with it as I sat back, choked on Sam's cigar smoke and revelled in their joy. Hundreds of cars passed us, full of Burnley fans racing us to the pub along the M62. Coaches overtook us at speed, displaying windows full of flags, happy faces and bare backsides, like a fleet of Club 18/30 cruise ships. It was the culmination of a season's hard graft and the players wanted immediate rewards.

'Portugal here we come!'

'When are we going, gaffer?' they shouted down the aisle.

I couldn't think much further than my first pint.

We arrived back at Turf Moor where the bus was mobbed. We drove around the ground looking for a safe place to allow the players off to collect their cars, but fans hunted their heroes in packs. Amongst the shrieks, they slammed their hands along the sides of the coach. I worried they'd turn the thing over just to get at us.

'Sod it,' I told Arthur, our driver. 'Take us up The 'Drum.'

My local pub would have to put an extra barrel on. As we approached The Kettledrum along the deserted country road that passes its front door, I realised I had made a cock-up. It was like Trafalgar Square on New Year's Eve. At least 500 people were shoe-horned into the lounge.

I'd finally been cornered for a radio interview at Scunthorpe but my guard was down. I'd inadvertently announced, 'We're going to get on the bus, go home and have a pint at The 'Drum.'

The whole of Burnley must have been listening. They'd all come to the pub, bringing their families with them.

We squeezed inside and drank beer for half-an-hour. Fleets of taxis arrived continuously as word circulated around the town centre that we were home. Each new arrival brought more details about the orgy of celebration that was taking place down in the town centre's main pubs.

It proved too tempting for the players. Shouting their farewells, they were escorted eagerly by supporters towards waiting cars and carried off to get pissed.

I was relieved. I was totally exhausted and wanted to go home to see Kath. She collected me and we tucked into a free Indian meal sent as a reward from the lads at the Shagoor, my favourite restaurant.

Elsewhere, the players were paraded around a dozen bars, fêted by blokes and fancied by their women. Wrighty, a member of London's trendy and exclusive showbusiness haunt, the Met Bar, was refused entry into a nightclub by a jobsworth on the door because he was wearing training shoes. Typical. But that was another grouse for another time.

I sat in the peace of our kitchen with Kath, picked at my chicken bhuna and contemplated the day. Scunthorpe was an experience I would never forget, but as soon as I'd cried in the dressing room on the phone to Kath, all I'd wanted to do was reach home. I was desperate to share the day with the person who had been through everything with me.

We laughed as we discussed the results. Then I remembered. Because we had won, Peter Taylor's Gillingham had missed out. I recalled the kind advice he gave me on the Turf Moor pitch after his side beat us 3–0. I reached over, got a pen and a piece of paper out of a drawer and wrote him a note:

> *Dear Peter,*
> *Keep going, son, you'll get it right eventually.*
>
> *Best regards, Stan.*

I hoped he would appreciate it. I'd fax it the next day.

* * *

'Mr Stan! Mr Stan!'

As I looked down from the top deck of our open-topped bus, I saw every waiter from the Shagoor, dressed identically, salute me as we flashed past. That's quality service!

We were all squashed together, balanced precariously among the seats as our hastily arranged promotion parade wound its way through 40,000 Burnley supporters who had packed into the town centre to see us presented to the Mayor.

I took my nephew, Michael, along and it was a remarkable sight. Children and adults scaled lamp-posts and traffic lights to get a better view. Huge banners were draped above our heads across roads we passed through.

Wrighty and Mitchell were spellbound. I watched as they waved to a group of alcoholics who acknowledged them by lifting their bottles of cider.

A carpet of claret-and-blue formed around the bus. Six

mounted policemen forced the crowd back to enable us to move forward towards the town hall. Wrighty tapped Mitchell on the shoulder. 'Imagine if we had *won* the league!'

He told me, 'This promotion is right up there for me, Stan. I've been to the very pinnacle of the British game but I'm on a high from winning.' He knew that many of his young new team-mates had won nothing before and he was glad to be amongst them and as happy as they were. He said, 'I know I played my part in it and that's what I came here for.'

Mitch admitted, 'I've played for England and in cup finals, gaffer, but now I've actually won something. And we did it against the odds.'

The civic reception was chaos. The square outside the Town Hall was packed with supporters who sang every song they knew and then made up some more.

Wrighty was buzzing. He bounded over to me and Kath to ask for his photo to be taken with us. 'I want it for my private album, Stan.' Alarm bells rang.

'Why, where are you going?'

I needed him next season. He was vital if we were to reach the Premiership. Wrighty laughed and wandered away clutching his camera. He had become a TV icon. Everyone wanted a piece of him. Would Burnley be as attractive next year as the set of *Hi De Hi*, or whatever was lined up for him by the BBC?

Barry approached and put his arms around me and Kath. 'Listen,' he said. 'I've booked you a lovely holiday to Los Angeles, Las Vegas and Florida. Have it with our compliments.'

It was a generous gesture and Kath beamed at the thought. But we both knew what we fancied.

'Look, Barry, any chance of cashing in the tickets and having a week in Portugal instead?'

At the same time, I kept a promise to my players and paid for them to holiday in Portugal, too, a week before I was due to arrive.

Despite my worries over Wrighty's long-term future, he was so desperate to join the lads on the trip he turned down a lucrative public appearance in New York promoting Nike sportswear so he could make the journey. Anything to get the sun on his back.

Wrighty arrived at Manchester Airport wrapped in a sheepskin coat, shivering with cold. As they boarded the plane, he glanced miserably at the dark clouds. He is a poor flier and forced himself to fall asleep soon after take-off. Later, he felt a nudge.

'Come on,' shouted Glen Little, 'we're getting off.'

As he disembarked, Wrighty shuddered. He collared Sam. 'You said it would be warm in Portugal. It's fucking freezing.'

Sam laughed in his face and the rest of the players took the piss mercilessly. While he had been asleep, the pilot had used the intercom and told passengers there was a problem with the plane's cargo doors. They had turned round and landed back in Manchester.

Wrighty officially quit later that summer, announcing his decision during an appearance on ITV's *Jerry Springer Show*. He had worn the Burnley shirt 17 times but had only started eight games.

He managed to hide his frustration well, but when we sneaked into an upstairs room at The Kettledrum for a farewell scampi and chips supper one night, he let it all spill out.

'I was gutted when I wasn't getting a start,' he told me. 'I couldn't let you know at the time but I suppose, after I scored at Gillingham, it just kicked in. It was brilliant.'

Wrighty admitted that he was unable to see past his disappointment whenever he'd been made substitute.

I had wider issues to address. After he had failed to score in his first four games, the pressure built to such a level it could have destroyed him and tainted his last days in the game. I was adamant that I would not allow one of my best friends in football to be hounded out in disgrace when I was his manager.

Confining him to the substitutes bench had thrown newspaper

hounds off his scent. When he finally scored at Gillingham, only reporters from local papers had made the trip. He was able to do his business away from the glare of Fleet Street hacks whose only job that spring was to write his obituary.

Wrighty said, 'Even in London, I've never met people like these Burnley fans before. If I walk down the High Street they come from everywhere. They are really fanatical, but the thing I'll remember most is the amount of Burnley shirts I've seen on the streets. Everyone wears them. It must be part of the school uniforms around here.'

Wrighty had only known me as number two to Steve Coppell at Crystal Palace. He had undergone a conversion. 'I can't imagine you ever taking orders from anyone now I've seen you in action,' he said.

There is no doubt that Wrighty is a better person for having lived in Burnley. When he'd arrived, he imagined locals lived like Oliver Twist. He was right in one instance. There are not too many Bentley Continental coupés in Burnley. There are not too many millionaires.

But people here are proud of themselves and proud of their football team. Wrighty understood he was privileged to be part of their lives.

He certainly became a part of my family. On my granddaughter Olivia's birthday, he went shopping with Mitchell, pushing a trolley around the Early Learning Centre like a married couple, oohing and aahing over teddies. He arrived at my house carrying the largest stuffed toy I have ever seen. It dwarfed Olivia.

'Every child should have a Pooh bear,' Wrighty said as he beamed and tickled Olly with its nose.

I told him over a pint on his last night, 'You know, Wrighty, if you live the kind of life you do – showbiz parties, TV presenting, fast cars – you should come to live in places like Burnley to appreciate how lucky you are. Mind you,' I admitted, 'it is always pissing down and pitch-black.'

As our next crucial season in the First Division progressed, there were many times when I prayed for Wrighty's return. It was my best ever chance of reaching the Premiership and my fortunes swung from triumph to disaster with every kick of the ball.

I suffered my most humiliating defeat ever, I was embroiled in a sex scandal, I cancelled Christmas and I fell out with Porterfield again. Worst of all, with one game left and needing a victory to reach the play-offs, I was forced to travel to meet the team managed by Neil Warnock.

By half-time in the big game, I was covered in blood after a punch-up that I have never acknowledged until now. With possibly just 45 minutes to save my season, it had kicked off big style and I'd been well and truly snotted. But you should have seen the other guy.

If I'd had a gun at Bramall Lane that Saturday afternoon, I would have shot someone.

10

'Scotch for Me, Souey ...'

BURNLEY, 2000–2001

'When do we play Blackburn Rovers?'

That was the only question in every Burnley fan's mind when the First Division fixtures were eventually released. Actually, that's a lie. Our supporters refuse to call them Blackburn. 'When do we play Bastard Rovers?' was more accurate.

It was to be the first time we had played our nearest rivals for 17 years. Since the last competitive match on Easter Monday in 1983, nearly two decades of jealousy, bile, hatred and mutual loathing had festered like a boil.

On 17 December 2000, we were due to meet again. I was worried about drowning in pus. All police leave was cancelled. Helicopter gunships were put on alert and Robocop would direct the traffic.

Even though it was only June, it was impossible to persuade supporters of either team to focus on anything other than the prospect of our two league clashes.

Just six miles apart along the M65, Burnley and Blackburn fans spent most of the 1970s and early '80s tearing lumps out of each other. The intense local rivalry is compared in its ferocity to the animosity felt between Celtic and Rangers or United and City.

In Accrington, the border town nestling between Burnley and Blackburn like a Berlin Wall of terraced houses, supporters of both teams mix in pubs and clubs where petty comments can spark full-scale riots.

When any team visits Turf Moor, their supporters always bait ours by singing, 'You're just a small town in Blackburn.' It works.

Before Jack Walker invested his millions into Ewood Park, our sides operated on similar budgets as small-town clubs desperately trying to compete with big-city rivals. Each side floated around the lower divisions and met regularly with honours equal.

Orgies of violence would precede, accompany and follow any game. Mobs of fans belonging to visiting teams made short trips to away matches by any means of transport possible, evading police patrols and trashing pubs.

Burnley fans pulled a corrugated roof off the full length of terracing behind one of the goals at Ewood Park in 1983 and hurled shards on to the pitch.

Rovers fans had their revenge when Burnley were losing a crucial play-off semi-final in 1991 against Torquay. With only minutes left and defeat inevitable, a light aircraft appeared over Turf Moor trailing a banner which read: 'STAYING DOWN FOREVER LOVE ROVERS – HA HA HA.'

Once Blackburn won the Jack Walker lottery, they left us in their wake.

Burnley fans clung to any crumb of comfort. When Rovers were knocked out of Europe by a team of postmen from Sweden, our town was unofficially twinned with Trelleborg and road signs announcing the decision appeared around the boundary.

When Rovers manager Brian Kidd asked for better support from their fans, Burnley supporters seized on an article in the

Guardian which declared, 'Blackburn is not a football town in the way that neighbouring Burnley is ...' The quote was re-printed and distributed on leaflets before the next home match.

Now Rovers had been relegated and had failed to return to the Premiership at the first attempt. As I hit the golf courses of Vale do Lobo in Portugal that summer, I knew I had to distract our fans or our whole season would be judged on results from two matches against one of the country's richest teams with the odds on victory stacked massively against us.

I signed some new faces. Lee Briscoe, a determined left-sided player and former England Under-21 international from Sheffield Wednesday. Gareth Taylor, a centre-forward from Manchester City. Northern Ireland international Phil Gray. Sunderland's tough-nut midfielder Kevin Ball. I even gave Vinnie Jones another chance to join us. He had just finished filming *Gone in 60 Seconds* and said from his home in Los Angeles that he would consider my offer.

He told ITV, 'If I'm not filming in September, I'm seriously thinking about going to Burnley. I'd love to help out a club which could be massive. It would be good for the crack.'

Did the *Isle of Man Courier* deliver to LA? I bloody hoped not. I could have kicked off our pre-season by swanning around Sweden but, instead, I flew the lads over to play in the Manx Tournament. We promptly lost 1–0 to the amateur Isle of Man side, allowing a schoolboy to score their winner. We battered them for 90 per cent of the match but still managed to become the first professional team to lose to them in 110 years.

As I was jostled by grinning buffoons during a pitch invasion after the final whistle, I told reporters, 'This result is of no significance.' Privately, my worst fears were realised.

Oh Christ! There was a huge gulf for my players to overcome if we were going to survive in the First Division. Were they up to it?

More bad news followed when captain Steve Davis stood on our leading goalscorer, Andy Payton, in training and broke his toe before the opening league match. Payton scored 27 in our promotion season. Now he was crippled.

As our first game against Bolton loomed, I began to think positively. I dumped an Aussie called Mark Robertson on to Swindon Town for £50,000 because he wanted a car and a house in his deal. I'd kept Bury afloat with far less resources than him. If we were going to survive we would do it my way. I had to be merciless.

With seven games gone, we had only been beaten twice and faced a tricky trip across the Pennines to Huddersfield. Goalkeeper Paul Crichton had played without an understudy for months in a situation I couldn't allow to continue. I signed lanky Greek international Nikolaos Michopoulos on a short-term contract from PAOK Salonica in order to have a look at him during a friendly game played behind closed doors, ironically against Huddersfield.

Nik was good. I brought him into training the next morning and he was expert at his drills, top class. The problem was, he could hardly speak a word of English. The language barrier was mutual. I couldn't even pronounce his name.

'You – yes, YOU are called Nik the Greek from now on, sunshine,' I told him. I have only ever called Nik by his full name once, at a press conference, and I sounded like John Prescott reading Dutch. Fans who couldn't afford to have his name printed on the backs of their shirts paid for 'NIK ETC' instead.

He only knew two words of English – 'coffee' and 'thank you'.

I left him with Jeppo for two minutes and suddenly he knew five more.

'It's fucking freezing here, gaffer,' he said.

Nik was an expert shot-stopper and was immediately on the bench as reserve keeper for the Huddersfield game.

First choice Crichton lived in Nottingham and I gave him permission to make his own way to the McAlpine Stadium by car. As I sat on the coach talking tactics with Sam, I received a mobile phone call.

'Gaffer, it's Crichts. I'm stuck in traffic.'

I told him straight, 'If you are not at the ground by 1.45pm, you're not playing.'

My code is strict and applies to any player. Do not be late.

At 2.15pm, Crichton burst into the dressing room, dripping with sweat. He had been unable to park and forced to run a mile to the ground. He looked at me appealingly but he knew he'd blown it.

'No chance,' I said. 'Don't get changed. Do not pass go. Sit in the stands. I don't want to fucking see you.'

If fans can get out of bed to get to games on time, it is not too much to expect players to be able to do the same. Nik had a great game and we won 1–0.

Chrichton? He never started another game for me and spent six months sat on his arse on the bench until I sold him to Norwich.

I signed Nik permanently, although dealing with his countrymen drove me to distraction. One day I was eating an egg mayonnaise butty in my office when the phone went. They tried to stall the deal. I dropped a blob of greasy egg on my new trousers and flung the phone and the butty simultaneously against the wall in frustration. I kicked the desk, the bin and my cupboard. I flung files on to the floor and then picked up the sandwich so I could throw it again.

Eventually, when the noise died down, Sam and Cliff poked their heads around the door.

'All right, gaffer?'

My office looked like a dirty protest at a battery hen farm. I went home, but not before the deal was done. To cap it all, as I tried to relax in my garden, a heron that lives near my house and has haunted me for five years swooped down and stole one of my prized fish. Again! Right in front of my eyes.

I borrowed a shotgun. I even slept with it loaded, ready to rush out at any hour to get the bastard.

Kath complained I looked like Elmer Fudd, but only the threat of a £10,000 fine for killing an endangered species forced me to pack away my firearm. I hope it chokes.

Our win with Nik at Huddersfield was followed by five matches in which we were unbeaten. We reached the play-off positions and fans went into a frenzy. We were more than ten points ahead of Blackburn. Predictably, our lot began to get carried away. Expectation levels, always high at Burnley, became ridiculous.

It was inevitable players would not be able to sustain such fantasies but I never expected the supporters to turn on our own team.

We were drawing 1–1 at home to Portsmouth and Paul Cook, my hard-working, left-sided Scouse midfielder was having a game in which his levels of effort outstripped his achievements with the ball.

Every player has them. Even Pele. The solution is to persevere. Keep running. Keep trying.

Some Burnley fans have never bothered to read the script. Too quick to judge, too quick to criticise, they hamper their own team with a burden of hope that wouldn't be out of place at Old Trafford. When they feel let down, the abuse can flow down from the stands like sewage in malevolent waves. I've seen Burnley players insulted to their face by our fans. I have seen grown men reduced to tears.

As Cooky continued to battle with his own disappointing form against Portsmouth, I ordered the fourth official to make a substitution.

Cooky misread the number on the board and assumed he was coming off. As he ran towards the touchline, a huge cheer swept the ground. Bastards!

Public humiliation is not a clause in any Turf Moor contract and the temptation to throw up two fingers and march to the tunnel in response to this kind of behaviour is immense.

When Cooky realised his mistake and I sent him back to the pitch, the same muppets who had cheered him off, booed him back on. Loudly.

He was in pieces. How supporters expect players to work hard for them in the future when they dish out this sort of stick is beyond me. If I had seen the ringleader, I would have raced into the crowd to strangle the fucker.

As the final whistle sounded, I walked across to put my arm around Cook. It was a gesture of support designed to neutralise the damage done by those so-called 'fans'. It was too late. The same player who had worked his balls off to earn us promotion just three months earlier was now distraught. He wasn't alone.

I'd brought Lee Briscoe on as a substitute during one match and you could hear the boos as far away as Bolton. He responded by scoring twice. The same people who had abused him then had the cheek to cheer his goals, which says everything about their principles.

Cooky responded well to his ordeal at his next game, a 3–2 win at Tranmere. Because I had launched a tirade against fans who choose to betray their own team, supporters bowed and sang his name to apologise for their more fickle mates.

I was busy, too, fighting my own battles on the touchline. We moved into fifth place as Christmas approached and the scrap became personal. When Neil Warnock brought his Sheffield United side to Turf Moor, we stuffed them 2–0.

Keith Curle – a player I respect and like – went over the top in a tackle on another of my other unpronounceable Greeks, forward Dimitri Papadopolous. I joined the fray which was close to my dugout, and grabbed Curle by the throat to pull him off while daring Warnock to walk the 20 yards to confront me. I never let the game get in the way of a good row.

During an unlucky 3–2 defeat at Birmingham, I heard Trevor Francis call his assistant Mick Mills to the touchline.

I asked them both, 'Fucking hell, what's *he* doing here?'

Psychological warfare in football can either be a precise weapon or a blunt instrument. I don't mind which.

We were fourth now, still ahead of Rovers and less than a month away from our first date. I was a fully fledged hero in town by now, if not quite a household name.

I was asked to open an Indian restaurant in Burnley centre. I arrived with the Mayor and tucked into tasty chicken tikka nibbles. When I pulled the string to unveil the plaque, I could only admire the lovely piece of stonework. The inscription read: OPENED BY THE BURNLEY MANAGER SAM TERNENT.

Sam?

'Look,' offered the manager, 'I'll get a chisel.'

'Don't fucking bother,' I said.

It's still there today.

Away from my public humiliations, I needed more ammunition to push for promotion and broke the transfer record to buy Stockport County's leading goalscorer, Ian Moore, for £1 million.

Blackburn lose that much down the back of the Boardroom sofa at Ewood, but it represented a massive investment for Burnley. At the last minute, Norwich tried to poach Mooro and invited him to their ground.

I telephoned his dad, Ronnie Moore, the manager at Rotherham. 'Get your lad back up here,' I told him. 'Norwich is too far to travel on a bus.'

I needed every able body available. We faced three crucial derbies in a row in the build-up to Christmas. First up were Preston.

We lost 2–1. The team was poor. Fans were gutted.

Second up were Blackburn Rovers.

Going into the match we were eighth on 38 points with Rovers a place behind us on 36. That, in itself, was a miracle.

Traditionally, Burnley are viewed as a bigger club than either Blackburn, Bolton or our other local rivals Preston.

Yet if anyone ought to have been feeling immense pressure as kick-off neared, surely it was their manager, Graeme Souness.

With his nuclear budget, bulging wage packets and the five-star opulence available at Ewood, Rovers fans expected him to buy a spot in the Premiership at any price.

Match day approached. The police were terrified. They feared mass disturbances. They feared a riot. They feared bloodshed. I think they were right.

I was invited to appear at a series of unprecedented joint press conferences with Graeme during the week preceding the clash in an attempt to calm emotions. He said all the right things. 'It will be difficult, as are most away games. The form book will be out of the window. It is about having the balls to go out and play.' Blah blah blah.

He knew they were expected to win. He also knew he would be slaughtered if they lost.

I played it down. I reminded fans how, since both sides had last met in the league, we had been one game from extinction at the bottom of the Fourth Division while they had won the Premiership. We were poles apart but it was impossible to dampen fans' expectations. Match day was chaos.

Police advised Blackburn fans not to travel to the game unless under escort. Rovers officials paid to hire a huge fleet of 40 luxury Shearings coaches to ferry their supporters to our ground.

Swathes of Burnley fans surrounded the buses as they arrived, desperately struggling against a cordon of police armed with 4ft-long truncheons.

When we normally arrive at the players' entrance 90 minutes before kick-off, the area is practically deserted. Against Blackburn, swarms of supporters in claret-and-blue milled about completely blocking the road.

The game was live on Sky TV and the atmosphere was gladiatorial. Kevin Ball almost chopped David Dunn in half with a tackle as the crowd bayed for blood.

We held our own until a minute before half-time when we gave away a crap goal to Jason McAteer.

As we failed to find an equaliser in the increasingly desperate second half, tensions rose. Burnley-born Andy Payton was targeted, isolated and ruthlessly picked off by Rovers fans with frightening intensity as they hurled coins and spat in his face.

With minutes to go we were frantic and the ball ran out for a throw-in. As we tried to retrieve the ball, one of their idiot players began to wrestle for it on the touchline. The crowd howled. Dozens lurched to their feet.

I thought, This is it, they're coming on to the pitch!

We were seconds away from a full-scale riot. I ran from the dugout towards their guy in a rage. I'd spent all week working with his manager and the police to calm the crowd down, only to see a dumb player press the trigger.

I ran to his side. 'What the fuck are you doing?'

Graeme yelled at me, 'I'll sort it, Stan.'

We got the ball back and played on.

Disaster struck. With seconds to go as we pushed forward to save a point, they stole behind us and scored their second.

As we shuffled into the tunnel after the final whistle, I saw Payton make a gesture to the Blackburn crowd gathered around the entrance to gloat and spit. Payts had stood on the terraces at Turf Moor as a Burnley supporter the time they flew over in the abusive aircraft. He felt this defeat as keenly as any of our supporters.

The lads were miserable in the dressing room, deafened by delirious Rovers supporters dancing in the stands above our heads and by roars and shouts from their players further along the corridor.

There was still time for things to get worse. As Blackburn fans were escorted to their coaches, a few dozen Burnley morons short on lamp oil tried to attack them. Frustrated after being beaten back by waves of riot police, the Burnley Suicide Squad as they are known charged into their own town centre and launched a wrecking spree, smashing scores of windows. We had lost a football match. They had lost their minds.

I wasn't to know it, but that afternoon was a picnic in the park compared to the nightmare that awaited us in the return fixture at Ewood in four months' time.

Once our fans hauled themselves back off their window ledges, the correct assessment of the Rovers defeat they needed to comprehend was that it had only cost us three points. We were still in the race for the play-offs.

Bolton were visiting us on Saturday and it was time to begin again. We lost 2–0.

Three derbies – Preston, Blackburn, Bolton ... three defeats. Merry Christmas everybody.

It was vital we put in a better performance on Boxing Day at Barnsley. Five thousand Burnley fans high on sherry and last night's lager braved the freezing weather to follow us. Barnsley won 1–0 with a last-minute goal capping a performance from my lot best described as bollocks.

Four defeats in a row. The worst run of my career so far.

My face was purple with rage as I tore into the players in the dressing room. I could tell from their stunned expressions they were surprised at the intensity of my reaction. God knows why. We'd had plenty of chances to win the damn thing before we offered it to them wrapped in ribbons.

I cancelled Christmas. 'Let's see if you Billy-fucking-big-times can be arsed doing a bit of hard work, eh?' I ranted. 'No days off. The holiday is over.'

Some of the senior players tried to make excuses but that only provoked me even more. 'Don't start feeling sorry for yourselves. There's 5,000 pissed-off people sat on buses now slagging you and me off. A lot of cats are going to get kicked tonight. I won't have it.'

We lost our next game, at home to Wolves, after taking the lead. Our run of defeats was now five. The fans turned on us again. This time they booed Ronnie Jepson who would have happily chinned the lot of them, one by one, if I'd let him.

During training, the players tried their familiar trick of ringing my son Dan to ask him to drop in with my granddaughter Olivia. She is one of the most beautiful things that has ever happened to me. I cried when Dan's beautiful wife Yogi gave birth to her. She compensates for the years I missed when my own children were growing up.

The lads know that I can't stay in a bad mood when she smiles at me so they take advantage. But I was wise to their ploy so I warned Dan off. The situation was too grave to involve my beautiful Olly.

Results by now were so poor I hardly dared read the local papers. When I finally plucked up courage, I found the front page of the *Burnley Express* dominated by news of a local couple who broke into Turf Moor on the eve of the millennium to have sex in my dugout and conceive a child. They actually had it off on my seat! At least someone else was getting shafted.

My next disaster struck at our lucky ground, Scunthorpe. Just a few months after winning promotion at Glanford Park on the last day of the season, we played the Third Division side in the FA Cup at the Turf.

We scraped a shambolic 2–2 draw with a last-minute equaliser to earn a lucky replay at their place, where we played no better.

I took Andy Payton off towards the end of extra-time because of a niggly hamstring pull and the Burnley fans – who had made bugger all noise all night – suddenly started booing me again. I gestured angrily towards them. Get stuffed. Supporters who barrack their own team don't deserve respect. I'm not frightened to take the lot of them on.

The match went to penalties and we lost, missing out on a lucrative trip to Bolton in the next round. I launched into the fans and told reporters, 'They are unbelievable. It's a long way to Scunthorpe. Do they think I came here to lose? Perhaps it's time up for me. Christ Almighty!'

The ref was going to get it, too. He turned down a blatant

penalty appeal during the first 90 minutes and I stormed around the corridor near the dressing rooms, looking for his hidey hole. A bulky steward blocked the way. I moved to barge past him but he placed a flabby hand on my chest.

'Sorry, pal, can't go in there,' he said.

'Can't go in there? I'm a fucking manager. You're not from the FA. I'm part of the game, let me in.'

'Sorry, pal.' He was adamant. He was also taking the piss.

Newspaper reporters stumbled across the scene just as I lost my rag and they recognised my frustration.

What option did I have? The jobsworth had manhandled me. Every nerve in my body screamed at me to knock him out. I looked up from my rant and rave to see Clive Holt peering at me from further up the tunnel. I caught his eye. His face registered horror and dread. I heard him say, 'I'm going outside.'

Clive was the duty director that night.

'Everyone else got out and away, Stan,' he said. 'Talk about leaving the sinking ship.'

Resigned to a night of frustration, we both made our way outside to get on the coach. Where was it? Not where I had told the driver to leave it, that's for sure.

As Clive ducked for cover, I marched along the pavement braving heckles from disgruntled Burnley fans and derision from Yorkshire locals. I finally spotted the bus, parked beyond a police cordon 50 yards away from the players' entrance. I stood and beckoned the driver to reverse. No reaction. I beckoned again, using two fingers instead of the whole hand. Nothing.

Reluctantly, I told the team to make their way along the pavement through a driving rainstorm.

Safely seated on the bus, I took out my frustration on the driver.

'Gaffer,' he appealed, 'the police wouldn't let me move.'

Police? 'Fuck the police,' I told him. 'When I say I want you somewhere, I want you there.'

Throughout the journey home, Clive and the team kept their

heads down. A season I had begun with realistic aspirations of attaining the Premiership collapsed with a crap run of form. My mood darkened.

A day later, after a telephone call from a fellow manager, I was apoplectic. He told me that he had heard Scunthorpe's manager, a gobby ex-Burnley player called Brian Laws, who fancied himself as the next Brian Clough, say that someone said that he should have been given my job.

I bear a grudge very well and this one festered for weeks. Eventually, I travelled to Bradford to watch their reserves play Liverpool and chose to have a cup of tea at half time. As I stood nursing my brew opposite chief scout Cliff Roberts and my son Chris, I noticed Cliff getting edgy. He shuffled his feet. He moved around to my left. It was almost as if he was trying to block my view.

I smiled at him, nodded and then peered over his shoulder.

It was Laws, standing in the corner of the lounge as though he hadn't a care in the world. I slammed down my cuppa, spilling tea.

'There's that snake,' I shouted, as I thrust Cliff to one side. 'Hey, you!' I yelled into Laws's face. 'That's my job you're talking about. If you want my job ... if you think you could do my job as well as me, come and see me.'

He mumbled, 'I haven't said anything.'

I didn't believe him. 'Never speak about me or my players again,' I said. 'And another thing. Next time, I'll knock your fucking head off.' Satisfied, I walked away.

Cliff and Chris stared open-mouthed. The rest of the room, packed until 20 seconds ago, had mysteriously emptied.

My trials continued. We lost our next game at Crewe 4–2, and then we played Crystal Palace at Turf Moor.

We lost that game, too, 2–1. Julian Gray scored their first and Clinton Morrison hit their winner with seconds left, even though we had scored first from Steve Davis. I was gutted. I was speechless.

I was also furious when their manager Alan Smith began his antics. Alan was part of Steve Coppell's backroom team with me at Palace. Yet, as their winning goal went in, he ran from his dugout to mine, cheering and dancing on the spot, like *Rising Damp*'s Rigsby on hot coals. It was a victory jig under my nose by the same guy who had befriended me and Kath as we made our way in London.

After the game, I got changed and walked towards the players' entrance. I saw Alan dash across the pitch to the Boardroom in his white suit. I walked down the tunnel. He saw me and said casually, 'I'll come and have a drink later, Stan.'

Kath, who stood alongside me, said, 'Just don't forget, Alan, what comes around, goes around.' Hear, hear.

I added my contribution. 'Don't bother with a drink, Alan. Fuck off.'

Despite the string of poor results, we still performed far better than anyone had predicted at the start of the season. I occasionally switched from my safety 4-4-2 formation to 4-3-3 to juice up the forward line. We remained comfortably in the top half of the table, a far cry from the panic which gripped the club the last time they'd hit the heady heights of the First Division.

Proof of a turnaround in our form came with a brilliant 2–1 home win against runaway league leaders Fulham. They took the lead, but we fought back and the big crowd were behind us 100 per cent.

With a trip to Huddersfield – who were going down – next on the agenda, I even started to relax. Bad move. Just days before our crucial match, my talented centre-half, Ian Cox, was hijacked by Ian Porterfield, who now managed Trinidad and Tobago. They had a World Cup qualifier against Jamaica.

I let Coxy fly out for a training camp earlier and did a deal with Porterfield that, as a result, he'd let him play against Huddersfield before calling him up. I told Coxy, 'If you want to go halfway across the world playing for some tinpot outfit in the middle of an ocean, fair enough. But you won't be playing for this team.'

Porterfield allowed Dwight Yorke and Shaka Hislop to play their league games before flying out, so what was the deal with Coxy? He eventually flew home late. I was forced to drop him for the next match, and he admitted, 'I'm knackered, gaffer.'

Trinidad and Tobago failed to set the world alight and Porterfield was sacked after they finished bottom of their qualifying group, with one point from five matches.

With Coxy eventually back in the ranks, my life, briefly, began to improve, even though the foot and mouth epidemic ravaging Britain forced us to close our training ground. We drew at Stockport County which put us on 49 points, one short of my pre-season survival target. After the game, the players wanted to celebrate staying up but we had plenty more to do. Finally, a win at Watford the following week ensured we were safe from relegation. In a league boasting Sheffield Wednesday, Wolves, Nottingham Forest, Blackburn, Fulham and Birmingham, it was no mean feat.

The players had worked hard to drag us within eight points of the play-offs. But now I wanted to push on to reach the Premiership. My ambition went beyond attaining First Division status for another season.

I made the mistake of publicly congratulating the players. They thought it was Christmas. We were stuffed 2–0 by an awful Sheffield Wednesday side and I told them afterwards, 'You were awful. If you can't beat teams like that then I'll sell the lot of you and bring people in who can.'

That would have been tricky. I hadn't had one offer for any of the players. That spoke volumes. However, I'd had a clearout in my first season when I'd sacked four lads during a match. This current bunch needed to believe I would do it again, especially considering our next game was the biggest for our supporters in years.

We were about to make the short journey to Blackburn Rovers

for our return fixture. The whole town talked of nothing else. Which was a shame. It was such a horror show that Stephen King could have written the match report.

Police warnings forced the kick-off at Ewood Park to be moved from Saturday at 3.00pm to Sunday at noon. The date? April Fool's Day. The omens? Not good.

Since our last meeting at Turf Moor, Rovers had overtaken us after showing form their investment in players warranted. They now challenged Bolton for the final automatic promotion place. Fulham were bound to be champions.

During the build-up, I was wheeled out for another series of press conferences with Graeme Souness to show a united front. We had to stop our rival fans tearing each other's heads off.

He looked tanned and fit. Rovers paid for their lot to spend the week sunbathing in Dubai to prepare for the game. We prepared Burnley style ... training every day in tropical Padiham.

On the day of the game, security fears meant our 5,000 fans had to travel on specially hired buses to Ewood Park. In contrast to Blackburn's subsidised service of sleek, matching luxury coaches to ferry their fans to our ground, Burnley supporters arrived bleary-eyed in the Turf Moor car park to be confronted by a motley collection of double-deckers, service buses and minicabs. I'm sure there was even an ice cream van on the end.

Fans, many fuelled on lager that had washed down their breakfasts, had to pay £3 to travel in a convoy that wouldn't have looked out of place in a *Mad Max* film. Cops queued up for overtime, and choppers patrolled the skies.

The weather was sunny, the pitch was excellent. The game was a disaster. The whole shambles was broadcast live on Sky TV, so my pain was magnified.

We were 3–0 down at half-time; 5–0 down by the end. They'd fluked three of them but the contest was over by the interval. As the second half progressed, I looked at the clock with 20 minutes to go and thought, This could be ten. Emerging with dignity became our sole aim.

As the goals went in, I marched to the edge of the technical area closest to the pitch, in full view of our fans. I am the manager. I wasn't going to skulk in the dugout like a whipped dog. I saw Rovers fans taunt our supporters behind the goal, holding up their hands displaying five splayed fingers. At one point, I noticed Graeme emerge from his dugout to stand close to the pitch. We are good pals. I shouted over, 'Scotch for me, Souey. A fucking large one!'

I've not touched a drop of whisky for years, but at that moment I could have drunk a whole bottle. And then another one to summon the courage to watch the action replay!

His players cost seven times as much as my squad. The gulf was massive. Since Jack Walker had begun to pump money into Rovers, we had done brilliantly even to be in the same league as them.

My one consolation as the final whistle blew was that if I had put the shower of shit I'd already thrown out of Burnley on to the pitch, it would have been 25–0.

The dressing room was silent. The players were numb. Andy Payton was gutted for the fans which included many of his mates. I'd certainly be giving Sainsbury's a wide berth for a while.

As tradition dictates, I made my way to Souey's office. I opened the door to find him holding court with Andy Gray from Sky TV, his assistants Tony Parkes and Phil Boersma, and also Kenny Dalglish who'd come to support his old Liverpool team-mate.

To their eternal credit, they talked about everything but the game, which was a bit like rowing away from the *Titanic* and not mentioning the iceberg. I sucked on a glass of warm white wine and said nowt.

* * *

Our only option was to come out fighting. We didn't have too long to prepare.

With all the relish the BBC displayed for the Queen Mother's funeral, Sky TV ensured they were at our next game, too, against fierce local rivals Preston at Turf Moor. They were scrapping with us for a play-off spot and clung tenaciously to sixth place. Defeat would end my dream of reaching the Premiership for another season.

The players needed little motivation. They knew their Ewood Park humiliation had been witnessed by millions of TV viewers in pubs up and down the country. Aside from their club, this game was about restoring their personal pride, too. They did the business in front of a capacity crowd and won 3–0.

Our supporters were euphoric. They allowed the frustration and humiliation from the Rovers match to erupt as they brought the house down. It was the turn of Preston's supporters and players to slink away.

It was still mathematically possible for us to reach the play-offs. Suddenly, we were flying again. On the way to Wimbledon, I looked out of the coach window to see we were being overtaken by the Bury team bus. I saw Terry sat at the front and called him on his mobile phone.

'You never allowed us to travel down like that the night before a game,' I shouted.

Terry said, 'The players are paying for themselves.'

I bet they were. I forgot Bury quickly. We won at Wimbledon and edged closer to that magical sixth place.

West Brom were next up at Turf Moor, another rival from the top of the table. Stress levels were high.

As I enjoyed a fag outside my kitchen door the night before the match, a taxi pulled up to bring a neighbour home. As it drove away, the driver wound down his window and shouted at me, 'Come on, you Baggies!' Cheeky bastard!

I started to run after his car but I'd had an Indian meal so my belt and trousers were undone. I could have been arrested for streaking or whacking him, so I wandered home to make plans for the match.

We were winning 1–0 on the day. Then they equalised in the last minute. It was all or nothing now.

We travelled to Norwich knowing we had to win to stay alive. We came from behind twice to take the game 3–2.

On the way home, as normal, we pulled up at the first off-licence we saw and I despatched Steve Davis inside with £50 to buy a bottle or two of wine. Win or lose, we could at least be civilised.

We dropped two points at home to Birmingham with a 0–0 draw but then beat Tranmere 2–1 to go seventh with two games left.

Our next match would decide our fate. If we lost at Sheffield United, and West Bromwich beat Huddersfield, all our season's work would be worthless.

United were managed by Neil Warnock. If ever a man would enjoy conducting my football funeral, it was him. I would do anything to stop Warnock having the last laugh at my expense. *Anything*.

By half-time at Bramall Lane, I'd been snotted big style. Blood oozed from my nose and formed a small puddle on the dressing room floor beside a discarded sock. The Burnley players sat around, staring at me in stunned disbelief.

After our frantic promotion at Scunthorpe, we had battled to within touching distance of the First Division play-offs at our first attempt – the closest I had ever come to reaching the Premiership as a manager.

A win against Warnock's mob would keep us in the race. A defeat and we were out. Bollocksed. Knackered. It would all be over.

Our physio was the first to spot me stride back into our room. He tried unsuccessfully to stem the flow of claret from my hooter.

'What happened, gaffer?' asked Glen Little.

'I've been in a fucking punch-up,' I explained. 'That's what you are up against,' I raged, pointing vaguely through the open door and out into the corridor. 'The ref's against you. The crowd's against you. And then you get people like that.'

They all craned their necks to see if a corpse lay outside.

'Mind you,' I said, 'if you think *I* look bad, I've made sure the other fella doesn't see the second half.'

It was always going to be a testy visit to Sheffield. After most football matches, directors hob-nob in Boardrooms while managers and their staff slum it, slurping bottles of beer together in draughty offices close to the dressing rooms. It's a chance to watch the classified football results filter through on Sky TV and rue missed chances during the match. Most football men enjoy these get-togethers as a chance to swap anecdotes and insults. I've never done that with Warnock. Our feud goes back years. I cannot abide the man. Let's say our personalities clash.

If I was alone with him for just one minute, I...

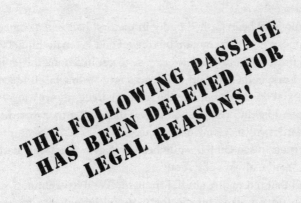

THE FOLLOWING PASSAGE HAS BEEN DELETED FOR LEGAL REASONS!

... so I would happily do it slowly, forcefully and with both hands.

Therefore, when we went in at half-time 1–0 down, I was not prepared to be rational. I was raging as I sat the players down and started talking.

'It's only one goal. You're still in with a shout of the Premiership. How much do you want it?' I didn't discuss tactics. Not yet. I hesitated because I thought I heard a noise on the other side of the emergency exit door. Was some big-eared spy listening in?

'What you've got to do,' I said, 'is stay calm. Just stay cool, calm and collected.' I began to walk slowly towards a large green metal door. Bolted to it was a sign with large red writing: STRICTLY PRIVATE: FIRE EXIT ONLY.

I motioned for the players to keep quiet, while I carried on talking. 'Just stay calm. That's the way to ...' I launched myself through the air, landed a two-footed kung-fu kick against the door and exploded outwards into the corridor. I saw a slinking figure fall backwards away from us both before he scurried away. 'You c**t,' I yelled as I ran after him.

He disappeared around a corner so I charged back into our dressing room and pointed at Paul Cook. 'Come with me. We'll go and see the ref.'

Cooky had been gashed badly in the first half when someone had gone over the top on him but the ref had given nothing. I was full of fire and needed a quick excuse to get in among the United lot, so I dragged Cooky off to the ref's room while he still bled.

'Look at this,' I shouted at the ref as I barged my way towards his room. I held Cooky's leg in the air displaying the wound.

I heard a voice. 'Come off it, Stan.'

I turned to see United's number two Kevin Blackwell staring at me. 'You're always at it, you!'

I call that red rag to a bull. I shouted, 'We'll have it now.'

I ran up, smacked him in the face and nutted him for good measure, banging him hard. He hit me back and my nose ruptured.

Here we go. I jumped on him and we fell to the floor, shoving the door to the ref's room wide open. From all sides, stewards and United staff pounced on to my back and tried to pull me off Blackwell. Eventually, they dragged me away.

I'd given him a quick crack and a couple of follow-ups. I hadn't had an option. He offered me out, so I hit him. Simple as that. If you are going to get in a fight, you don't wait for them to strike first.

I made my way back to our dressing room. Cooky had wandered back on his own moments before, his face pale after witnessing the punch-up. He'd told the lads what had happened but I don't think they believed him until I turned up with my nose bleeding.

'I've given him a right fucking hiding,' I said. 'He won't see the second half. I've sorted him out big style.'

When the physio started sticking plasters up my hooter and covering himself in blood, too, the players started pissing themselves.

'Just get out there and do them.' We tried hard to find an equaliser, but United frustrated us. Then, just as we pushed forward in numbers, they broke away in injury time and hit a second. Fifteen thousand of their fans laughed and cheered. 'Piss off, Stan. See you here next season, eh?'

Under-achievers mocking their betters. How pathetic. I steamrollered towards the tunnel. God help anyone who said a word out of line. Kevin Ball approached me as we left the pitch.

'I'll wait for you outside our door,' he offered.

Bally's one of the handiest players I've ever met. If it was going to kick off, I was glad to have his backing. 'Cheers, Bally,' I said. 'OK. Let's see what happens.'

The tunnel was packed with stewards and police. One copper laid his arm on my shoulder and beckoned me to one side. He said, 'I was there at half-time. Not a bad right hook you've got there, Stan.'

I smiled and looked up to see one of Warnock's staff videoing me. He followed me around with a camera for minutes, just in case I had it out with someone else.

It was time to go. West Brom had only scraped a draw against doomed Huddersfield but it was enough for them to secure the last play-off spot. We had battled hard until the last game of the season. I had motivated a team of free transfers, Bosman signings and a couple I had paid money for to beat some of the best teams in the country. I was exhausted.

I turned up at The Kettledrum that night covered in bruises. Kath had been scratched by our granddaughter Olivia and we sat there over our drinks looking like domestic violence victims.

I've had a friendly beer with Blackwell since our fight but I won't look Warnock in the face. Forget him. I had one match left and then I could have a summer break. I'd earned it. I was going to Portugal with the players. Only ... it turned out that I wasn't. I was going to hospital, at 5.00am, in an ambulance, at 80mph. And the *Sun* newspaper would announce to the world: BURNLEY BOSS TERNENT HAS HEART-ATTACK.

11

'Can You Work around the Duck?'

BURNLEY, 2001–02

We won our last game, a meaningless one at home to Watford, 2–0. Ironically, on the same afternoon, our rivals West Brom lost. We finished one agonising place and two annoying points behind them.

If it hadn't been for Bob Taylor's last-gasp equaliser when we played them two weeks earlier, we would have been sixth, in their place. My back door to the Premiership through the First Division play-offs was slammed shut again.

I watched our last match at a first-class ground bathed in sunshine and packed with Burnley fans. I ought to have been happy. We were beating bigger and better teams than us regularly. I had put Burnley back in the top ten of the country's best-supported teams per head of population. Middlesbrough were top with 23 per cent of their residents watching the team. In Burnley, 14.4 per cent of our 90,000 residents came regularly to Turf Moor, better figures than Sunderland, Blackburn, Manchester United, Newcastle and Liverpool. Season ticket sales of 12,500 were at a record high. The country was taking Burnley seriously again.

Yet the frustration at our failure to progress up the leagues hurt. My stress had been critical for two consecutive seasons. I'd suffered skin rashes, burning indigestion and developed a mop of dashing, but depressing, grey hair.

Before the game against Watford, I presented a piece of glassware to their manager Graham Taylor to mark his last game in charge. Throughout the ceremony, I could see our fans gurning at him. Here was a man who risked his health to succeed in this business, yet was vilified by the press and the public.

Let's face it, if some journalist put my head on a turnip he'd have to remove the first vegetable that came to my hand afterwards from up his own arse!

I consider myself equal to Graham and many other managers who already work in the Premiership. I am prepared to sacrifice anything for just one season to pit my wits against the best managers in Britain. I had already begun preparations for another crack at it. I was confident.

The players were in holiday mode but the night before our end of season trip to Portugal I felt sick. Far too ill to travel. I phoned Sam to put him in charge and Kath packed our lads Chris and Dan off with him. They could look after themselves.

'I'll catch you up,' I told the boys as I waved them off. I went straight to bed, bent double with chronic nausea.

'You are an awful colour,' Kath decided as she came up the stairs behind me. I looked in the bathroom mirror and met a man who looked much older than 55. My face was puffed with fatigue and greyer than my hair. I collapsed on to the bed and tried to sleep. I must have dozed briefly but I woke in agony. I groped for the bedside clock and saw it was just after midnight.

Stabbing pains ripped through my chest. I struggled to breathe and woke Kath as I gasped in agony. I could hear her shouting, 'Stan? Stan? What's wrong?' but I was too numbed by cramps to respond.

An ambulance rushed me to Burnley General Hospital. As I was deposited in the casualty department, I heard the paramedic say, 'Suspected heart-attack.'

I was convinced I was going to die. Heads turned, fingers pointed, mouths gaped. Within 30 minutes of my public appearance in a wheelchair, the press besieged the hospital reception desk. Was I dead? Was I alive? Was I having a head transplant?

I was hooked up to a machine that went 'ping' for an hour before doctors transferred me to an intensive care ward. To avoid Burnley's equivalent of the paparazzi, they wrapped me in a bedsheet and wheeled me through corridors around the back of the hospital. I looked like Ghandi.

As we passed the kitchens, I sniffed mashed potatoes and thought, once more, that I was going to die. I spewed bile into my lap and gurgled for help. We reached the bed and I struggled to breathe but no one paid any attention.

'Is there any danger of any help?' I asked.

A consultant arrived and checked me over.

'I'm knackered,' I admitted and he KO'd me with an injection. I slept for a few hours as Kath sat by my bed.

I woke around 5.00am and reached for her hand.

'I thought you were going to leave me,' she said.

I laughed, shrugged and then thought, Sod it, machismo has its place and it wasn't here. We both had a little sob but were forced to compose ourselves quickly when a sizeable crowd of sightseeing patients gathered at the foot of my bed. They acted like rubberneckers at a motorway pile-up.

I was still heavily nauseous and globs of bile erupted from my mouth as they watched. The medics fannied around. I lost patience and shouted, 'Will somebody give me something to stop me spewing. And draw those bloody curtains!'

As the nurses wheeled me away for tests, I asked Kath, 'Should I wear a dressing gown?'

She said, 'Judging by the amount of people waiting to see you, I'd put it over your head.'

As they hoisted me out of bed, one Burnley fan walked up and said, 'Are you all right, Stan?'

'Oh aye,' I said, 'that's why I'm in this fucking wheelchair.'

They checked my heart. They rammed a camera down my throat. Christ, if they wanted to see stomach contents they just had to check my chin. It was coated in the stuff. The specialist returned after supper and sat on my bed. 'It's not a heart-attack, Stan,' he announced, and smiled. 'It's a stomach ulcer.'

I asked a million questions and he answered the lot. Then he said, 'You need to rest.'

I asked one more question. 'Can I go home?'

Kath rang the lads. She woke them at 6.00am on the Algarve. 'Chris? It's your mum. Listen, your dad won't be coming out there. He's in hospital with a stomach ulcer.'

The timing was perfect. Two hours later over breakfast, they bought the Mediterranean edition of the *Sun* which announced in bold headlines: BURNLEY BOSS TERNENT HAS HEART-ATTACK.

Both boys were upset and wanted to fly home. Kath spent an hour on the phone trying to convince them that I was OK and they should stay. The players panicked when they read the news. So did my old Bury Chairman Terry Robinson.

Early the next morning, he barged into my bedroom unannounced after finding the kitchen door unlocked. He was crying. 'Don't you ever do that to me again.' He had returned from a holiday at 3.00am and checked CEEFAX headlines before he went to bed. He'd read TERNENT IN HEART SCARE and he hadn't slept a wink.

Others were not so sympathetic. Peter Reid telephoned soon after Terry had left. 'So you've pulled through, eh? Fuck me.'

Radio Lancashire also came knocking. I told them solemnly, 'I know I may disappoint everybody, but it seems I'm going to be all right.'

All right? Would we really be all right?

I patched myself up during the summer, rested at home and annoyed my family. Kath booked us a trip to America to stay with our pals, Bob and Patti Martin and their son, Alexander. Bob is a former chairman of Bradford City and a general hanger-on, who allows me to use him as a sounding board as we drift on his yacht off the Florida coast. This year, the trip was delayed for three days as I chased a new signing. Peter Crouch is sensational in the air and not too bad with his feet. He played against us for QPR and I rated him. If you put pegs on his legs they'd look like a washing line but he could withstand a tackle.

He was rated at £1m but I was due to spend a bit of cash. The majority of my team I lined up for my second assault on the Premiership had cost next to nothing — Nik the Greek in goal, free transfer; Dean West, poached from Bury, free transfer; Arthur Gnohere, hand-picked from France, free transfer; Lee Briscoe, refugee from Sheffield Wednesday, free transfer; Graham Branch, recruited from Stockport County, free transfer; Gordon Armstrong, another Bury lad, free transfer; Paul Cook, free transfer; Gareth Taylor, resurrected after being rejected by Manchester City, free transfer; Mitchell Thomas, older than Jimmy Saville's hairdo, but a free transfer.

Crouch would cost us a packet but, as a talisman, he was worth every penny. I persuaded him to come north and we sat in my kitchen to discuss his move. He liked the look of the place. So did his agent. Crucially, I thought, so did his wife.

Then, the next night, 300 white blokes and 300 Asians restaged the Battle of Stalingrad in Burnley town centre and the deal was off.

Days after a race riot had portrayed nearby Oldham as a backward hick town torn apart by primitive hatreds, it happened in Burnley. Thank you very much, lads. Communities hurled themselves at each other, disguised by masks and armed with petrol bombs. My deal to sign a new striker was killed stone dead.

TV cameras on the scene relayed images of terror, aggression and downright bestiality to every TV set in Britain. Mr and Mrs Crouch obviously subscribed to Sky News. As police and council workers damped down the glowing embers in the remains of a pub and half-a-dozen houses, I got a call from Crouch's agent. If I didn't mind too much, the deal was off. Peter was going to sunny, peaceful, Portsmouth instead.

Selling Burnley suddenly became more difficult than ever. I felt like the manager of Beirut United. I would drive players used to appearing in the Premiership towards Turf Moor down a flyover through the centre of town called Centenary Way. If they glanced to the left they saw a neon advertising sign for a 'Restarunt.' Not good.

That summer, I got close to signing Danny Dichio, Shefki Kuki and Graham Alexander from Preston North End. But every deal collapsed.

Alexander got as far as my kitchen before he turned us down. It didn't matter, anyway. He wasn't my kind of signing. He wore an earring.

*   *   *

Top by Christmas.

We were top of the league, favourites for promotion before Boxing Day, eight points clear of the team chasing the final play-off place. Manchester City, West Brom, Wolves, Birmingham, Coventry, both Sheffield clubs and Nottingham Forest were left in our wake.

I watched Mark Lawrenson point out on *Grandstand* that only one team in the history of the First Division since the war had failed to achieve promotion after leading the league at Christmas. Game on.

We won 15 of our first 25 games, drew five of the others and lost just five. Away wins at Sheffield Wednesday, Birmingham, Preston, Coventry, Millwall and Crystal Palace ensured we were feared.

We suffered the obligatory 4–2 home defeat to Manchester City but we overcame it to reach the top. Fans got excited. The press began sniffing around. Football people began to take notice.

While at Burnley, I had been linked to positions at Sheffield Wednesday and Derby County but I wasn't interested. Now, as we raced towards the Premiership after a 25-year absence, I had an interesting conversation.

I'd gone to spy on Barnsley and bumped into Charlie Woods. I owed Charlie one. He was the scout I spivved when I signed Steve Davis from Luton. Since then, Charlie had left White Hart Lane and joined Bobby Robson at Newcastle. As we watched Barnsley lose together, he told me that Mick Wadsworth had just quit as Bobby's assistant to take up the same role under Stuart Gray at Southampton.

'I could do that job,' I said.

Charlie turned to face me. 'Would you be interested?' he asked.

I thought for a minute, nibbled on my pie, smiled and said, 'I might be.'

My achievements over the previous eight years — taking into account the budgets I've had to work with — were better than any football league manager apart from Alex Ferguson.

But Newcastle was not for me. Not yet. I wanted to play them next season at Turf Moor. I wanted to prove I was better than some Premiership managers who survive by reputation and not achievement.

As we scaled Division One and perched on top, it seemed, at last, my ambition was fulfilled and Turf Moor life was almost perfect.

Then the police called to tell me that my star striker had driven while drunk and been found by officers hiding in a house.

Andy Payton is a legend in Burnley. A local lad with a solid, square jaw and an accent straight off the darts team at the Rovers Return, he is hero-worshipped by most of the town and envied by the rest. He joined the staff as a 15-year-old schoolboy when Brian Miller was manager. Then came John Bond.

Fans blame Bond for sending the club on a downward spiral and dismal form during his spell as manager. He watched Andy play one game, a 5–3 win when he scored a hat-trick ... and then got rid of him.

To prove Bond wrong, Andy eventually rejoined us in 1998 via Hull, Middlesbrough, Celtic, Huddersfield and Barnsley, averaging a goal every other game along the way.

I was his manager at Second Division Hull in the early '90s when he was so prolific as a 22-year-old we almost had to build a new stand to house scouts from Arsenal, Wimbledon, Spurs, Manchester City, Leeds, Manchester United, Celtic and Aston Villa who queued up each week to watch him.

Lennie Lawrence won a tug of war to buy him for Middlesbrough, and then promptly sold him for £650,000 to Liam Brady, who desperately wanted Payts to play for Celtic.

Andy was the leading scorer at Parkhead in his first season with 20 goals in 25 games. When he joined Barnsley, he became *their* top scorer and, in my first two seasons at Burnley, Andy led our hit list, too.

He had also, as Andy admitted to me one morning, 'twatted' a bloke in broad daylight in a row over his ex-wife in an incident involving a golf club and a shop window on a street in his home town of Padiham. A year later, he ran off from the police when they stopped his car.

Now, as we faced our toughest run-in to a season for 25 years, he crashed his VW GTi into a wall and ran off to his estranged partner's house only to be dragged out by cops, handcuffed and escorted bare-chested down to the nick to spend a night in the cells.

With Andy, you always get goals. You can also get grief. Each time he ballsed it up, I gave him a sympathetic ear and helped him through his personal traumas. I was happy to live with his latest cock-up, too, but within hours of his arrest, news of the incident swept Burnley and the directors were soon on the phone. They wanted to meet.

Talented individuals are not allowed flaws in these days of stifling political correctness. They have to be perfect. So, after the third time Andy had landed himself in court in two years, I had to be *seen* to act.

He admits he was lucky he wasn't sacked. Andy believes his neck was spared because of all the goals he scored and he is probably right. Instead of the boot, I farmed him out on loan to Blackpool.

Fans were furious and blamed me for sabotaging Payts's career. There was so much animosity, the only person who could tell them I was blameless was Andy himself and he chose the best way possible, in the match-day programme.

Since managing Payts at Hull, I became his mentor. I advised him on transfer deals and even acted as his agent. I travelled with him to Oakwell to hammer out his move to Barnsley.

When he was asked, 'Who has been the biggest influence on your career?', he answered, 'Stan Ternent.'

The players slaughtered him for a football crime far more heinous than chinning a bloke — arse-licking.

But Andy and I both know the truth. He has scored over 80 goals for Burnley in 150 games, becoming one of the club's top 20 all-time scorers. He is also a target of envy. His mates are local lads and, whenever Payts goes out in town, he is pestered by drunken idiots, jealous of his success. Normally he copes. Occasionally he snaps.

Now, because even I couldn't protect him this time, we were forced to manage without our leading scorer who was exiled to a month's hard labour at the seaside. Our form began falling apart as early as Boxing Day. And we didn't even play!

We prepared well for our trip to Rotherham. I had even banned our forward, Ian Moore, from having Christmas dinner with his dad, Rotherham manager Ronnie, in case he slipped out our tactical secrets over the turkey. But just two hours before kick-off, the game was postponed due to a frozen pitch, and our rhythm stuttered.

A win that day could have increased our lead at the top where we had been for six weeks. Instead, our bogey team Manchester City won and closed the gap on us, and they were our next opponents.

We lost 5–1. Another predictable, depressing defeat.

I tried to limit the damage. We played well in the first half. Glen Little missed a penalty that could have levelled the score. Instead, we conceded the game and the momentum to Kevin Keegan's team again.

We faltered further, winning only one out of our next seven league games. The fight for promotion was punishing. By the time we won again, a scrappy 2-1 victory at Crewe at the end of February, we had slipped to fifth in the league.

During a 1–1 draw at home with Nottingham Forest, I put our new £1m striker, Robbie Blake, on at half-time to shake it up, but within 15 minutes I hauled him off. I told him to say he'd had a stomach strain but, in reality, I'd made a tactical error and I wasn't prepared to allow it to develop into a disaster just to avoid my pride getting hurt. We needed a quick fix for our promotion bid or we'd had it. We needed inspiration on the pitch. The fans needed inspiration off it. I had to prove that Burnley had the balls for a fight, the money to mount a challenge and the ambition to succeed.

I sat at home after our next home game, a miserable 1–0 defeat to Birmingham City, watching my favourite *Auf Wiedersehen, Pet* video, when I had an idea. 'Kath, don't disturb me for a minute will you, love,' I shouted to her, 'I'm just going to call Gazza.'

* * *

'You can't send him out on to the pitch looking like that.' Jimmy Five-Bellies stood in front of me, beaming from ear to ear and looking twice the size of my back four.

He had come to Turf Moor as Gazza's spy to investigate our facilities and sample the atmosphere. But I couldn't let the fans see him yet because Gazza was still an Everton player. I kitted Jimmy out with the biggest bobble hat I could find and jammed it down on to his head. When I had finished, it looked more like a balaclava with three chins.

Next, I made him wear an extra-large manager's coat. *Voilà!* Ten-Bellies!

He sat next to our scout Cliff Roberts in a cordoned-off section amongst the away fans. With any luck, any of our supporters with eagle eyes would think he was a new signing. Maybe not. A new chef? Perhaps.

My efforts were wasted. Jimmy emerged from the players' entrance on to the main road outside, which was heaving with Burnley fans after the final whistle, whipped off his bobble hat and began signing autographs.

He watched us draw 1–1 with Norwich and I saw him wince as, at the end, some spoiled, clueless fools among our fans booed. Loudly.

'I thought that was a bit harsh,' Jimmy told me afterwards. A bit harsh? Those idiots jeopardised everything.

I stormed into my house that night, convinced any potential deal for Gazza was blown. 'Sign fucking Gazza? You think he'd come to play here with those tossers in the crowd?' I expected the deal to be a long shot, but I didn't dream our own supporters would sabotage it.

Gazza was a frustrated Everton squad member, relegated to the bench by manager Walter Smith, when I first imagined he might fancy a heroic spell to push us to promotion. His career, with so many highs for Newcastle, England, Spurs and Lazio, was ending in ignominy at Everton.

Just as I did with Ian Wright, I offered another of the greatest players this country has ever seen a chance to go out in style and, more importantly, a chance to go out in the headlines.

We first met in Barry Kilby's plush conservatory. Gazza sipped Chablis and his best pal Jimmy had mineral water. I told him, 'I just want you to play football.'

Gazza is a vulnerable soul. In his blind desire to be part of the only game he knows, he has fallen prey to all manner of hangers-on who abused him. I understood his weaknesses and accepted them.

I told him straight, 'It's obvious you're not off booze completely. If you want to go bang on it, book into a clinic and then check yourself out on a Friday to come and play for us, I don't mind.

'If you've been on the piss all night, tell me. I'll pick a team to suit you for 30 minutes. I'll do what you want. Just play. If you're knackered, I'll take you off.'

Gazza had recently been reunited with his wife Sheryl and, as our discussions broke up, I spoke to her briefly on the phone.

'He just needs to play,' she said.

Gazza is an uncomfortable spectator. He found it hard to cope when he was dropped at Everton and not told why. I reassured Sheryl, 'He can have plenty of time with you and just come here to play.'

Gazza missed the greasepaint, whether it was with Burnley, Rochdale or Real Madrid. I couldn't believe he wasn't besieged by offers once he'd become an outcast at Everton. He looked in great shape. Besides, I only needed him for 90 minutes a week. If you deal with Gazza, you have to recognise that he is public property and, as far as I was concerned, he could hide away for the rest of the time.

I didn't give a toss about his drinking stories. If you're in a booze clinic, get a 24-hour pass out. I know plenty of players who have wowed football just hours after stumbling home pissed.

Whingers lined up to savage Gazza for drinking in the Hong Kong dentist's chair before Euro '96, but he answered them in the best way, against Scotland, by lifting the ball over Colin Hendry's head and volleying one of the greatest Wembley goals ever.

Bollocks to the lot of them!

I made him feel wanted by Burnley. 'I can see you in the play-off final at Cardiff, Gazza, conducting my orchestra with the roof shut.'

He jumped to his feet. Gazza had already spoken to Andy Townsend, Chris Waddle and Ian Wright, all of whom recommended that he should play for me. 'That's it,' he declared, 'I only want to play for Burnley.'

Music to my ears. But I had to be practical. 'Hang on,' I warned him. 'What if Fergie suddenly wants you for his last few Champions League games? Never say never. Just go and see Walter as a friend. Talk to him man to man. You're one of the greatest players the world's ever seen. You need to play football, Gazza, and be able to go and see Sheryl when you want. Look after yourself. Go to Walter as a friend and tell him, "Play me or I'm off." '

A day later, I discovered that Walter Smith was not playing ball. I called to see if Gazza was available and he told me straight in his clipped Scots accent, 'The lad wants to play for his place.'

That was about it. He gave nothing else away. Deal off.

Yet 48 hours later, Everton played West Ham and Gazza wasn't even on their bench. He had become a non-person at Goodison and I became increasingly frustrated. By now we had lost to Walsall and had slipped to sixth in the table. I forgot the glitz, the souvenir shop revenue and the media interest I knew would accompany Gazza to Burnley and focused on my real reason for signing him. I wanted Gazza at Turf Moor on ability alone. He had the potential to influence my dressing room and inspire my team along the finishing straight. He was a winner when I needed 11 of them. It was a cold, calculated football decision.

Sadly, Walter Smith came to the same conclusion. After ignoring Gazza for months, he suddenly decided to pitch him into his midfield for Everton's FA Cup quarter-final at Middlesbrough. As I saw my potential genius run out at the Riverside Stadium, I mentally killed the deal off.

Walter Smith told the press afterwards, 'I am keeping Gazza until the end of the season.'

We would have to go it alone. I tried to reach Walter by phone to make one last attempt at changing his mind but, after the Middlesbrough defeat, he disappeared to Scotland with his pal Archie Knox.

Gazza's agent, Ian Elliott, pestered Everton Chairman Bill Kenwright but he did not respond to messages left on his mobile phone. It soon became clear why silence reigned. Walter had been sacked.

Kenwright had been busy finding a replacement he felt could keep Everton in the Premiership. Gazza's future and Burnley's promotion hopes were of little importance at crisis-hit Goodison. This was the time to take advantage.

Kenwright appointed Preston manager David Moyes as Smith's replacement and I decided to act. I persuaded Barry Kilby to ring Kenwright and insist on a chance to sign Gazza. At the same time, I urged Gazza to confront Moyes on his first day in charge and say, 'I can't understand why I'm not playing. I want to leave.'

Both Moyes and Kenwright were desperate for Gazza to stay but, after a fateful conversation with the star just hours after the new manager had arrived at the ground, Moyes was wise enough to accept that the player wanted out. I told Gazza to come to my house to discuss our deal.

He wanted a weekly wage, appearance money and a lump sum if he was a substitute and didn't play. With his agent in tow, we hammered out the package.

Kath had other priorities. She began to panic over a huge steak and kidney pie she had made for our tea.

'Stan,' she called as she dragged me away from our negotiations.

'What is it?'

'It's the pie,' she said.

'What about the pie?'

'Well,' she said, 'it's supposed to feed six but I'm worried that Five-Bellies will think it's an individual portion.'

I stomped back to our discussions. The agent Ian Elliott was off his food, anyway. He had pulled me to one side earlier, away from Gazza and Jimmy, and said, 'I cannot wait for this deal to be done. I've been living with them on Merseyside for two weeks and it's killing me. Last night Gazza made me a sandwich and I've been up all night on the bog. I went 14 times. They mixed five high-strength laxatives in with my fucking tuna.'

We were ready to sign the deal 24 hours later but were forced to wait for Barry Kilby to return from a business trip in London. Gazza was booked into the nearby Oaks Hotel but he, Jimmy and Ian had returned to my house to sit and kick their heels in the kitchen. My lad Chris arrived and broke the tension. 'Jimmy, do you fancy a pint?'

Five-Bellies moves fast for a fat lad and was at the back door like a whippet after a chip.

Chris drove him a mile up the road to The Kettledrum for a peaceful pint. After an hour, Jimmy called Gazza on his mobile phone. 'It's dead quiet up here, man. Come on up.'

Gazza stood and prepared to set off, with Ian as his minder. I warned them both, 'If you walk in that pub, the news will be all over town in ten minutes. There will be so many people outside it will make Mafeking look like a picnic.'

Gazza laughed and left. As he walked into The 'Drum, I heard the sound of jaws hitting tables even back at my house.

'Gi'us a pint, love,' he said. Predictably, three of the regulars suffered whiplash injuries because of the speed with which they dug out their mobile phones.

Gazza, Chris, Ian and Jimmy sat near the gents with their backs to the rest of the pub, but their efforts to avoid attention were pointless. The pavement outside turned into a taxi rank as cabs zeroed in from all over town. The front door rattled like a turnstile.

Grown men bowed before him. Requests flooded in. 'Gazza, Gazza, sign my packet of Lambert and Butler, will you?'

As Gazza sipped on a glass of white wine, blokes kissed him. One had his best disco shirt autographed in black biro. Dozens of people developed sudden bladder retention problems and formed a queue for the gents which snaked past his table. Chris knew that, as the lager flowed and more supporters added to the crush, things could get out of hand. He said, 'Come on, Gazza, we're going.'

They left through the kitchens to avoid the rush at the front door. As Gazza passed through the dining area, the landlord placed a curry in front of a customer. Gazza nicked a popadum and darted out. Seconds later, he reappeared at their table. 'Mind if have another one?' he asked and ran off with their plate.

Like Wrighty before, Gazza discovered in one night the levels of blind devotion that would be offered to him if he joined Burnley. That night, as he made his way back to the hotel, Bill Kenwright called to make a last attempt to persuade him to stay at Everton. Gazza would not budge.

As he returned to my house next morning to meet Barry and sign his contract, Manchester City called his agent. Now even Kevin Keegan wanted Gazza. Thankfully, he had made up his mind and only had eyes for Burnley.

We signed him officially at 8.45am and I whisked him down to the training ground to meet the players. In 24 hours, we were playing Preston North End, our closest play-off rivals, in a TV match at Turf Moor. News that Gazza had joined us leaked out and the media swarmed all over the place. Our skipper Steve Davis shook hands with Gazza and introduced him to the squad.

'They were a bit quiet, a bit apprehensive,' I said to Steve afterwards.

'Well, he's a legend, isn't he, gaffer?' he said.

With a legend on board, how could we fail? We moved Gazza to the Dunkenhalgh Hotel near Accrington where he spent the night with Sheryl and his son Regan as we prepared for our big game.

I returned to Turf Moor alone. I walked out on to the pitch, took a bottle from my pocket and sprinkled more precious Holy water on to all four corners and both penalty areas. If Preston won tomorrow, they would close the gap on us at the top and our confidence could be fatally undermined.

Gazza wasn't eligible to play, so for our biggest game of the season so far, I decided I needed to rely on a different legend.

I woke on the morning of the game at 5.00am and jerked upright in bed, a thousand tactical formations flowing through my mind. I am tormented on match days. I become intolerant. When Kath goes to the supermarket, I instruct her, 'Don't buy loud cereal.'

Close to kick-off against Preston, we were joined by Gazza in the dressing room. The noise from thousands of their visiting supporters echoing down through the roof was deafening.

He shook hands with the lads, patted them on their shoulders and shouted words of encouragement in order to be heard above the constant refrain from above of 'PNE ... PNE ... PNE ...'

He had given a pre-match press conference and now it was the turn of our fans to salute their new hero. I wanted him to parade across the pitch to the directors' box where he would watch the game with Sheryl and his lad. I called a bloke from our media department over to the tunnel to sort out the arrangements.

'Listen, Gazza is available at 6.00pm to wave to the crowd and walk across the pitch in front of the ITV Digital cameras.'

'We'll have to get back to you.'

'You what?' I said, incredulous, trying to focus amid shouts of 'Ternent, you wanker!' from the visiting supporters.

'I said we'll have to get back to you, Stan,' the media suit said.

'Their mascot, Deepdale Duck, and ours, Bertie Bee, are having a race before kick-off so we'll have to fit Gazza in.'

'Let me get this straight,' I said. 'I've just signed one of the world's greatest players and you want me to work around some fucking duck?'

Unbelievable!

Gazza was finally allowed out, and to slightly more interest than stuffed animals jumping through hoops. He received a standing ovation from our sections of the ground which were filled to capacity. The crowd soared from our average of 15,000 to over 18,000, but plenty of the Preston muppets booed him.

I watched Gazza make his way waving and smiling, then I turned right to head on to the pitch towards my dugout. After four paces I stopped, turned promptly on my heels and marched straight back to the dressing room. Some dirty sod had spat in my face.

Burnley spit? I could cope with that ... maybe. But I refused to watch the match dripping in Preston phlegm.

Gazza jumped on to his seat in the stands to celebrate our first goal. When our second went in, a streaker ran on to the pitch with 2–0 painted on his arse. He ran to the Preston fans, waved his backside in their faces and then charged back towards the stand. Our mascot Bertie Bee, an 8ft insect with an oversized black-and-gold head, rugby tackled him on the edge of the box, flinging him into the air and displaying his knackers to TV viewers all over Britain. Gazza thought he'd come to a lunatic asylum. He told reporters after we'd run out 2–1 winners, 'I'm going to love it here. Stan's mad like me.'

Almost 20,000 fans packed the Turf for Gazza's début, a disappointing 1–1 draw with Bradford City. We allowed them to equalise through some sloppy defending, yet we still clung to fourth place. It wasn't fatal. Yet.

Two wins and a draw out of our last six games would be enough to secure my coveted play-off spot.

Next up was Warnock's Sheffield United. I could not forget that they posted a spy outside the dressing room the last time we'd played at Bramall Lane. If they wanted another fracas, I was ready.

After our short journey over the Pennines and a ten-minute break at a service station on the M1, we arrived. When the coach pulled into the car park behind their main stand, I saw a crowd of over 500 United fans gathered around the players' entrance, held back by police crush barriers.

As I stepped off the bus, they started. 'Fuck off, Ternent,' ... 'Boo!' ... 'Get stuffed back to Burnley ...'

I laughed in their faces. I trotted through the doors and shouted, 'The truth hurts,' as their insults faded away.

We piled into the cramped dressing room, forced to wrestle for space amongst stainless steel kit cases overflowing with boots, studs, bulk packs of chewing gum and soft drinks. The players changed, spitting and snotting on the floor at will. Typically, the queue for the bogs began at the same time as my team talk.

'Come on out of the khazi, lads!' I shouted.

Gazza made his way around the room, switching off all the plug sockets beneath the benches. Nerves.

'Have you wiped your arse on this towel?' It was Paul Weller who had a hygiene query for our kit man.

I worked the room with Sam, probing, begging, urging, pushing the players. 'How much do you want it? This is the nearest you'll get.'

I never drink before a match, although I know plenty of managers who go on to the pitch bollocksed with alcohol. Today, I gave one of my lads who was looking a bit pale a tot of whisky.

'I know the pitch is crap. Pele couldn't play on it. But you can. You're better than this lot.'

We were, too. Except that day. We were 2–0 down at half-time, 3–0 by the end.

We were abused by their fans throughout. Our squad members who hadn't made the bench were forced to change seats after knuckleheads in the crowd threatened them.

Sam came out to stand shoulder-to-shoulder with me on the pitch-side but I sent him back into the dugout. I appreciated his gesture but managers have a duty to take the shit as well as champagne.

After the game, I gave my moping players 20 minutes to make the bus and went for a beer with Blacky, the bloke I had walloped, hard, in the mush the previous season. He passed me a bottle of Heineken from the fridge in his office and we talked over stale ham butties about everything but the game. It passed for a kiss-and-make-up in football circles.

Warnock left. Pronto.

On the journey home, I phoned Terry, my former Chairman at Bury. He was now Chief Executive at Sheffield United and before the game had asked Sam to persuade me not to 'fuel the fire' with Warnock.

I told him, 'If you've got anything to say to me, do it to my face.'

As we waited for our next chance to cement our play-off place at home against Wolves, I held court. Each Friday I gather the players in the Turf Moor dressing room to dish out fines for misdemeanours during the week — bad fashion, bad tackles, bad haircuts, bad parking, bad language, bad behaviour and being a downright pillock are just some of the offences I punish.

It began at Bury after someone nicked my shoes. They'd disappeared from outside my dressing room one afternoon so I'd called an instant court. Each offence needs a witness. If a player is charged and disagrees he can appeal to the rest of the squad. If the appeal fails, his fine is doubled.

I knew the identity of the shoe thief at Bury and accused him to his face. 'Lenny Johnrose, where are they?'

'I haven't had your shoes, gaffer.'

He didn't know about my star witness. 'Come with me, the lot of you,' I ordered.

The squad followed me along the corridor outside the dressing room until we arrived at the smallest office in the complex. I barged inside with Johnrose at my side and the rest of the lads fought to get a view over his shoulder.

'What's that?' he asked nervously.

'CCTV. Gotcha.'

I flicked a switch and a clear picture of my dressing room door appeared with the shoes laid neatly outside. Within seconds, a silhouette of a black player emerged into the frame and walked off with the pair.

'Well?'

'Well what, gaffer?' said Johnrose.

'That's you.'

'No it isn't.' He was adamant.

By now, 20 sweating bodies were crushed into a room the size of a lift. I was struggling to breathe.

'Back up,' I shouted.

Johnrose maintained his defence and named every other black player in the squad. The TV picture quality was so poor it could have been any of them. He got away with it. My cases would never be so flimsy in future.

The courts at Burnley became just as heated, even if fines were no more than £10. The first words our French defender Arthur Gnohere learned in English were, 'Not guilty, gaffer.'

On one occasion, Brian Flynn, who helps me out with a spot of coaching, accused Kevin Ball.

'What for? Ball bristled.

'Bad driving,' claimed Flynny. 'You overtook me at some traffic lights.'

Bally escaped with a classic defence ploy. 'How would you know? You're too fucking small to see over the steering wheel.'

Now it was Gazza's turn. I'd already fined him for illegally handing out my doughnuts on an away trip. The lads made sure they dug into his ribs, too. Since his arrival, they'd been terrified of his reputation as a practical joker and got stuck in first. They snipped his shoe laces in half and cut the toes off his socks.

During the court session, I said, 'Looks like they've got it in for you.'

'Ah, don't worry, gaffer,' said Gazza, 'it's all taken care of.'

A look of horror swept the players' faces. It was as if Graham Norton had bent over in the showers and sung 'Please Please Me'. They desperately tried to reconstruct the events of the day as Gazza sat grinning. Then they remembered.

The tea!

As they arrived for training that morning, Gazza had been waiting with a full pot of tea, liberally filling plastic cups for everyone, some of them more than once.

The lads were chuffed. They had their own fully-fledged celebrity waiter. This was the life.

'What was in the tea, Gazza?' they asked.

He grinned. 'Fart powder, lads. Fucking heaps of it.'

* * *

Morale was high as the Wolves game arrived. We were still in fourth place for the fifth game in a row. Results elsewhere went in our favour. It was time we moved up. Or so I thought.

We were 3–0 down by half-time. A crowd of 22,000, most of them ours, couldn't believe their eyes. I took Gazza off during the interval as we sat in the dressing room and listened to their supporters singing through our roof. We won the second half 2–0 but it wasn't enough. Three more crucial points had disappeared.

I flipped after the match and interrupted my shower to rampage around the dressing room. At one point, while I wore nothing but a damp towel around my neck, I bollocked Nik the Greek using obscene pidgin English for letting in a goal at his near post.

Later, when I calmed down and managed to put my underpants on, I had a beer with Wolves manager Dave Jones. TV pictures confirmed that a goal scored for us by Gareth Taylor in the first few minutes should not have been disallowed. It would have changed the game. I was furious with the ref and confronted him in the tunnel.

He looked terrified but, even when he saw he'd cocked up, he never owned up. I gave him zero marks in my report that is sent to the Football League. I always do.

Wolves were scrapping for the second automatic spot with West Brom behind Manchester City and needed the three points as much as us, so when I pointed the mistake out to Jones, he laughed and said, 'I don't give a toss.'

I left Gazza on the bench for the next two games, an away draw at Portsmouth and a 2–0 home win against Gillingham. We stayed in fourth place.

Our penultimate game was at Grimsby Town, who needed to win to avoid relegation. It was hard to imagine a bigger blow than the Wolves game, but this was it. Once more we were 3–0 down by half-time. My dream began to slip away.

With one game left, at home to Coventry, we dropped to sixth spot, level on points with Norwich. We had to score one goal more than them in our last match to beat them to stay in the play-offs.

We had only been out of the top six twice all season. It represented unparalleled success for Burnley and me. Yet it would count for nothing if we failed to beat Norwich to that spot.

The Turf Moor pitch was rubbish by this stage. Only a council roller would make it playable.

Norwich were at home to Stockport County and had barely kicked off when news filtered on to the Burnley terraces that Stockport's goalkeeper had been sent off after 50 seconds. Amazingly, County, who were already relegated, hung on and we scored!

For a brief moment, we were in the play-offs. Agonisingly, Norwich scored, too, and suddenly we were bollocksed. We were both 1–0 up. Whoever scored next had made it.

County did their bit and defended their goal valiantly as

Norwich bombarded them with crosses. Back at Turf Moor, we won a free kick on the edge of the Coventry box. Perfect for Gazza. This was his moment of destiny. So far he had failed to score. As he lined up to take the kick the crowd went silent. It was fate. It was predestined.

It was saved. Coventry's Swedish international keeper Magnus Hegman made a miracle stop.

Minutes later the ref blew again. Another free kick on the edge of their box. Another beautiful Gazza special.

Another heartbreaking save.

I think we knew then the game was up. We huffed and puffed and the crowd huffed some more but the final whistle cut our throats.

I slumped on to the pitch. Supporters were crying. We trudged off to the dressing room. There was no noise. It had been a dream for Burnley. It was a career for me.

I walked around the pitch as my players did a lap of honour. I waved to the crowd and applauded them. Some thought I was quitting. At that moment, I was.

Ian Wright had telephoned me the night before, concerned about my health, after seeing me on television.

He said, 'I worry for you. Football means so much to you I don't want anything to happen.'

When I waved to the Burnley fans after I failed on that final day, I agreed with him. My next 'heart-attack' could be a real one.

Sir Alex Ferguson spoke about me on TV. 'Stan is one of the great characters in football. He's a strong man, one of the good guys in the game.'

A nice epitaph. But later that night, I went to The Kettledrum with Gazza and Five-Bellies to say our goodbyes. We laughed about football. We laughed about life. We laughed about the good luck we shared which allowed us to make a decent living at this wonderful, violent, threatening, stupid, glorious, frustrating, painful, selfish and bizarre game.

STAN THE MAN

Over my fifth pint of Thwaites best bitter, I thought fondly of Turf Moor and knew, despite Wrighty's fears, I would be back.

After all, where else would I go for a hard life every Saturday?

Extra Time

Did I say hard life?

It just got harder. The rats at ITV Digital have deserted the Football League and left Burnley with a £4.6m black hole in our accounts. I let six key players leave the club before this season began and now I can't afford to replace any of them.

The chairman has had to pay £1million out of his own pocket and I've been asked by the Board to accept a pay cut in order to help keep Burnley afloat.

We can't afford hotel bills any more. My lads had to sit on a bus for a 500-mile round trip to Ipswich to play a night match. I was banned from the touchline for two games after daring to speak to the ref following last season's Wolves game when our promotion hopes died.

My seat on the bench was auctioned to fans to raise funds. To cap it all, we lost our first four games and plummeted to the bottom of Division One.

This time though, no one is shouting 'Sack Stan.' No one is booing the players. History has, thankfully, taught us that much.

After the fourth successive defeat, Kath marched on to the pitch and sprinkled another shower of our precious Holy water. Immediately, we went 12 matches unbeaten and reached within sniffing distance of the play-offs as well as beating Spurs in the Worthington Cup. The players are scrapping. Supporters are digging in.

A long, exhausting, tortuous, stressful, mean, unpredictable winter stretches ahead. But while we have a penny in the pot and a chuckle in our boots I promise this ... the dream is still alive.

Stan
Turf Moor
December 2002